NFL HEROES

George Johnson & Allan Maki

NFL HEROES

The 100 Greatest Players *of* All Time

Updated Second Edition

FIREFLY BOOKS

A FIREFLY BOOK

Published by Firefly Books Ltd. 2022

First printing

Library of Congress Control Number: 2022935188

Library and Archives Canada Cataloguing in Publication
Title: NFL heroes : the 100 greatest players of all time /
    George Johnson & Allan Maki.
Other titles: National Football League heroes
Names: Johnson, George, 1957- author. | Maki, Allan, author.
Description: Second edition. | Includes index.
Identifiers: Canadiana 20220206481 | ISBN 9780228103479 (softcover)
Subjects: LCSH: Football players—United States—Biography. |
    LCSH: National Football League. | LCSH: Football—United States. |
    LCGFT: Biographies.
Classification: LCC GV939.A1 J64 2022 | DDC 796.332092/2—dc23

Published in the United States by
Firefly Books (U.S.) Inc.
P.O. Box 1338, Ellicott Station
Buffalo, New York
14205

Published in Canada by
Firefly Books Ltd.
50 Staples Avenue, Unit 1
Richmond Hill, Ontario
L4B 0A7

Cover and interior design: Stacey Cho
Page production: Sam Tse

Printed in China

We acknowledge the financial support
of the Government of Canada.

As always, to my wife, Rita, and daughters, Michela and Sabrina, who keep me sane, whole and happy.

— G.J.

To my grandson Brady, who has become a serious football fan and occasionally asks me to tell him what the NFL was like in the old days — like 2015 or thereabouts.

— A.M.

CONTENTS

Introduction

WHILE GUESTING ON SIRIUSXM NFL Radio's *'Let's Go!'* segment back in mid-September of 2021, Tom Brady ruminated on legacy, professional life span and the inevitable passing of the proverbial torch.

"I don't remember this many rookies playing," the 44-year-old seven-time Super Bowl champion mused wistfully that day.

"Even the second-year guys. Tua [Tagovailoa], [Justin] Herbert, [Joe] Burrow, Trevor Lawrence. [Justin] Fields played a little bit. Trey Lance played a little bit. Zach Wilson is playing. Mac Jones is playing.

"That's a lot of young quarterbacks.

"Gone are the days of Drew Brees, Peyton Manning, Philip Rivers, Eli Manning. You know, those are the guys I'm used to hearing about.

"I'll be forgotten here soon. I'll move on and they'll be onto someone else but that's just the way football goes.

"As does life."

Brady needn't fret unduly about being remembered. How on earth could anyone forget?

And his decision to continue playing — after an astonishingly brief spell in retirement — leaves us with the enticing possibility of even more memories to come.

Tom Terrific's right about one thing, though. Nothing, no one, lasts forever.

They're mostly gone now, of course, the touchstones of a generation.

Only Aaron Rodgers, a league MVP again at 38, and 33-year-old Russell Wilson stubbornly continue to resist the march of time.

Fear not, though.

Able replacements to spark the imagination, establish new rivalries, have already arrived. A virtual cavalcade of them.

As Super Bowl LVI loomed inside SoFi Stadium in Inglewood, California, this past February, its main protagonist, for instance, was a 25-year-old in just his second year as a starting quarterback.

QB Joe Burrow of the Cincinnati Bengals is only one of those who'll be vying for the bling, individual and collective. But he's surely among the brightest.

"He's got ice in his veins," Cincy tight end C.J. Uzomah trumpeted on Super Bowl media Monday, six days before kickoff. "The utmost confidence. We have him in the huddle, we have his mind and his ability to analyze defenses and just be a leader. Just a presence. Ice-cold-blooded killer out there dissecting defenses. It's great.

"It's why I call him 'Franchise' — he is a franchise player; he can turn an organization around. It's not one person, it's a team game, but he is a vital part of why we are where we are.

"I love Joe.

"He's the man, dude."

They could with varying degrees of validity make the same claim in K.C., or Buffalo, or Foxboro, or Dallas or any number of other cities across the NFL landscape.

The Bills' Josh Allen and 2019 MVP Lamar Jackson of the Baltimore Ravens are but 25 years old. Daniel Jones of the New York Giants and Arizona starting chucker Kyler Murray, 24; Herbert of the Chargers, New England's Mac Jones, Jalen Hurts of the Philadelphia Eagles and Miami's Tua all an evolving 23.

Trevor Lawrence, the future of the Jacksonville Jaguars? A shaggy-maned babe at 22.

On the "old-guy" end of the new-era quarterbacking spectrum, there's Patrick Mahomes, already a Super Bowl winner and undisputed poster boy for this dynamic new generation. He's 26. So, too, DeShaun Watson of the Houston Texans.

Why, even the senior citizen on the far edge of this emerging generation, Dak Prescott of the Cowboys, could hardly be described as geriatric. Not carrying a 1993 birth certificate.

This is a rich, perhaps singular, smorgasbord of talent.

Whether it's Mahomes somehow escaping an unruly mob or Travis Kelce rumbling over the middle, Allen choreographing seven touchdowns in seven drives during a playoff game last season against the Pats, Herbert tossing a rookie-record 31 touchdown passes or Jackson tucking the ball away and rushing for 1,206 yards in 2019, most ever by a quarterback en route to MVP laurels, the possibilities seem endless.

Burrow, the cool kid from Ames, Iowa, who bounced back after tearing an ACL in his freshman season to not only direct his team to the Super Bowl but also scoop up Comeback Player of the Year honors, may have been foiled in his bid for a Mahomes-like second-season championship, subdued 23–20 by a smothering L.A. Rams defense.

Don't wager large against seeing him back on Super Sunday again. Soon.

"We're a young team," said Burrow, postgame. "You like to think that we'll be back in this situation multiple times over the course of the next few years. We'll take this and let it fuel you for the rest of our careers.

"Yeah I think it's going to propel us into next year and we are going to have a really good off-season and we have a lot of hard workers in that locker room that is going to attack this off-season like they did last year.

"Obviously, we are not satisfied with what we did this year. We are going to keep getting better and attack next year with the same intensity."

Standing in his way, their way, will be Mahomes, Allen, Murray, Herbert, Jones, Prescott, et al.

And, for at least one more season, Tom Brady.

What makes this particular incoming generation of quarterbacks so compelling is its depth. They'll be butting helmets against each other for the next decade, minimum.

Some will ascend the heights. Some will not. But watching how it all plays out promises to be a helluva good time.

Just as no one could replace' Johnny U, Broadway Joe, Dan Marino, Brett Favre, Peyton Manning or Joe Montana, no one will be able to replace Tom Brady when, in fact, that day does arrive.

But when it does, there'll be no reason to ache for the past.

A brilliantly blue horizon is here, already, smack-dab in front of our eyes. ◼

Kansas City Chiefs quarterback Patrick Mahomes holds up the Vince Lombardi Trophy after the Chiefs' 31–20 victory at Super Bowl LIV.

Top 10 Greatest Players of All Time

TOM BRADY QB

G	Att	Comp	Yds	TD	Int
318	11,317	7,268	84,520	624	203

The Gold Standard

THE "OFFICIAL" RETIREMENT, IF YOU WANT TO CALL IT that, lasted all of 40 days.

"These past two months, I've realized my place is still on the field and not in the stands," tweeted Tom Brady, audibling as well as ever, on March 13, 2021.

On February 1, Brady had announced with a drumroll that he would, at 44, finally be stepping away from football.

Even at the time, under the circumstances, it didn't seem plausible.

Ten Super Bowl appearances, after all. Seven championships. Five ultimate-game MVP laurels. Fourteen Pro Bowl trips.

Tom Brady, of course, collects Super Bowl rings the way people collect Funko Pop! figurines; he has become to the QB position what Sinatra is to popular song or Hemingway to clean, lean prose.

Records? He's got more gold platters than Elvis. Most passes thrown. Most passes completed. Most yardage. Most wins at the position. Tied for most titles among QBs alongside Otto Graham. Most this. Most that.

When Brady signed with the Tampa Bay Buccaneers after two decades of helping transform the New England Patriots into a juggernaut, the buzz of a new challenge, being away from the cocoon of Foxboro, was palpable.

"Excited, humble and hungry ... if there is one thing I have learned about football, it's that nobody cares what you did last year or the year before that ... you earn the trust and respect of those around through your commitment every single day," wrote Brady on Instagram, after signing a two-year, $50 million deal.

Tom Brady holds the Lombardi Trophy after Super Bowl LV on February 7, 2021.

"I'm starting a new football journey ... I have always believed that well done is better than well said, so I'm not gonna say much more — I'm just gonna get to work!"

And he did just that, piloting the Bucs to their second Super Bowl victory, the first since 2003, in front of the home Florida fans at Raymond James Stadium.

"You want to get this far, you've got to get the job done," Brady said postgame on a videoconference. "We did it."

He usually does.

Tom Brady, of course, hasn't simply set a standard. He became THE standard. What's been so amazing is the lack of drop-off in brilliance over the years. Even at his age, when most guys suck in their stomachs at the gym, Brady led the NFL in passing in 2021, with 5,316 yards. Ahead of youngish whippersnappers like Mahomes, Herbert, Jackson, Prescott and Burrow.

"I met him when he was 32 years old, when I was 20 years old, and he hasn't had a single drop off since I've met him. He's never lost the throwing power, he's never lost his skills," longtime sidekick Rob Gronkowski marveled during the 2021 season. "This guy has it every single day, week in and week out, game in and game out."

The tall, cool Californian has been profiled on *60 Minutes*, has been lampooned on *The Simpsons* and *Family Guy*, and has hosted *Saturday Night Live*. His wife is Brazilian supermodel Gisele Bündchen. His signature No. 12 jersey sells more than any other player's.

Brady defines what it is to be a star.

But peel back the layer of fame for a moment, and you'll understand it's more about substance than style.

"A lot of time I find that people who are blessed with the most talent don't ever develop that attitude," he said of his inner drive. "And the ones who aren't blessed in that way are the most competitive and have the biggest heart."

Belying his upper-middle class upbringing in San Mateo, California, Brady developed an almost obsessive desire early on to succeed, to push for more.

"I had the worst temper when I was little," he once confessed. "I could never stand to lose in anything. I kicked through glass windows and threw video-game controllers at the TV and broke more tennis rackets than I could count. It got to where nobody ever wanted to play with me."

Now it's gotten to the point where nobody wants to play against him.

Brady emerged from unheralded NFL beginnings — he was the 199th overall pick in the 2000 NFL Draft, out of the University of Michigan. A fortuitous blending of the right talent, the right coach (the crusty, crafty, incomparable Bill Belichick) and the right team resulted in the closest thing that the modern game has seen to a dynasty.

"I still have the image of Tom Brady coming down the old Foxboro Stadium steps with that pizza box under his arm," recalled Patriots owner Robert Kraft years ago to Boston's CBS TV affiliate.

"A skinny beanpole, and when he introduced himself to me and said, 'Hi, Mr. Kraft,' he was about to say who he was, but I said, 'I know who you are, you're Tom Brady. You're our sixth-round draft choice.'

"And he looked me in the eye and said: 'I'm the best decision this organization has ever made.'

"It looks like he could be right."

Without a shadow of a doubt.

When Brady took over from the injured Drew Bledsoe in 2001 and led the Pats to the team's first Super Bowl championship, in what was a huge upset for the prohibitively favored St. Louis Rams, the one question on the lips of all but the most diehard football fans was, "Who on earth is this Tom Brady?"

Only a few years later, you'd have been hard-pressed to find anyone in North America who didn't know the name or recognize the face.

Over the years, he's gone from strength to strength, using disappointment as motivation and rising like Lazarus to smite his ever-dwindling number of doubters.

The Super Bowl in the first year of his new adventure was only further proof of his position at the very summit.

After signing a one-year extension following Tampa's 33–19 curb-stomping of reigning Super Bowl champion Kansas City, Brady and the Buccaneers swashbuckled their way to a 12-5 record in 2021 and the No. 1 seeding in the NFC.

But things began to unravel early in Tampa's first playoff assignment, versus the L.A. Rams. Falling behind 27–3, Brady and the Bucs someone managed to claw back to even in the fourth quarter, but

a dramatic walk-off field goal consigned them to an unexpected defeat.

During the postgame celebrations a little less than a year earlier on the same field, amid all the ticker tape and fanfare, the new king of south Florida had left no doubt as to his immediate plans.

"I'll be back," he promised.

There was none of that ironclad certainty in Brady's remarks following the loss to the Rams. Instead he spoke of family and shifting priorities, leaving the door to furthering an incomparable career both half open and half shut.

In the end, though, after further consideration, he opted for fully open.

In most any line of work, those both in or out of the public eye, what sets the absolute elite apart isn't necessarily size or strength or speed.

It's appetite.

"You wanna know which ring is my favorite?" Brady once responded to the inevitable, clichéd question.

"The next one." ■

College: University of Michigan
Drafted: 2000, New England Patriots, 199th overall
Years active: 2000–present
Top honors: Super Bowl Champion (2001, 2003, 2004, 2014, 2016, 2018, 2020), Super Bowl MVP (2001, 2003, 2014, 2016, 2020), NFL AP MVP (2007, 2010, 2017), NFL AP Offensive Player of the Year (2007, 2010), NFL AP Comeback Player of the Year (2009)
Hall of Fame induction: N/A

JIM
BROWN RB

G	Att	Yds	Avg	TD
118	2,359	12,312	5.2	106

If Superman *Were a* Running Back

MANY TIMES, WHEN OPPOSING PLAYERS TACKLED JIM Brown, they would congratulate themselves on doing such a smash-up job. They'd watch him slowly get to his feet and pause for a moment before walking back to the Cleveland Browns' huddle looking like a 1,000-year-old man.

There was a chance it could happen that way two, three times in a row. But eventually, Brown would burst through the defensive line, crash into the linebackers — at 6-foot-2 and 232 pounds, he was as big as them — then outrun the defensive backs all the way to their end zone, or at least deep into their territory.

And then, like before, Brown would trudge back to his teammates looking worn and exhausted. His opponents weren't certain what to make of it. Was he truly vulnerable? Was he wanting the other side to believe

he had no more breakaway runs left in him?

If there was ever a moment of uncertainty or hesitation, Brown exploited it throughout his remarkable career, one which saw him retire as pro football's then all-time leading rusher with 12,312 yards. He currently ranks 11th behind such luminaries as Emmitt Smith, Walter Payton, Barry Sanders, Eric Dickerson and Tony Dorsett. (It should be noted that the backs who played after Brown did so in 16-game regular seasons; Brown played in both 12- and 14-game seasons during his nine years in the NFL.)

And yet, despite his ranking, there are football people and NFL fans who still regard Brown as the prototypical NFL running back: strong, powerful, fast. Gone from the game for over five decades now, his name still resonates whenever people speak of the top players of all time. Washington Redskins' Hall of Fame middle linebacker Sam Huff once said that the only way to handle Jim Brown was "to grab, hold, hang on and wait for help."

Brown left such a legacy that he was voted the best pro football player of all time by *Sporting News* in 2002. A quote attributed to an unnamed defender, perhaps merely fanciful but nonetheless dead accurate, gives a fair impression of the man's impact: "That Jim Brown. He says he isn't Superman. What he really means is that Superman isn't Jimmy Brown!"

Brown spent his youth on St. Simons Island, off the Georgia coast, and was raised by his great-grandmother. His father, a boxer nicknamed "Sweet Sue," wanted nothing to do with his son and left the family when Brown was still an infant. As for his mom, Theresa, she left to do housework for a family in Manhasset, Long Island. Mother and son were reunited in Long Island when Brown was eight, and they shared a rocky relationship in the single room they lived in. Theresa would go out on the town or invite men over, and Brown, critical of her dating habits, would get into fierce fights with his mother. With

College: Syracuse University
Drafted: 1957, Cleveland Browns, 6th overall
Years active: 1957–1965
Top honors: NFL AP MVP (1957, 1958, 1965), First Team All-Pro (1957–61, 1963–65), NFL Champion (1964)
Hall of Fame induction: 1971

nowhere else to turn, Brown got involved with a gang called the Gaylords.

Football pulled him out of trouble. "It changed my life," he said. "Otherwise, I could have been some kind of gangster."

When he reached college age, Brown went to Syracuse University, where he excelled in a variety of sports — football, lacrosse, basketball and track and field. That explains why he was inducted into the Pro Football Hall of Fame in 1971, the Lacrosse Hall of Fame in 1983 and the College Football Hall of Fame in 1995. Some of his NFL records are still on the books: most seasons leading the league in rushing (eight times in nine years) and the only player with a career average of more than 100 rushing yards per game. In 1964 he carried the Browns to the NFL title.

"You gang-tackled him, did whatever you could, give him extracurriculars [a punch followed by a squeeze]. He'd get up slow, look at you, and walk back to the huddle and wouldn't say a word, just come at you again, and again," said Chuck Bednarik, who played for the Philadelphia Eagles. "You'd just say 'What the hell? What's wrong with this guy, for heaven's sake? When is he gonna stop carrying the ball? How much more can he take?'"

The answer: anything any defender had to give.

Brown gave this bit of advice to Baltimore Colts tight end John Mackey: "Make sure when anyone tackles you, he remembers how much it hurts."

Gone from the game for over five decades now, his name still resonates whenever people speak of the top players of all time.

"He lived by that philosophy," said Mackey, "and I always followed that advice."

Brown was also into acting — as in television and movie acting. It was an emerging aspect of his life and, in the end, he severed his relationship with the Browns and the NFL to pursue it.

In the summer of 1966, Brown was supposed to be at Cleveland's training camp. Instead, he was filming *The Dirty Dozen*. The team's owner, Art Modell, ordered Brown to report to training camp and practice with his teammates. Brown refused. The Browns announced they were going to fine their star player for every day he missed. Brown thought it over, then announced his retirement at the age of 30. He filled his days and weeks with movie and television appearances and by donating time and resources to various charities. He began giving aid to small communities like the one he grew up in. He worked with kids caught up in the gang lifestyle by introducing them to the Amer-I-Can program, which he founded in 1988.

It was his social conscience that earned him new fans and words of praise.

"I had two heroes growing up, John Wayne and Roy Rogers," former heavyweight boxing

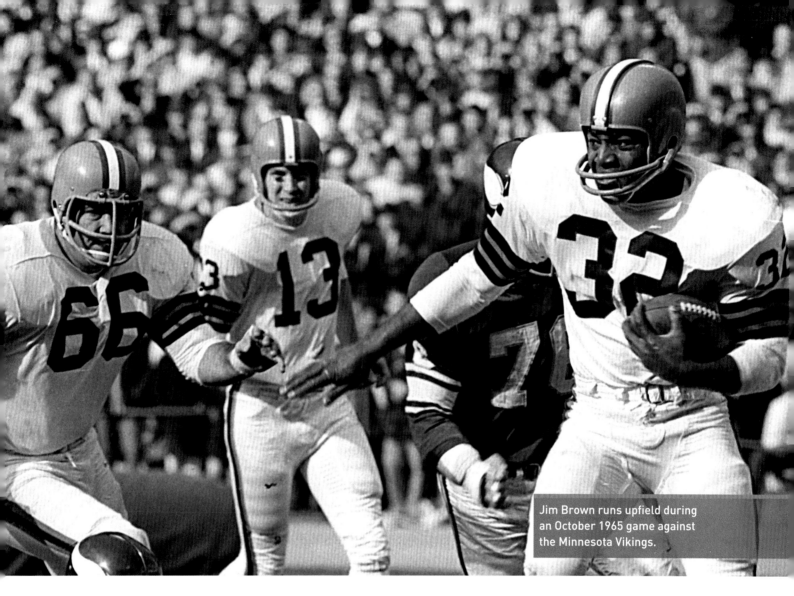

Jim Brown runs upfield during an October 1965 game against the Minnesota Vikings.

champion George Foreman admitted. "Then one day I saw Jim Brown."

Spending most of his life in the public eye has spotlighted Brown's both good and question- able endeavors. Brown made the cover of *Time* magazine in 1965, but, on the flip side, he posed nude for *Playgirl* a decade later. Over the years, Brown has been tied to numerous assault allegations. He was charged with assault and battery in 1965; the charge was dropped. He was charged with rape in 1988; that charge was dismissed. He was found guilty of vandalism for smashing his wife's car with a shovel. He then received an extended six-month

sentence for not attending his court-ordered counselling sessions, though he was released after three months. In 2002 director Spike Lee made a documentary on Brown's career and life called *Jim Brown: All-American*. The movie showcased how stubborn and angry the running back could get, even though he made a point of not showing his emotions during games.

Washington linebacker Sam Huff once told a story that captures perhaps all the aspects of Brown's personality, from deceptive to dynamic. It took place in one of the many battles they waged as punish- ing runner and bruising tackler.

On Brown's first carry in this

particular game, Huff plugged the hole and held Brown to no gain. As Brown hauled himself into the Cleveland huddle, Huff hollered, "Brown, you stink!"

On the second carry, the same thing happened. Huff got the best of Brown and shouted again, "You stink."

"The third time Jimmy carried," said Huff, "he dove into the middle, but nobody stopped him. He got a couple of key blocks and exploded past me and the secondary and raced 65 yards for a touchdown.

"Trotting back to the Browns' bench, he turned toward me, and I could see a big grin on his face. Then he shouted, 'Hey, Huff. How do I smell from here?'" ∎

DICK
BUTKUS LB

G	Int/Yds	TD	FR
119	22/166	1	27

Born *to* Be *a* Bear

"**I** WOULDN'T EVER SET OUT TO HURT ANYBODY," DICK Butkus said one time. "Unless it was, you know, important — like a league game or something."

The ferocity, the anger, that unparalleled rage to be the best and to get it done at any cost: it all passed into the realm of sporting legend long ago. The story of Dick Butkus apparently trying to bite Miami guard Larry Little in a pileup and then take a nip at an official, whether true or not (Butkus denied it, saying, "I'm a football player, not a gourmet"; Little affirmed it and the official never gave his view of the situation), has taken on almost mythic proportions. In another game, against Detroit, he was accused of provoking three on-field fights and poking a finger through the facemask and into an eye of Lions tight end Charlie Saunders.

If the name Johnny Unitas embodies cool efficiency, Lynn Swann balletic grace and Brett Favre inspirational toughness, only one word comes to mind when you mention Dick Butkus: pain.

"It makes me mad sometimes," Butkus once complained. "Some people think I have to get down on all fours to eat my couple pounds of raw meat every day. Nobody thinks I can talk, much less write my name.

"I guess people think the Bears keep me in a cage and let me out on Sunday afternoons."

He could hit like an ornery mule, fill a gap in the defensive line and strike fear in the heart of anybody daft enough to hold onto the football for any significant length of time. His image, that of the wild man with a moustache in the Chicago Bears' No. 51 dead-of-night blue jersey, defined an era.

Dick Butkus makes the tackle against the Packers.

Some memorable quotes have been uttered about Butkus's play over the years: Green Bay running back MacArthur Lane once said, "If given a choice, I'd rather go one-on-one with a grizzly bear. I pray that I can get up every time Butkus hits me." NY Giants scout Joe Walton said, "He plays the middle like a piranha," while fellow All-Pro Deacon Jones of the Rams' legendary Fearsome Foursome quipped, "Every time he hit you, he tried to put you in the cemetery, not in the hospital."

Pittsburgh quarterback Terry Hanratty spoke for all quarterbacks of the era when he said, "If he doesn't tackle you, you can still hear him coming. You know he's going to be there eventually. It's savage." While teammate Ron Smith said of Butkus, "He'll be all right as soon as he has his couple cups of blood."

Put simply, Dick Butkus made brutality attractive. That was the beauty in the beast.

Born and raised in the Roseland section of the south side of Chicago, from Lithuanian stock and one of nine kids, Dick Butkus was seemingly born to be a Bear. Butkus has always credited his hunger for success to being a poor kid who wanted more.

Eventually he and his city would become synonymous, inseparable in the public consciousness. Small wonder the City of Big Shoulders wrapped its arms around this native son.

At 6-foot-4 and 245 pounds, Butkus could not only roam from sideline to sideline, but also possessed superb instincts for reading a play — skills he was never given full credit for. Drafted in the first round by his hometown team and handed a reported $235,000 contract to keep him away from the rival AFL, he led the Bears in tackles, interceptions, forced fumbles and fumble recoveries during his rookie season. Not only did he inspire the Bears' defense, he *was* the Bears' defense.

"I never thought any player could play as well as writers write that they play," marveled L.A. Rams coach Tommy Prothro. "Butkus comes as close as any I've seen."

During his career, the big Bear would make 22 interceptions from the position and recover 27 fumbles. What set him apart from virtually every other linebacker of his era (with the exception of Green Bay icon Ray Nitschke) was a voracious appetite for physical contact, for confrontation. He absolutely loved to be challenged to one-on-one battles.

To stoke the inner fire, he would use an old but effective parlor trick.

"When I went on the field to warm up," he recalled, "I would manufacture things to make me mad. If someone on the other team was laughing, I'd pretend he was laughing at me or the Bears. It always worked for me."

And it worked against whatever team Chicago was supposed to play that afternoon.

Alex Karras, one of the meanest hombres of the Butkus era, paid homage to the king of linebackers when he said, "He's one of those rare superstars, like Wilt Chamberlain or Lew Alcindor [Kareem Abdul-Jabbar] in basketball or Gordie Howe in hockey in his great years, where just by being on the field, the game changes. If you had 11 like him going against you, you wouldn't get any points on the scoreboard. Ever."

Unfortunately, the Bears of the Butkus era often weren't up to his extraordinary level, so he had to make do with individual accolades. He was a five-time First Team All-Pro selection and an eight-time Pro Bowler — his only miss coming in his ninth and final season. It was the first time in his career he played fewer than 13 games.

A series of knee injuries forced Butkus to retire in 1973. But he'd packed more into those years than less-motivated men had in 15. He was inducted into the College Football Hall of Fame and joined the legendary Red Grange as one of only two players whose jersey numbers have been retired at the University of Illinois.

The Pro Football Hall of Fame was, of course, a lock in 1979, in his first year of eligibility. When the Illinois Fighting Illini unveiled

He could hit like an ornery mule, fill a gap in the defensive line and strike fear in the heart of anybody daft enough to hold onto the football for any significant length of time.

a statue of their most famous alumnus four decades later, the then-76-year-old Butkus was in typically fine form.

"You ask yourself, 'Why, man?'" he marveled. "I did what I thought I was supposed to do. I had fun knocking the s— out of people. So if it was that unusual, I guess you take it."

More than the accolades and the honors, though, we are left with the visceral memory of No. 51: eyes ablaze, arms flying, looking like a madman escaped from the asylum, putting his body on the line to lay another thunderous smack on a ball carrier. That image is the essence, the spirit of the indomitability of pro football.

"With the highest respect," said former teammate Mike Ditka on one occasion, "I've got to say that Dick is an animal."

The quintessential Monster of the Midway. ▪

College: University of Illinois
Drafted: 1965, Chicago Bears, 3rd overall
Years active: 1965–1973
Top honors: First Team All-Pro (1965, 1968, 1969, 1970, 1972)
Hall of Fame induction: 1979

DEACON JONES DE

G	Int/Yds	FR
191	2/50	15

The Man Who Never Sacked

THIS IS HOW THE NFL SAW IT: David "Deacon" Jones spent 14 years at defensive end, appeared in eight Pro Bowls, was named to the league's 100th-anniversary team and was inducted into the Pro Football Hall of Fame in 1980 — and not once did he sack a quarterback.

He may have scored two safeties, made two interceptions, recovered 15 fumbles, ran back two kickoffs and kicked an extra point. But tackle a quarterback for a loss?

No way. Never happened. Not even for the Los Angeles Ram who invented the term "sack" and a nasty helmet-cracking technique known as the head slap, which begs the question: if Deacon Jones is considered one of the most dangerous pass rushers the NFL has ever seen, just how revered would he have been had the league recorded quarterback sacks as an official statistic back when he played in the 1960s and 1970s?

Pro Football Weekly went through every statistic from every game Jones played and found such gawdy numbers as Jones twice recording 22 sacks in a 14-game season and totaling 173.5 sacks in his career. That number was eventually surpassed by Bruce Smith, who reached the 200 mark, and Reggie White, who finished his career with 198.

It wasn't until 1982 that the NFL began keeping official tabs on sacks. Anyone who played prior to that year was left with a collective zero next to his name, even if his name was synonymous with terrorizing offensive lines from New York to California. In a 1999 interview with the *Los Angeles Times*, Jones explained the meaning of the word sack: "You take all the offensive linemen and put them in a burlap bag, and then you take a baseball bat and beat on the bag," he said. "You're sacking them, you're bagging them. And that's what you're doing with a quarterback."

Former New York Giants defensive end Michael Strahan and add T.J. Watt of the Pittsburgh Steelers hold the acknowledged record of 22.5 sacks in a 16-game season. "According to Deacon, he has like 3,000 sacks. And it grows each year," Strahan once said. "Those guys who played before they had all the stats, they do have some kind of legitimate gripe."

Anyone who played against Jones would agree that he was a menace ahead of his time. He stood 6-foot-5, weighed 272 pounds and had long arms that he used to his advantage — enabling him to head slap an opponent so they'd lose their concentration for a split second. Jones told people he learned that by watching Muhammad Ali box. Jones's leopard-like speed added another element to his game, allowing him to catch his opponents off guard. He could make tackles from sideline to sideline, all over the field. Rams coach George Allen best described Jones by saying that "he played with sheer abandon."

College: Mississippi Vocational College
Drafted: 1961, Los Angeles Rams, 186th overall
Years active: 1961–1974
Top honors: First Team All-Pro (1965–69)
Hall of Fame induction: 1980

If Deacon Jones is considered one of the most dangerous pass rushers the NFL has ever seen, just how revered would he have been had the league recorded quarterback sacks as an official statistic back when he played in the 1960s and 1970s?

Added to that, he was part of what was the first truly dominant defensive line in NFL history, the Fearsome Foursome, which also included Lamar Lundy, Rosey Grier and Merlin Olsen in its glory days.

"We started the trend. We proved that defensive lines can control the game," Jones said in an interview with ESPN.com. "I don't think you'll find, even now, four men who had as much talent and doled out as much damage and devastation as our group. After our group came the Purple People Eaters, the Steel Curtain, Dallas's Doomsday team and that Baltimore [Ravens] team. The dominant teams all had great defensive lines, and we had something to do with that trend. That's why they've changed so many rules. They don't want games controlled by defensive lines."

Jones, who was hailed as the Secretary of Defense, was never shy about highlighting his football skills. What was far more remarkable was everything he endured to make it as a pro football player. Growing up in Florida in a family of 10, Jones picked watermelons and pitched them into trucks to earn money. In town, he couldn't drink from the same water fountains as whites. He couldn't use the same restrooms as whites. He

had to sit in "black only" sections in restaurants. He had to stay in the black wing of the local hospital when he needed an operation.

When Jones enrolled at South Carolina State, he took part in a march protesting the treatment of black youths who had been arrested for eating at a lunch counter. Jones said the police and fire department dispersed the marchers with hoses and dogs, and that he was pinned against a wall by a blast of water. For taking part in the march, and for having poor marks due to him skipping classes, Jones lost his football scholarship and enrolled at Mississippi Vocational (now Mississippi Valley State), where he and other football players were rounded up by the police and told to leave and never return.

The Rams were only so-so on Jones at the time of the 1961 NFL Draft. There wasn't a great body of work for them to evaluate. They ended up taking him in the 14th round, 186th overall. When he got to training camp, he knew he had to make an impression. Fueled by an overwhelming desire to prove himself in the mostly white world of professional football, Jones pillaged blockers and plundered quarterbacks and became a Pro

Deacon Jones has little Mike Garrett in his grip and the ball is flying loose in 1971.

Bowl regular for seven consecutive seasons, from 1964 to 1970. He earned an eighth Pro Bowl invitation in 1972 as a member of the San Diego Chargers.

He finished his career with the 1974 Washington Redskins, where he partook in two indulgences. First, before every home game at RFK Stadium, Jones would spit on the statue of George Preston Marshall, the former team owner who refused to sign black players for as long as he could; second, Jones got to kick an extra point in his final game. It was the Redskins' George Allen, who had coached Jones with the Rams, who let the veteran lineman attempt a conversion, and it was good.

The culmination of Jones's life experience was to pass along opportunities to young students from inner-city neighborhoods to help them prosper. The Deacon Jones Foundation, which Jones and his wife established in 1997, gives underprivileged teenagers an opportunity to go to university and become leaders and volunteers in their communities. That way, they can give back and help the next generation succeed. It was a project that Jones, happily in retirement, tackled as hard as he had any quarterback.

Following Jones's death on June 3, 2013, the NFL created the Deacon Jones Award to be given to the player who records the highest number of sacks per season. It was a well-deserved and long-overdue honor for one of the game's toughest defensive players — something Jones knew about himself.

"I'm probably the toughest [expletive] here," he once said. "Ain't no question about that with me. I'm the toughest guy here ... I'm clean. I mean, I ain't got no marks on me. I don't know nobody else who can say that who came out of any sport. I ain't got no marks on me, so I've got to be the baddest dude I know of."

Officially or unofficially. ■

JOE
MONTANA

G	Att	Comp	Yds	TD	Int
192	5,391	3,409	40,551	273	139

The
Comeback Kid

H E WAS JOE. THE COMEBACK KID. BELIEVER IN LOST causes.

"He's like Lazarus," San Franciso 49ers teammate Tim McKyer said one time. "You roll back the stone, Joe limps out — and throws for 300 yards."

What set Joe Montana apart from virtually every other quarterback was his flair for the dramatic, the theatrical. His face should've been plastered on the cover of *Playbill* as often as *Sports Illustrated*.

There isn't an illusionist alive who wouldn't kill to know Joe Montana's secret. He convinced his audience that he could, in fact, manipulate time. Take it in his hands, turn it over, bend it, shape it, and make it do his bidding — quite a trick. Salvador Dali's *Persistence of Memory* had nothing on this guy.

In Joe's mind, nothing was out of reach. No deficit too great. No mountain too daunting. He gave the impression that he could climb Everest in trainers and a windbreaker.

When the screws were tightest, that's when he was at his best.

"Quarterbacks, the best ones, like that time of the game, when you know you're going to drop back and throw it and they know it, too," Montana said once. "That cat-and-mouse game for a quarterback?

"Nothing like it."

His amazing 31 fourth-quarter comebacks are why *Sports Illustrated* voted him its all-time clutch quarterback in 2006.

In four Super Bowl appearances, he collected four rings — tied with Terry Bradshaw and second only to Tom Brady, by the way — completed nearly 70 percent

Joe Montana passes during the San Francisco 49ers' 38–16 victory over the Miami Dolphins in Super Bowl XIX.

of his passes, and didn't throw a single interception in 122 attempts. In three of those games he was named MVP, stepping back only once to allow his favorite receiver, Jerry Rice, to command the spotlight.

Beyond the cool and the list of accomplishments, early on there was something of the underdog in the cowboy who would go on to conquer the City by the Bay — and that was appealing, too.

He began his collegiate career at Notre Dame, listed seventh on the quarterback depth chart. In 1977, only three years later, he led the school to a national championship.

It seems ludicrous now, but Montana was considered too slight and his arm strength was rated only "average" by NFL scouts, who'd charted his days with the Fighting Irish. Even a wild comeback win in the 1979 Cotton Bowl, with Montana completing the winning TD pass with two seconds to play — foreshadowing things to come — wasn't enough to completely convince the skeptics.

He lasted until the third round in his draft year, chosen 82nd overall by the 49ers. The rest, as they say, is history.

With Bill Walsh's legendary West Coast Offense, the kid from New Eagle, Pennsylvania took over control of the team in 1981 and went about efficiently setting a new standard for the position. Ironically, the play that began the Montana legend — the 6-yard pass to Dwight Clark in the Dallas Cowboys' end zone with less than a minute to play, that thrust the 49ers into Super Bowl XVI — wasn't planned. The moment remains an image

frozen in time: Clark leaping high in the air to snare the ball, forever to be remembered by NFL fans as simply "The Catch." Montana later admitted he'd been trying to heave the ball out of the end zone so he could regroup on the next snap. If that isn't being touched by the heavens, nothing is.

Exactly how anointed Joe Montana was would be all too apparent in 1989. In the closing moments of Super Bowl XXIII, Montana drove the 49ers an improbable 92 yards and threw a 10-yard touchdown pass to John Taylor with 34 ticks left on the clock to give the 49ers a 20–16 win over the Cincinnati Bengals. The man himself endeavored to explain his knack in the clutch:

"It's a blur," he admitted. "I hyperventilated to the point of almost blacking out. I was yelling so loudly in the huddle that I couldn't breathe. Things got blurrier and blurrier."

The next year, Montana followed that up in Super Bowl XXIV with an even more dominating performance, shredding the Denver Broncos for five touchdown passes in a 55–10 rout.

He just kept topping himself.

When he finally retired in 1995, Joe Montana held NFL playoff records for completions, yards and touchdowns, as well as for a single season (1989), and owned the second-highest-rated passing efficiency in league history.

He had, by then, played briefly with the Kansas City Chiefs. No matter — he remains as quintessentially 'Frisco as the Coit Tower, cable cars, Fisherman's Wharf, a cappuccino in North Beach or

stopping to browse at City Lights bookstore.

Typically, in exiting, he spread the praise around as easily as the football. "The beauty of Bill's system was that there was always a place to go with the ball," Montana said, with typical humility. "I was just the mailman, just delivering people's mail. And there were all kinds of houses to go to."

When he walked away from the game he had come to embody, Joe Montana cited his young family as a major reason.

"When I was playing, I missed my two girls' [activities]," he said at the time. "They look up, and myself and my wife are not there. To me, it's more important to be home with my boys. The Super Bowl is a great event, but I've moved on with my life. I want to be there for the boys."

Two of those boys now play Division I college ball.

Besides, he'd spent enough years being there for his other boys — for coach Bill, for Jerry, Roger, John, Dwight and the rest. Fifteen years was enough. In the end, you could say, Joe Cool ran short of urgency. He never ran out of time. ∎

College: University of Notre Dame
Drafted: 1979, San Francisco 49ers, 82nd overall
Years active: 1979–1994
Top honors: Super Bowl Champion (1981, 1984, 1988, 1989), Super Bowl MVP (1981, 1984, 1989), First Team All-Pro (1987, 1989, 1990), NFL AP MVP (1989, 1990), NFL AP Offensive Player of the Year (1989)
Hall of Fame induction: 2000

WALTER
PAYTON RB

G	Att	Yds	Avg	TD
190	3,838	16,726	4.4	110

Sweetness,
and Then Some

FOR WHO KNOWS HOW MANY CHICAGOANS, IT WAS THE first time they had ever heard the words "primary sclerosing cholangitis." They were serious-sounding words — so serious they brought down the Bears' greatest running back in a way no NFL tackler ever could. That's why the NFL and its Chicago fans have made it a tradition to find a moment every November 1st since 1999 to pay homage to the man they called Sweetness: Walter Payton, who died from a rare liver disease at age 45.

Jim Harbaugh, a rookie with the Chicago Bears in 1987 and the current head coach at the University of Michigan, said upon Payton's passing, "Sweetness ... there may not have been a better nickname for a player."

Payton was every bit a running back. He could grind it out, lugging the ball six, seven times in a row, or he could snap off a lengthy romp by going outside, gaining the corner and speeding down the sidelines. If that didn't work, he could catch the ball or even throw it. He was that versatile, and fans loved him for it.

They loved his workman-like approach to how he played the game. In 13 years, he missed only two games. He was a constant — there when the Bears were miserably mediocre at best, and there in 1985 when the team rolled through the regular season and playoffs to win its first Super Bowl by 36 points. On all occasions, Payton did everything he was asked to do and did it to the apex of his abilities.

Payton usurped Jim Brown's record for most rushing yards in a career (Brown's record stood at 12,312). Payton's count was 16,726 yards, though Emmitt Smith currently leads the field with 18,355 yards. Payton also

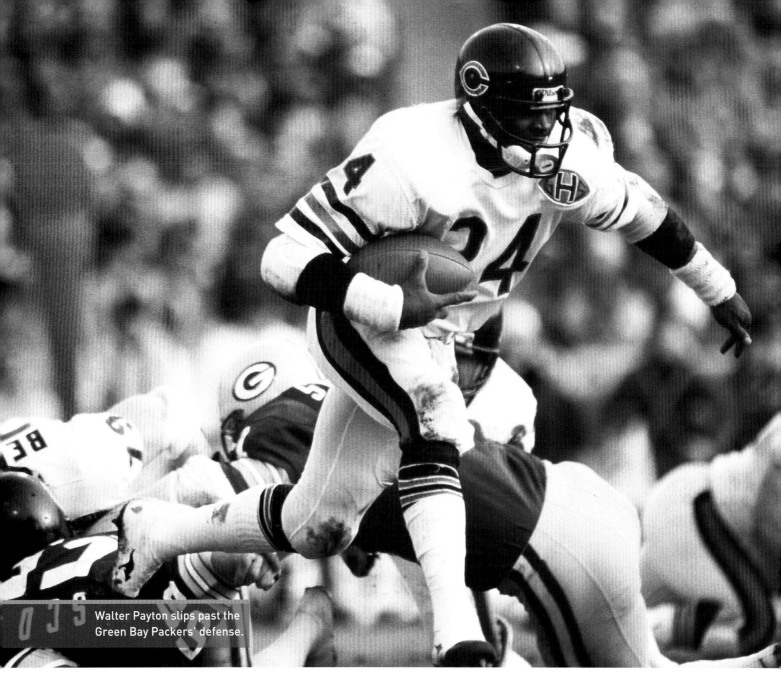

Walter Payton slips past the Green Bay Packers' defense.

held the one-game rushing record with 275 yards. That record has since been eclipsed by a handful of players, and now stands with Adrian Peterson and his 296-yard showpiece in 2007.

At 5-foot-10 and 200 pounds, Payton was not a big back, although he did have tree trunks for legs and an indomitable will. The sight of his patented high-stepping kick as he pranced away from defenders never failed to excite the home crowd. Amazingly, Payton was as good a blocker as he was a runner,

and as good a receiver as he was a blocker. He could throw the ball as a change of pace and, in a pinch, punt.

It was during his college days at Jackson State University that Payton was tagged with the nickname Sweetness — some say for his skills, others say for his personality. In 1973, as a junior, he scored a school-record 24 rushing touchdowns and was named Black College Player of the Year. He won the award again in 1974, his senior year, and finished fourth in the

Heisman Trophy balloting for the most outstanding player in NCAA football.

Selected fourth overall by the Bears in the 1975 NFL Draft, Payton's first pro game was a spectacular dud. He carried the ball eight times and gained zero yards. In the final regular-season game played that year, he had 20 carries for 134 yards. It was becoming clear that there was something unique about the young man from Jackson, Mississippi. In *The Football Book*, Paul Zimmerman of *Sports*

Illustrated recalled an astonishing feeling he had while interviewing Payton one unforgettable night. "His eyes sparkled in that half-light," Zimmerman wrote, "and I got this weird feeling there was a glow around him, that he was giving off sparks, that there was some kind of fire burning inside, lighting him up. It was the fire of pure energy."

Payton would use that burn to full advantage: he was the 1977 NFL MVP, a nine-time Pro Bowler, the 1977 Pro Bowl MVP and a 1985 Super Bowl champion with the Bears. Ten times he ran for 1,000 yards or more in a season. He caught 492 passes, too. He was also voted into several Halls of Fame, including the College and Pro Football Halls.

Typical of Payton's insatiable drive, when he eclipsed Brown's career rushing mark, he sent up a flare for all those who would follow.

"I want to set the record so high that the next person who tries for it," he said, "it's going to bust his heart."

Nothing could bust Payton's heart. Everything else might wear out, eaten away by the ravages of disease, but not the heart. That stayed strong until the end. Even at home, away from the crowd's roar, Payton remained unshakeable in his faith and commitment to his community. His name lent support to many causes, including a heightened awareness of the need for organ donors.

His name was also lent to two top football awards: the Walter Payton Man of the Year honor, which celebrates an NFL player for exceptional work both on the field and in the city where he lives, and the Walter Payton Award, which goes to the most outstanding offensive player in the NCAA Division I Football Championship Subdivision. These awards continue to bear his name.

In his final months, Payton held an emotional press conference to discuss his illness. As difficult as it was to see his once-powerful physique turn gaunt and weak, it also gave strength to those dealing with terminal illnesses. Out of his skeletal frame, an immense bravery shone brightly — a bravery beyond running between the tackles on fourth down and a yard when everyone in the stadium knows the quarterback is handing you the ball.

"Am I scared?" Walter Payton said at that press conference. "Hell, yeah, I'm scared. Wouldn't you be scared? But it's not in my hands anymore. It's in God's hands."

Nine months later, he was in God's hands.

At his memorial service, held at Soldier Field, his family and hundreds of friends turned out so they could bid farewell to a legend.

"Many of you knew my father as a football player and as a businessman," said his son Jarrett, then 18, who now runs the Jarrett Payton Foundation in support of Chicago's youth. "I knew him as my dad, and he was my hero. My mother, my sister and I will miss him, but we know he's in a place where there's no sickness, no pain."

The service lasted for more than two hours and included a moving speech from defensive tackle Dan Hampton, who was known in his time as the Danimal and was Payton's teammate for nine years.

"I've got a little girl, she's four years old," Hampton said. "Ten years from now, when she asks me about the Chicago Bears, I'll tell her about a championship. And I'll tell her about great teams and great teammates and great coaches and how great it was to be a part of."

Hampton's voice began to quaver. "But the first thing I'll tell her about is Walter Payton." ▪

He was a constant — there when the Bears were miserably mediocre at best, and there in 1985 when the team rolled through the regular season and playoffs to win its first Super Bowl by 36 points. On all occasions, Payton did everything he was asked to do and did it to the apex of his abilities.

College: Jackson State University
Drafted: 1975, Chicago Bears, 4th overall
Years active: 1975–1987
Top honors: First Team All-Pro (1976, 1977, 1980, 1984, 1985), NFL AP MVP (1977), NFL AP Offensive Player of the Year (1977), Walter Payton Man of the Year (1977), Super Bowl Champion (1985)
Hall of Fame induction: 1993

JERRY
RICE WR

G	Rec	Yds	Y/R	TD
303	1,549	22,895	14.8	197

The Best There Ever Was

J OE RICE WASN'T ONE FOR EXCUSES OR ALLOWING HIS boys a few more minutes of extra sleep.

Every summer day, at 5 a.m., he'd be up and hauling his boys out of bed so they could go to work with him.

Joe was a mason, and young Jerry's job was to catch the bricks his brothers tossed at him so he could hand them to his dad for placing. Sometimes Jerry stood on a wooden scaffold two stories high and caught bricks until his hands were calloused but sure. A typical day went to sundown in the unforgiving heat of a Mississippi July and August.

That was how it began for Jerry Rice, the greatest all-around football player of our time. Without knowing it, everything he learned and did as a child and everything he yearned to perfect as a teenager was the foundation for what he would accomplish in the NFL.

It was all laid out in Crawford, Mississippi, just like the bricks his father used to set row by row, one on top of another.

There have been hundreds of great football players over the decades, men who aspired and inspired with an equal passion. Rice was one of those who kept doing his best game after game, season after season, until he retired, and the numbers showed that he had accomplished what no other receiver or football player had ever done.

The sixth son of Joe and Eddie B., Rice didn't just set records, he etched them in granite. He didn't just outdistance his closest challengers, he humbled them. In many key offensive categories, he presides at the top, hopelessly out of reach for the next best player — as good as that player may be.

From his mind-blowing 22,895 career receiving yards (Larry Fitzgerald, next on the list, is more than 5,000 yards behind) to his 208 career touchdowns (Emmitt Smith is second with 175), to his 274 consecutive games of catching at least one pass (Art Monk is second at 183), Rice defied all coverages with seldom seen mastery.

For his efforts, he won every award that mattered — NFL Offensive Player of the Year, Super Bowl champion and Super Bowl MVP. Once, when asked to comment on his many achievements and accolades, Rice replied, "It was about the way I played the game. I played the game with a lot of determination, a lot of poise, a lot of pride and I think what you saw there ... was an individual who really just loved the game."

The love of football came to Rice early in his childhood. He and his brothers played sandlot games the way they chased the horses that ran wild in the countryside — for fun, with reckless abandon. His first taste of organized football came in 10th grade after he was caught skipping school. The story

College: Mississippi Valley State University
Drafted: 1985, San Francisco 49ers, 16th overall
Years active: 1985–2004
Top honors: NFL All-Rookie Team (1985), First Team All-Pro (1986–90, 1992–96), NFL AP Offensive Player of the Year (1987, 1993), Super Bowl Champion (1988, 1989, 1994), Super Bowl MVP (1988)
Hall of Fame induction: 2010

goes that Rice played hooky one day, only to be caught by his high school principal, Ezell Wickes. When Rice saw the principal, he took off like a frightened colt.

The next day, Rice was called into Mr. Wickes's office and strapped for his transgressions. Still, the principal was so impressed with Rice's running ability that he talked to the school's football coach, who convinced Rice to play.

Rice relied on his natural gifts and capacity for work to become an all-state receiver, but he attracted no interest from the major universities. Only one school offered him a scholarship, so he went to Mississippi Valley State, a Division 1-AA school. There, he became one of the most prolific players in the U.S. by starring in coach Archie Cooley's run-and-shoot offense that averaged more than 55 points per game in one season. It was Cooley who said of Rice, "He can catch a BB on a dead run at night."

The San Francisco 49ers were so taken by Rice's catching ability that they traded up in the 1985 draft so they could select him as a target for quarterback Joe Montana. It was a decision that paid off many times over, especially in the critical games where Rice rose to new heights — and so did his numbers.

In 1987 he caught 22 touchdown passes, a record that was broken in 2007 by Randy Moss of the New England Patriots. But here's the catch: Moss scored his 23 touchdowns in 16 games. Rice did his 22 in just 12 games (the 1987 season was shortened by a players'

As sure as the sun sets in the west, Jerry Rice could catch a football.

strike). Not only that, Rice's 22 touchdowns came off of 65 catches, which meant one of every three receptions went for a major. For good measure, Moss scored on a short run, giving him 23 touchdowns for the season.

The next season, in Super Bowl XXIII, he caught 11 passes for 215 yards and a touchdown and was named Super Bowl MVP. In Super Bowl XXIV he caught seven passes for 148 yards and scored three touchdowns. In Super Bowl XXIX he caught 10 passes for 149 yards and scored three touchdowns again, this time with a shoulder he had separated earlier in the game.

Rice never stopped working on his game. His practice regimen was legendary, and he constantly studied game film, creating drills aimed at exploiting the weaknesses in the defensive backs assigned to cover him. When Montana moved on, Rice and quarterback Steve Young kept the show rolling. When Rice left for the Oakland Raiders at age 39, he maintained a remarkable level of consistency. In his three seasons there (2001–2004), Rice averaged 79 catches for 1,078 yards and six touchdowns. As sure as the sun sets in the west, Jerry Rice could catch a football.

He joined the Seattle Seahawks four games into the 2004 season and attended the Denver Broncos' training camp in 2005 before choosing to retire. By then, the name Jerry Rice stood

Jerry Rice catches a 44-yard touchdown pass against the L.A. Rams.

for unbridled excellence. He set the bar so high it may never be cleared.

From making the hardest catches look easy to forcing himself to run more sprints because he had to be better than everyone else, Rice proved to be a hard-working stickler. He had no choice. That was the way it had to be for him, the way he was raised as the country kid who caught bricks before galloping after his ambitions with a football tucked under an arm.

In Jerry Rice, what we saw was an individual who truly loved the game and played it like no other. ■

LAWRENCE TAYLOR LB

G	Int/Yds	Sk	FR
184	9/134	132.5	11

Not Merely a
Game-Changer,
but a Sport-Changer

BEING KNOWN BY A NICKNAME IMPLIES A CERTAIN degree of fame. But instant, widespread recognition from your initials alone? That, brother, takes the cult of celebrity to a whole different level.

Such a force of nature was L.T. in his No. 56 in New York Giants blue that it wasn't uncommon to see him shed his block from the outside linebacker position so effortlessly that it looked as though he was a man among boys. He'd then explode into the backfield, drawing a bead on the QB, who might as well have had a "Sack Me!" sign taped to his jersey.

Then ... impact! Followed by the aftermath.

The Lawrence Taylor saga, so familiar to football followers, is symbolic of that age: full of controversy, suspensions, sex and self-destructive drug use. It's also overflowing with exponential impact and achievement.

Not that L.T. ever did things the easy way.

During a 1993 interview on *60 Minutes*, Taylor admitted to sending prostitutes to opponents' hotel rooms the night before games in order to tire them out. He confessed that he had used samples of teammates' urine to beat league drug tests and to being hooked on cocaine.

But if L.T. couldn't seem to get out of his own way beyond the white lines, no one seemed able to get in his way when he was on patrol between them. He is arguably the most dominant single defensive player the league has ever known.

Double-teaming Lawrence Taylor seldom worked, if ever. More than dominating his side of the ball, he actually dictated the way offenses lined up. He never felt beaten on a play. Teams were forced to make

If L.T. couldn't seem to get out of his own way beyond the white lines, no one seemed able to get in his way when he was on patrol between them.

special provisions for him. Bill Parcells called Taylor the greatest player he ever coached.

"You try to stay within the rules for the sake of the game," said Taylor one time, "but you can always turn up the intensity."

Intensity was never an issue for Lawrence Taylor. He always seemed stuck on maximum overdrive. The title of his autobiography — *LT: Over the Edge* — pretty much summed it all up. His life. His game. His persona.

Taylor and New York took a shine to each other the moment the raw but gifted linebacker was drafted out of North Carolina, second overall in 1981. (The New Orleans Saints opted for Heisman Trophy–winning running back George Rogers with the top pick. He all but fizzled after a great rookie season.)

College: University of North Carolina
Drafted: 1981, New York Giants, 2nd overall
Years active: 1981–1993
Top honors: NFL AP Defensive Rookie of the Year (1981), NFL AP Defensive Player of the Year (1981, 1982, 1986), First Team All-Pro (1981–86, 1988, 1989), NFL AP MVP (1986), Super Bowl Champion (1986, 1990)
Hall of Fame induction: 1999

Giants general manager George Young was so taken by Taylor's abilities that even before the draft, he predicted Taylor would be better than NFL legend Dick Butkus.

"Sure, I saw Dick Butkus play," Young said. "There's no doubt in my mind about Taylor. He's bigger and stronger than Butkus was. On the blitz, he's devastating."

Later, when Taylor's dominance had been established, Young would proclaim: "He is the Michael Jordan of football."

Not merely a game-changer, but a sport-changer.

"Lawrence Taylor, defensively, has had as big an impact as any player I've ever seen," said TV pundit John Madden. "He changed the way defense is played, the way pass-rushing is played, the way linebackers play and the way offenses block linebackers."

The young L.T. and his new city had much in common. Both were bigger than life, badder than bad, exhilarating, intoxicating, and infested with a wild, self-destructive streak. It was love at first sight.

Not one to ease into anything, the new kid in town proved to be an immediate sensation, being named the league's 1981 Defensive Player of the Year in his rookie season — his first of three nominations. In 1986 he upped the ante by being named NFL MVP. Only two other defensive players have been so honored. The NFL didn't start recording sacks until Taylor's second season in 1982. So if you factor in the nine and a half sacks he was unofficially credited with in his rookie year, he amassed 132.5 in

184 games — an incredible ratio.

That he lasted 13 years and was so productive, given his drug and alcohol problems, is nothing short of astounding. In a perverse way, it served to underscore what a giant talent fans in New York had been privileged to watch.

A 1988 game against the New Orleans Saints is widely remembered for personifying Taylor's almost fanatically competitive attitude. Suffering from a torn pectoral muscle, the single-minded linebacker put aside the pain and wore a sling/harness to keep his shoulder in place.

He only recorded seven tackles, three sacks and forced two fumbles that day.

The year Taylor became eligible for Hall of Fame induction (1999), debate sprang up that perhaps his bad-boy image, and all those indiscretions he so readily admitted to, should keep him out of Canton. The shrine of the game, they argued, was reserved for immortals, not immorals.

"If they don't vote me in the Hall of Fame," Taylor countered defiantly, "then they need to close that place down."

They did. And they don't.

They might have argued all day long and into the night about Lawrence Taylor's off-the-field misdeeds, but there was simply no way around all those sacks, the 10 Pro Bowls, the individual awards and two Super Bowl rings. His career, however compromised by his off-field actions, screamed out for such recognition.

No one could dispute that he had established a new standard for the linebacker position.

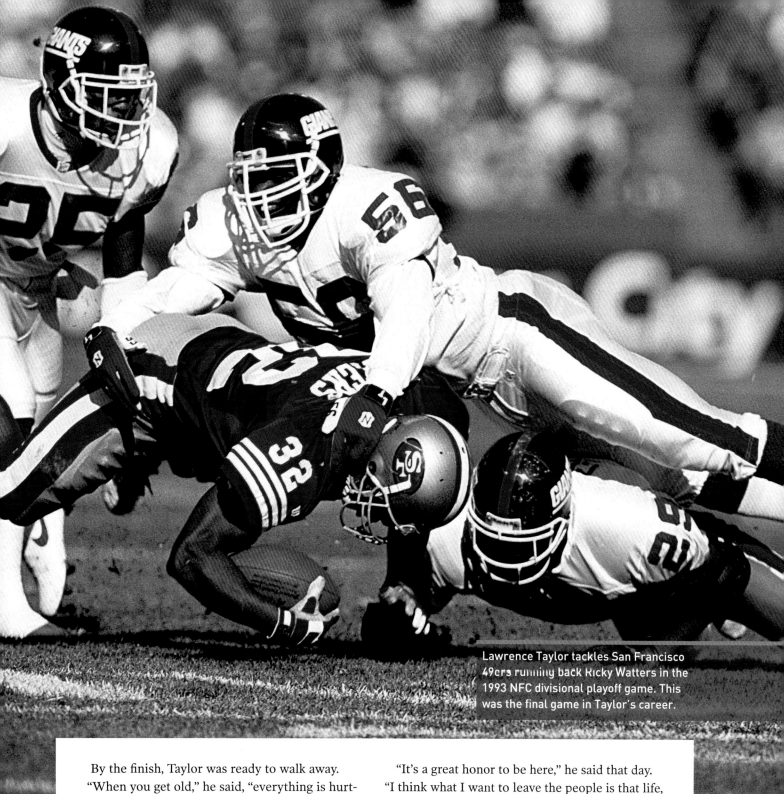

Lawrence Taylor tackles San Francisco 49ers running back Ricky Watters in the 1993 NFC divisional playoff game. This was the final game in Taylor's career.

By the finish, Taylor was ready to walk away.

"When you get old," he said, "everything is hurting. When I get up in the morning, it sounds like I'm making popcorn."

Ever the rebel, L.T., by then drug-free and living clean, arrived for his induction in Canton in 1999 decked out unconventionally in a black T-shirt under his yellow Hall of Fame sports jacket, instead of the customary shirt and tie. Oh, and he was wearing sandals. But when the time came to speak, the longtime annihilator spoke eloquently and from the heart.

"It's a great honor to be here," he said that day. "I think what I want to leave the people is that life, like anything else, can knock you down.

"You know, anybody can quit. Anybody can do that. A Hall of Famer never quits. A Hall of Famer realizes that the crime is not being knocked down. The crime is not getting up again."

Six years later Taylor looked back on the ride.

"L.T.," he mused, "died a long time ago. And I don't miss him at all.

"All that's left is Lawrence Taylor." ∎

JOHNNY UNITAS QB

G	Att	Comp	Yds	TD	Int
211	5,186	2,830	40,239	290	253

The Golden Arm

PERHAPS TIGHT END JOHN MACKEY SUMMED UP THE man and his aura best: "It's like being in the huddle with God." Johnny Unitas, the kid from the tough streets of Pittsburgh, made something of an unlikely deity.

Those sloped shoulders. Crooked legs. Shy grin. Bowed right arm from throwing so many passes. The high-topped black football boots and that trademark crew-cut. So iconic was Unitas that in one episode of *The Simpsons*, more than two decades after he had retired, grandpa Abe Simpson exclaims, "Now, Johnny Unitas ... there's a haircut you could set your watch to!"

He was, simply put, better than anyone at the position who came before him and a part of the education of any quarterback who followed. A virtual institution of higher learning: Johnny U.

Unitas arrived in Baltimore in 1956 after playing for the semi-pro Bloomington Rams. He had been earning six dollars a game, on a field strewn with rocks and shattered glass that had to be sprinkled with oil before every game to keep the dust down. He was also working as a pile driver for a construction company at the time to make ends meet.

The man dubbed Golden Arm was no stranger to hard work. He grew up in a single-parent home after his father died when he was only five years old. His mother worked two jobs to support four children. Unitas later said he learned more from her than any coach.

After a standout collegiate career at Louisville, he was famously drafted in the ninth round, but then released by the hometown Pittsburgh Steelers in 1955.

Apparently, the Steelers had too many quarterbacks to offer him a decent look. After being cut, a downcast Unitas hitchhiked home. "Unfortunately," recalled Steelers owner Dan Rooney, in one of the greatest understatements in all of sport, "we did not give him a chance." It was an oversight a city and its franchise would long lament.

Not that the Baltimore Colts were falling all over themselves to sign some kid named Johnny Unitas. The Colts coach at the time, Weeb Ewbank, recalled that an anonymous fan sent a letter to the team extolling the virtues of this lanky, rawboned quarterback. Ewbank figured "What the hell!" and offered the guy $7,000 if he stuck around. "I always accused Johnny of writing [the letter]," Ewbank would later joke.

On October 21, 1956, Johnny U tossed his first-ever NFL pass, which was picked off and run back for a touchdown. He then ran into teammate Alan Ameche on the next possession. Chicago recovered the fumble and scored. Another botched handoff later would set up yet another Bears'

College: University of Louisville
Drafted: 1955, Pittsburgh Steelers, 102nd overall
Years active: 1956–1973
Top honors: First Team All-Pro (1958, 1959, 1964, 1965, 1967), NFL Champion (1958, 1959), NFL AP MVP (1959, 1964, 1967), Walter Payton Man of the Year (1970), Super Bowl Champion (1970)
Hall of Fame induction: 1979

No one tougher, no one smarter, no one more courageous has ever played the position. Johnny Unitas defied eras.

major. Baltimore lost 58–27 that day — hardly an auspicious debut.

Undeterred, Unitas would go on to lead the Colts to three NFL championships, win three MVP awards, log 10 Pro Bowl appearances and receive five All-Pro citations, becoming the quarterback standard for decades. He would be the first man to throw for 40,000 yards in a career. His 47 consecutive games with at least one touchdown toss — a record mentioned in the same breath as DiMaggio's 56-game hitting streak or Glenn Hall's 502 consecutive games tending goal for the Chicago Black Hawks — wasn't broken until 2012, 52 years after it was set.

Johnny U helped usher in the modern, TV-dominated NFL in the so-called "greatest game ever played": the December 28, 1958, championship clash against the New York Giants at Yankee Stadium. With only 90 seconds to work, Unitas completed four passes to set up a game-tying field goal. "We've got 80 yards to go and two minutes to do it in," a teammate remembers him saying on the field to start the march. "We're going to find out what stuff we're made of." Unitas later engineered an 80-yard drive in sudden-death overtime, capped by Ameche's 1-yard touchdown plunge. Telecast live and coast-to-coast on NBC, the drama of that game ushered in a new era of mushrooming popularity for the NFL. It also

made Johnny Unitas a star. "I don't know what he uses for blood," said former quarterback Sid Gillman, "but I guarantee you it isn't warm. It's ice-cold."

Not one to brag or boast, there was still a quiet, undeniable self-belief in Unitas, felt in the huddle or when in the man's presence.

"There is a difference between conceit and confidence," Unitas once famously said. "Conceit is bragging about yourself. Confidence means you believe you can get the job done."

To today's football fanatic, the No. 19 in blue might seem something of a relic from a bygone time: the short, slipped steps of a pure old-time pocket passer. Don't be fooled, though. No one tougher, no one smarter, no one more courageous has ever played the position. Johnny Unitas defied eras.

He also defied medical logic. There's something heroic, even romantic, about those who suffer for their art. And Unitas suffered. This was a man as tough as tungsten, just like his hometown. Broken ribs. Punctured lung. Shoulder contusions. Knee surgeries. He ripped a tendon in his right arm almost off the bone and missed most of the 1968 season. He ruptured the Achilles in his right foot playing paddleball with teammate Tom Matte at a YMCA in April 1971 and was supposed to be sidelined for six months.

Johnny Unitas sets for play in a game against the Oakland Raiders.

He made it back in half the time. "What made him the greatest quarterback of all time wasn't his arm or his size, it was what was inside his stomach," said former Giants general manager Ernie Accorsi, who worked with Unitas during his final years in Baltimore.

And defiant? You didn't screw with Johnny U.

"A guy broke through the line, hit him, pushed his head in the ground," recalled teammate Bubba Smith. "He called the same play, let the guy come through and broke his nose with the football.

"I said: 'That's my hero.'"

Johnny Unitas retired in 1973, holding 22 records at the time ("I could have played for two or three more years. All I needed was a leg transplant," he joked at the time). He'd completed 2,830 passes for 40,239 yards and 290 touchdowns. He was voted into the Pro Football Hall of Fame six years later. In 1999 *Sports Illustrated* voted him the fifth-best player of all time, second among quarterbacks only to Joe Montana. But the old-timers — those who'd been there, seen it all unfold and remembered — knew

better. On September 11, 2002, while working out, Johnny Unitas died of a heart attack at the age of 69. Baltimore mourned. A nation that had become obsessed with the game, a game he helped reinvent and popularize, stopped to pay tribute.

"IIe couldn't throw a screen pass like Y.A. Tittle. He couldn't run like Fran Tarkenton. He couldn't throw like Sonny Jurgensen. He was a sickly-looking guy," Hall of Fame linebacker Sam Huff said in tribute. "But John, he was the general. He was absolutely awesome under pressure." ■

REGGIE
WHITE DE/DT

G	Int/Yds	Tkl	Sk	FF	FR
232	3/79	1,111	198	33	20

Sundays, Sacks and Service

THE GREEN BAY PACKERS OF 1993 KNEW THEY NEEDED an upgrade: a player with talent and character, a leader on defense who could incite his teammates. Packers head coach Mike Holmgren knew exactly who could provide that — Reggie White, the 6-foot-5, 300-pound Baptist minister who lived like a saint but played like a demon.

With White ready to leave the Philadelphia Eagles, the Packers believed they could sign the veteran pass rusher as a free agent. They had no connections to White, but Holmgren figured it was worth a try. So, on a whim, he called White and left him a message.

"I said, 'Reggie, this is God. I want you to play in Green Bay.' Then I hung up," recalled Holmgren. "Fortunately, he had a good sense of humor. He recognized my voice and we were able to sign him."

Four years after joining the Pack, White helped Green Bay to a pair of Super Bowl appearances, earning a championship ring for beating the New England Patriots in Super Bowl XXXI. The victory reaffirmed White's reputation as the Minister of Defense, one of the premier defensive linemen of his time, with only the Buffalo Bills' Bruce Smith providing a real comparison.

On his first try at retirement, White lasted a year and then made a comeback with the Carolina Panthers. On his second retirement bid, he knew it was permanent. He set about doing his ministerial work to benefit the less fortunate, and he was making good things happen. Four years after his departure from the field came the news that shook the football world — on December 26, 2004, Reginald Howard White was found dead in

Reggie White pressures the quarterback in a September 1993 game against the Philadelphia Eagles.

his home in Cornelius, North Carolina. Cause of death: cardiac arrhythmia. He was 43.

People figured there wasn't anyone or anything that could slow White down, much less stop him from reaching the quarterback, from strapping on his pads (no matter how banged up his body might be) or from voicing his opinion on a wide range of subjects, however controversial.

"He may have been the best player I've ever seen," said Packers quarterback Brett Favre in tribute. "Certainly, he was the best I've ever played with or against."

Those sentiments were echoed throughout the NFL. Quarterback Rick Mirer, another former teammate (and later opponent), remembered his dealings with White: "I had the pleasure of getting hit by him several times. The way he just threw around 300-pound guys, I've never seen anyone do that. He was just head and shoulders above anybody else I saw. He just ... dominated."

Overall, the list of the Minister's sack victims is extensive. Seventy-five different quarterbacks felt his wrath. Phil Simms, the one-time New York Giants star, was dropped a record 15 times by

For doing his job so thoroughly, White generated a degree of fearful respect among opposing players. Intimidation was something he worked on.

White; Neil Lomax was dropped 13. Over the years White hunted down the great ones, from Troy Aikman (7 times) and John Elway (5.5) to Dan Marino (2), along with the likes of Danny Kanell and Blair Kiel — two players whose main claim to NFL fame is that they made it onto Reggie's list.

White finished his 15-year NFL career with 198 quarterback sacks. Add in the 23.5 he recorded during his two years with the USFL's Memphis Showboats, and White's sack count rises to 221.5. Smith holds the NFL record with 200, in part because he ended up playing four more seasons than White.

For doing his job so thoroughly, White generated a degree of fearful respect among opposing players. Intimidation was something he worked on.

"When I'm on the field, I want to do my best to intimidate the guy in front of me. I want to do my best to have him intimidated before I play him," White explained. "That means this week I have to play a good enough game so [his next opponent] will have a look at it [on tape] and say, 'Oh man, look what he did to him.'"

Ordained an Evangelical minister, White was a personal and professional contradiction to many. The relentless sack master between the lines was a gentle, peaceful man off the field. Never afraid to voice an opinion or to underline his

conviction, White angered and upset many with his outspoken, fundamentalist views on homosexuality. He was accused of being archaic and hate-mongering.

"God," he said once, "places the heaviest burden on those who can carry its weight."

White could carry plenty, which is what made his death so hard to accept. He had, in life, seemed something close to invincible. In his chosen profession, he remains unmatched. In 1999 *Sporting News* ranked him 22nd on its list of the 100 Greatest Football Players. In 2005 three teams — the University of Tennessee, the Eagles and the Packers — all retired White's famous No. 92. Rightly so, given how many numbers he put in the record books.

His nine consecutive seasons with at least 10 sacks remains an NFL record. Twice he was named the league's Defensive Player of the Year. He was also selected to 13 consecutive Pro Bowls and named to the NFL's All-Time team roster in the league's 100th season.

At his Hall of Fame induction ceremony at Canton in 2006, White's wife, Sara, and son, Jeremy, delivered the acceptance speech for a husband, a father, a minister and a football player. Jeremy, echoing the feelings of so many there that day, said: "Reggie will be remembered by some as the man who sacked quarterbacks on

Sundays ... But to others, he will be remembered for his faith in God. And yet to others he will be remembered as a father, a friend and a husband. Even though Reggie is not here to receive this great honor the NFL has allowed him to receive, I know he is with us. He is with us in spirit, but most of all he is with us in our memories. As long as we continue to remember anyone we have lost, they are never completely gone. They are with us."

For Favre, it will be the funny memories that will stay in his mind for as long as he lives.

One happened during a preseason practice. A young offensive lineman, Mirko Jurkovic, grabbed White by the jersey and hauled him down. White told Jurkovic to quit the holding, and the upstart rookie shouted back, "Hey, f— you, Reggie."

Favre recalled what happened after: "Reggie digs in, you know, and then 'set, hut.' And he clubbed Mirko, and it was a domino effect, and all five guys [offensive linemen] just fell down ... And Reggie says, 'God loves you, Mirko. But don't ever hold me again.'" ∎

College: University of Tennessee
Drafted: 1984 (Supplemental Draft), Philadelphia Eagles, 4th overall
Years active: 1985–2000
Top honors: First Team All-Pro (1986–91, 1995, 1998), NFL AP Defensive Player of the Year (1987, 1998), Super Bowl Champion (1996)
Hall of Fame induction: 2006

Offensive Icons

DAVANTE
ADAMS WR

G	Rec	Yds	TD
116	669	8,121	73

THIS ABOUT SAYS IT ALL. CHAD JOHNSON, THE receiving artist formerly known as Ochocinco, took one look at the video of Davante Adams running his practice routes, saw him take apart his defensive teammates with a diamond cutter's precision, and it was simply too much for Johnson to bear.

So he cried. Tears of admiration. Then he posted his reaction on social media so everyone could appreciate the beauty in the details he had watched.

That was just before the start of the 2019 NFL season, back when even the Green Bay Packers weren't 100 percent certain about Adams — was he a fragile soul troubled by injuries and a bad case of the dropsies or a player on the brink of superstardom? In 2018, he had notched 111 catches for 1,386 yards and 13 touchdowns. Yet he slid backward in 2019 with another injury that cost him four games, thereby limiting him to 83 catches, 997 yards and five touchdowns.

It was the last time Adams would let any doubts get the better of him.

In 2020, in only 14 games, he made history by totaling 115 receptions and 18 touchdowns, two numbers that had never been paired by the same receiver in the same season. And it wasn't just the enormity of the statistics he posted that announced his ascension, it was how he fashioned them, how quickly he could leave defensive backs beaten and bewildered, over and over again.

"He's really quick. He doesn't have any wasted moves in his releases," said Washington Football Team receiver Terry McLaurin. "It's almost like [he's] unguardable."

He was for Los Angeles Rams cornerback Jalen Ramsey in the 2021 playoffs. Of the several key grabs

Adams made that day, his most damaging came when his pre-snap motion took him from one end of the offensive line to the other and back to where he started. Locked into man-to-man coverage, Ramsey followed Adams there and back but had to avoid running into his own players. That left Adams unguarded for a Green Bay touchdown and Ramsey yelling at his teammates.

"That's definitely what you want," recalled Adams. "You want to see guys turn on each other or not communicate in situations like that because you can see it starts to mess with them."

Adams didn't have the entrance he wanted in the NFL. After a sensational career with the Fresno State Bulldogs, where he gained 3,030 yards and scored 38 touchdowns in just two seasons, he declared his eligibility for the 2014 NFL Draft and waited for his name to be called. In the second round, with the 59th pick, after eight receivers had already been selected, Adams was claimed by the Packers. [Of those eight, only four, including Odell Beckham Jr. and Mike Evans, were on an NFL roster at the end of the 2021 regular season.]

Adams' first year was hopeful but at times lackluster. In the Packers' receiving corps, he ranked third behind Jordy Nelson and Randall Cobb, which meant he wasn't a go-to guy for quarterback Aaron Rodgers. That relationship took time and needed to be built on trust.

On that road to bonding, Adams had some stumbles; he injured an ankle and a knee and wasn't always effective. In his sophomore season, he scored just one touchdown. He vowed to better prepare himself for the 2016 season. His workouts earned him the unofficial title as the Packers' off-season MVP. And he began to

Davante Adams makes a catch during an NFL Divisional Round playoff game on January 22, 2022.

carve out a reputation for doing all the little things right in his quest for greatness.

Rodgers took notice and began throwing more passes to Adams. By 2019, Rodgers to Adams was a Green Bay staple and the best quarterback/receiver duo in the league. They operated on a higher plane, often communicating by a look or a nod or a simple hand gesture. As Rodgers explained it, there were the plays put down on paper and the plays that Adams ad-libbed on the fly.

Rodgers learned to trust his receiver, who had a skill for coming off the line of scrimmage and instantly gaining separation from his defender. Adams would take a

hop step and then cut one way like a basketball player doing a crossover dribble. He'd then run his pass route with smooth efficiency before snatching the ball with a set of hands that had been cured of their unreliability.

All of that was on display in a 2020 game against the Philadelphia Eagles, when Adams scored on a 9-yard pass. The touchdown toss was the 400th of Rodgers' career. In splendid symmetry, it was the rookie Adams who had caught Rodgers' 200th touchdown pass. It was also the first touchdown of Adams' career.

The Rodgers-Adams partnership was dissolved early in the 2022 free-agency period when the

quarterback signed a $150 million contract extension that left the Packers receiver short on his financial wants. Green Bay then traded Adams to the Las Vegas Raiders for a pair of draft picks. The deal reunited Adams with Raiders pivot Derek Carr. The two had been teammates at Fresno State for two years. ■

College: Fresno State
Drafted: 2014, Green Bay Packers, 53rd overall
Years active: 2014–present
Top honors: First Team All-Pro (2020, 2021)
Hall of Fame induction: N/A

TROY
AIKMAN QB

G	Att	Comp	Yds	TD	Int
165	4,715	2,898	32,942	165	141

"**A** USPICIOUS" WAS HARDLY THE BEST WORD TO DESCRIBE Troy Aikman's NFL baptism. "Promising" and "assuring" didn't make the cut, either.

As the Dallas Cowboys surveyed the wreckage of their 1989 season, the prospect of a Hall of Fame career for their rookie quarterback — three Super Bowl rings, half a dozen Pro Bowl appearances and more wins throughout the '90s than any other quarterback — seemed laughable.

Aikman, the boy wonder No. 1 pick from the UCLA Bruins, had lost his first 11 games as a Dallas starter. The 'Boys flatlined to 1-15 that year under a new coach, Jimmy Johnson, who had controversially replaced the celebrated Tom Landry.

The smell of doom hovered over Big D like the stench from an abattoir.

"I know how difficult my rookie year in the NFL was," Aikman said years later, "and I know how competitive the sport is."

But those who wrote off the Cowboys after the horrors of '89 underestimated the ambition of owner Jerry Jones, the savvy of coach Jimmy Johnson and, most foolishly, Troy Aikman.

In 1990, ignoring the naysayers, Aikman brought the Cowboys back to respectability and into playoff contention. The next season, despite being injured, he bounced back to start an NFC Divisional postseason game. The Cowboys were beaten 38–6 by the Detroit Lions that day. But the seed of onrushing success had been planted in Irving, Texas.

The golden years of Troy Aikman began in 1992, when the 'Boys won 13 games in the regular season and ran the table come playoff time, brutalizing the Buffalo Bills 52–17 in Super Bowl XXVII in 1993.

The quarterback that the critics had so openly questioned only three years earlier passed for 273 yards and four touchdowns en route to being named the game's most valuable player. No one would ever doubt Aikman again.

Consistency would become his trademark, and he'd retire with a completion percentage of 61.5, the third-highest career figure in history at the time, behind only Steve Young and Joe Montana. He may never have put up the same kinds of passing yardage numbers as, say, Dan Marino. But then Marino never had a running back like Emmitt Smith to hand the ball to.

For Aikman, running the show, not being the show, was always the priority.

There would be still more Super Bowl glory: in 1994 against the beleaguered Bills again, 30–13, and a 27–17 decision over Pittsburgh in 1996.

By now, Aikman was the toast of Dallas. He exuded a folksy charm. It was impossible not to warm to the man. When asked about being selected as one of *People* magazine's 50 Most Beautiful People, for instance, he was typically self-deprecating: "I thought, 'Well, they don't know that many people.'"

During his final seasons, Aikman absorbed a ferocious physical pounding. In December 2000, while rolling out to throw a pass, Washington linebacker LaVar Arrington drilled the unsuspecting quarterback. That jolt triggered Aikman's 10th concussion, and it would be his final NFL play.

The hit left a dent in his helmet. Its aftermath left a hole in his heart.

Troy Aikman sets to pass.

Still wanting to play but unable to find a team to take a chance on someone who had given so much at such great personal cost, Aikman retired the next year.

He left behind him a decade of excellence: 90 wins (the most, to that point, by any QB in a ten-year span), six consecutive Pro Bowl appearances and a place on the Cowboys' Ring of Honor alongside his buddies in the famed Triplets offensive set-up: Emmitt Smith and receiver Michael Irvin.

"In my mind," said Jimmy Johnson, "I always judge a quarterback by how he plays in the big games. How does he perform in the playoffs? Troy Aikman always came up big in the big games."

On February 4, 2006, Aikman took his place in the Pro Football Hall of Fame. Standing at the podium during the induction ceremony, his thoughts must've drifted back to that first season.

"I'd like to share something that a close friend used to tell me back when I was playing," he told the audience. "When times are tough — maybe we'd lost a close game, I'd thrown the deciding interception or the grind and the rigors of the season were beginning to take their toll on me — he would say this: 'Sometimes we have to remind ourselves that these are jobs we've always dreamed of having.'

"For as long as I can remember, all I ever wanted to do was play pro sports. A lot of kids want that, but only a few actually get there. I was able to live a dream. I played pro football."

College: University of California, Los Angeles
Drafted: 1989, Dallas Cowboys, 1st overall
Years active: 1989–2000
Top honors: NFL All-Rookie Team (1989), Super Bowl Champion (1992, 1993, 1996), Super Bowl MVP (1992), NFL Walter Payton Man of the Year (1997)
Hall of Fame induction: 2006

MARCUS
ALLEN RB

G	Att	Yds	Avg	TD
222	3,022	12,243	4.1	123

THERE ISN'T MUCH THAT MARCUS ALLEN DIDN'T win in football. A California high school championship with him scoring five touchdowns in a 34–6 final? Did that. An NCAA national championship with the University of Southern California, plus the Heisman Trophy for being the most outstanding player in collegiate football? Did that, kept the jersey.

What about an NFL Rookie of the Year award, the NFL MVP award, winning the Super Bowl and being named Super Bowl MVP? Yup, those too. And then, when all was said and done, there was being named to the College Football Hall of Fame as well as the Pro Football Hall of Fame.

Is achieving all that even possible?

Yes, it is. And here's the thing: Allen could have done more if only he hadn't been stapled to the bench and given less playing time than he had early in his career.

It's strange to say, but for all he accomplished with the Los Angeles Raiders, Allen once found himself listed as the team's fourth-string running back. He was either a blocker or a back-up to the likes of Bo Jackson, Eric Dickerson and Roger Craig. Him, Marcus Allen, the first player to enter the Pro Football Hall of Fame having gained more than 10,000 yards rushing and 5,000 receiving.

The irony of Allen's rise and fall with the Raiders is that it involved the same person — the almost all-powerful, certainly all-paranoid owner and general manager Al Davis, he of the oil-spill hairdo and Terminator sunglasses, who tormented every NFL commissioner who held office while he moved his team up and down Interstate 5 in California.

Big Al was in court the day of the 1982 NFL Draft, monitoring the Raiders' plan to relocate to Los Angeles from Oakland. Holding the 10th pick overall, the team had its choice of running backs: Darrin Nelson, Gerald Riggs, Walter Abercrombie, Barry Redden and Allen. The Raiders' scouting staff chose Allen as the best of the bunch.

"Is that what you guys want?" Davis reportedly said. "Fine."

Allen turned in a rookie performance that was sweeter than fine. In the strike-shortened 1982 season, where teams played a nine-game schedule and then went to the postseason, the Raiders watched their first-year tailback rush for a league-leading 697 yards and 11 touchdowns. It was the start of a beautiful friendship; it just didn't last long.

"I think [Davis] tried to ruin the latter part of my career, tried to devalue me," said Allen. "He's trying to stop me from going into the Hall of Fame. They don't want me to play."

Based on Allen's accomplishments, it was hard to fathom Davis benching the runner who posted a then-record 74-yard touchdown run as part of the Raiders' 38–9 victory over the Washington Redskins in Super Bowl XVIII. (Allen finished with 209 yards of total offense and was named MVP.) Allen's touchdown is still considered one of the most memorable in Super Bowl lore.

Five years later in a 1989 regular-season game against the Arizona Cardinals, the Raiders' assistant coaches were told not to play Allen. Terry Robiskie took his headset off so that he wouldn't hear Davis or anyone else yelling in his ear. Then Robiskie put Allen in the game with the Raiders at the Arizona 4-yard line. Allen took the handoff and soared over a pile-up of 300-pound linemen right into the end zone for the winning touchdown.

Allen said that after the game Davis "gave me a dirty look." It was the measure of his distaste for Allen that Davis would rephrase the Raiders' mission statement to "Just lose, baby."

When Allen couldn't work out a contract with the Raiders, Davis called his former franchise running

There isn't much that Marcus Allen didn't win in football.

back "a cancer to the team." Allen took the hits, but let it be known he wanted out. So it was that in 1993, the face of Raider Nation became a key component in the Kansas City Chiefs attack, right alongside former San Francisco 49ers quarterback Joe Montana.

Allen rediscovered his love for the game while playing for Kansas City. Six years later, he was named to the Pro Football Hall of Fame. Davis attended, sitting onstage and supposedly offering some weak applause. In his acceptance speech Allen thanked "Mr. Davis for drafting me ..." then moved on.

In the fall of 2011 Davis was found dead in his room at the Hilton Oakland Airport Hotel. He had suffered a massive heart attack at age 82. The football world mourned the passing of the game's last rebel. Team officials contacted Allen, asking him if he'd light the memorial fire in tribute to Davis.

Allen accepted. It was the end of era. ■

College: University of Southern California
Drafted: 1982, Los Angeles Raiders, 10th overall
Years active: 1982–1997
Top honors: NFL All-Rookie Team (1982), NFL AP Offensive Rookie of the Year (1982), First Team All-Pro (1982, 1985), Super Bowl Champion (1983), Super Bowl MVP (1983), NFL AP Offensive Player of the Year (1985), NFL AP MVP (1985)
Hall of Fame induction: 2003

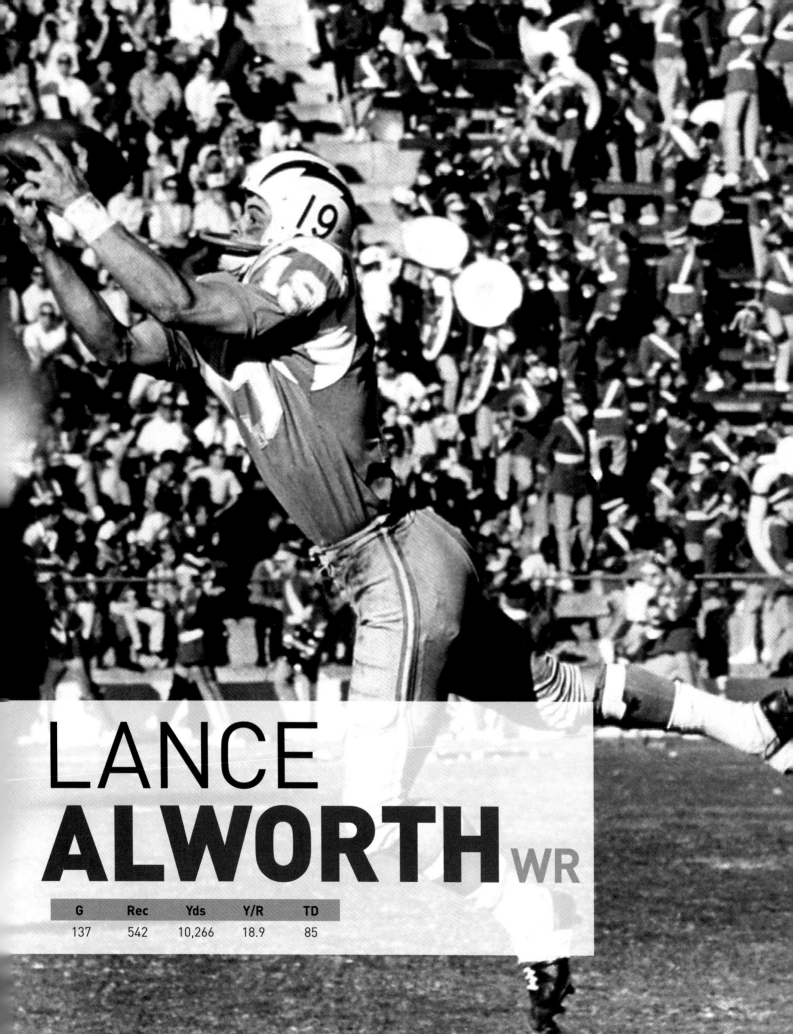

LANCE
ALWORTH WR

G	Rec	Yds	Y/R	TD
137	542	10,266	18.9	85

IT WAS HIS EYES, THEY SAID. THEY were big and brown and quick to see all. It was the way he ran, they added. With speed and agility.

"He could leap like a deer," said San Diego Chargers teammate Ron Mix. "Boing! Boing!"

And just like that, the extraordinary receiver for the American Football League's San Diego Chargers became known as Bambi.

"He could literally leap like a deer," insisted Mix. "It was unbelievable."

Possessed of an almost balletic stride, great leaping skills, sure hands and an ability to cover 100 yards in 9.6 seconds, Alworth would leave an indelible mark on the game through 11 seasons.

At 6 feet tall and weighing 184 pounds, he may have been undersized to play receiver, but Alworth was the perfect complement to Chargers quarterback John Hadl. They formed one of the great collaborations of their time (the 1960s into the 1970s) or any time.

Al Davis, then a Chargers assistant coach, saw Alworth play for the University of Arkansas and coaxed him into signing with the AFL club in 1962 rather than the NFL San Francisco 49ers. He knew full well San Diego had landed more than just a great receiver.

"Lance Alworth was one of the maybe three players in my lifetime who had what I call 'It,'" said Davis in 1978. "You could see right from the start that he was going to be a superstar."

Fitting perfectly into the West Coast sun-and-surf lifestyle, Alworth flourished. His talents were undeniable to everyone except his father Richard, who always pushed his son to do more and be better. Even to those who openly

mocked the AFL's overall quality, Alworth was as electrifying as that lightning bolt on the sides of his helmet; he came to symbolize the San Diego franchise and even the offense-first AFL itself.

Alworth helped San Diego win an AFL title in 1963, hooking up with Tobin Rote on a 48-yard touchdown pass to slay the Boston Patriots. He caught at least one pass in 96 consecutive games and still holds the record for most games (five) with 200 or more yards receiving.

Alworth apparently never did like the nickname Bambi, but even he had to admit that Chargers fullback Charlie Flowers caught the essence of his style when he tagged him with the famous moniker.

"He looked like a kid of 15," said Flowers. "He had real short hair and brown eyes. And he reminded me of a graceful deer when he ran."

Oh, he ran. He ran and ran, running superb routes past opposing secondaries. It seemed as if he never stopped. There was an uninhibited freedom about the way that Alworth flew down a field that caught people's imaginations. Add that to the elegance and the incomparable grace, and his star quality would be hard to overemphasize.

It'd be difficult to argue that Alworth wasn't the best receiver in all of pro football in 1965. That season, Alworth caught 69 passes for 1,602 yards and 14 touchdowns, averaging an astounding 23.2 yards a catch. There were fireworks ready to go off whenever Hadl dropped back to pass and Alworth made his move.

Bambi finished out the final two seasons of his career in Dallas. He won a championship ring there, catching the first touchdown pass in

the Cowboys' 24–3 conquest of the Miami Dolphins in Super Bowl VI.

Over those two seasons in Big D, however, Alworth only latched onto 49 passes and wasn't particularly enthralled with the way coach Tom Landry deployed him. He decided to retire and did so on top. He left on his own terms, with the admiration of his peers, having given more than a decade of keepsake catches to fans of two leagues.

Naturally there were honors aplenty to come. Alworth was enshrined in the Breitbard Hall of Fame at the San Diego Hall of Champions Sports Museum, and his No. 19 became the second number ever retired by the Chargers. To this day, he remains one of the most popular Bolts of all time.

Six years after walking away from the game, Alworth was inducted at Canton, the first player from the renegade league so honored by the football establishment. But his heart — his legacy — lay in California, not Ohio.

"This is about as good as it gets," he said about the day of honors bestowed on him in San Diego. "It's a humbling experience. Being inducted into the Hall of Fame was special, but being honored at home means even more."

Lance "Bambi" Alworth: forever a Charger.

College: University of Arkansas
Drafted: 1962, San Francisco 49ers, 8th overall
Years active: 1962–1972
Top honors: AFL First Team All-Pro (1963–68), Super Bowl Champion (1971)
Hall of Fame induction: 1978

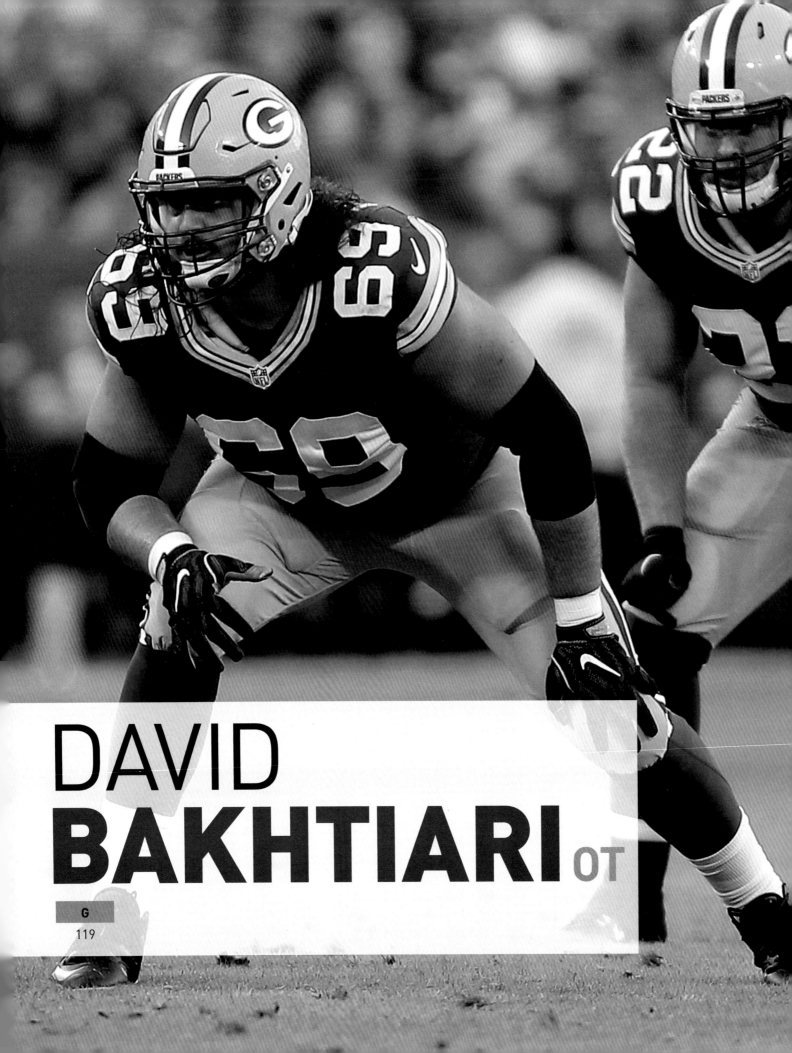

DAVID
BAKHTIARI OT

G

119

HIS NAME IS DAVID AFRASIAB Assad Bakhtiari, but it's easier to call him by his nom de football, Mr. Consistency. Game in, game out, season after season, he is the standard by which all NFL offensive tackles are measured. Proof of that was abundantly clear in 2020.

It was calculated that in the 758 offensive plays he participated in for the Green Bay Packers, Bakhtiari was penalized only four times and allowed just one sack. A Secret Service detail couldn't have offered quarterback Aaron Rodgers better protection, considering he threw 526 times, completed 70.7 percent of his throws, gained 4,299 yards and rang up 48 touchdowns.

Rodgers couldn't have reached those numbers without Bakhtiari playing on the left side, covering the quarterback's blind side.

"I think he has Hall of Fame potential," said Rodgers of Bakhtiari in 2018. "He's an incredible player. He's been a rock for us. When he's over there, you really feel comfortable with him locking down pass rushers throughout the game."

Since his first start in the 2013 NFL preseason, the 6-foot-4, 310-pound Bakhtiari has played with a reliability beyond his years. His peers say he has wonderful footwork, has put out a lot of effort in the weight room and has developed more strength and stamina as he's grown into his position. That drew the mightiest mention anyone in Wisconsin could come up with when in 2018 Bakhtiari became the first Green Bay offensive tackle in more than 50 years, since the legendary Forrest Gregg, to be chosen as a First Team All-Pro. Yes, we're referring to that Forrest Gregg, dubbed by the immortal Vince Lombardi as the

finest player he had ever coached — and Gregg was a right tackle.

Bakhtiari has taken advantage of every situation he's been afforded. At his high school in San Mateo, the California-born son of Persian and Icelandic descent was able to excite the college scouts who had heard of this left tackle who could carry a run offense on his back. That got the teenager a scholarship at the University of Colorado, where Bakhtiari continued his football education.

After bypassing his senior year at Colorado, Bakhtiari declared himself eligible for the 2013 NFL Draft. He was rated a late-second to third-round pick. Things played out as expected in a draft where offensive tackles were plentiful and good. Three were chosen in the first four picks, with the Kansas City Chiefs taking Eric Fisher first overall.

When Bakhtiari's name was finally called, it was the fourth round and he went to Green Bay as the 109th player taken overall. Eight other tackles had been taken before him. Even some of the Packers' scouts and personnel people weren't sure about what they had just drafted. The majority questioned Bakhtiari's style as a finesse blocker, suggesting that he was soft and wasn't strong enough to fire off the line on a run block and pancake his rival. (*Pancake* is a term used when a blocker knocks a defender on his back, leaving him flatter than a plate of waffles.)

Bakhtiari spoke with his parents concerning his future plans and also had talks with his brother, Eric, who had been a linebacker with the Tennessee Titans and San Francisco 49ers. The younger brother took the advice to heart and had a powerful showing at his first pro training camp.

Then fate entered the equation. Bryan Bulaga had been Green Bay's starter at left tackle, but a hip fracture cost him seven games in 2012 and a torn knee ligament all of 2013. That allowed Bakhtiari to move in on the left side of the Packers' offensive line. He got so comfortable that he took over the starting position there. (As for Bulaga, he was moved to right tackle and found his home there.)

It didn't take long for the Packers to realize their rookie left tackle had the stuff they were looking for. Former Green Bay defensive end Mike Daniels had his concerns put to rest on Day 1 of that 2013 training camp.

"The first day I did go against him and he rolled me back about six yards," said Daniels. "He's a long guy. Strong kid. You can tell he's been well-coached ... He's got that real nice, cool personality, but when he gets on the field he turns into a psychopath."

A very rich psychopath. On November 15, 2020, the Packers made Bakhtiari the highest-paid offensive lineman in NFL history with a four-year contract extension worth $105.5 million. Little more than a month after that, he blew out his ACL and was done for the rest of the season. Knowing how hard he rehabilitated himself in the weight room, Pro Football Focus rated Bakhtiari the top offensive tackle heading into the 2021 season. ■

College: University of Colorado
Drafted: 2013, Green Bay Packers, 109th overall
Years active: 2013–present
Top honors: First Team All-Pro (2018, 2020)
Hall of Fame induction: N/A

ODELL
BECKHAM JR. WR

G	Rec	Yds	Y/R	TD
96	531	7,367	13.9	56

H E HAS ALWAYS HAD A STYLISH LOOK, FROM THE VARIED haircuts and colors to his Zeus-like beard, but there's as much grit to Odell Beckham Jr. as there is glam. You don't become one of the top receivers in the NFL without a willingness to take a hit to make a play.

And you don't keep proving yourself a top receiver if you don't overcome your injuries. OBJ has done that as well as anyone who has ever caught a football for a living.

In his first three seasons with the New York Giants, the mercurial Beckham took his smacks and maximized his skills to surpass 200 catches and 4,000 yards faster than anyone in NFL history. Then he fractured an ankle. Then in March of 2019 he was traded to Cleveland in a multiplayer exchange that included the Browns' first- and third-round draft picks. It was a monumental deal that went to pieces the following season when Beckham's left knee imploded.

He worked his way back into the starting lineup only to feel underused and underappreciated. He responded by forcing his release from the Browns so he could sign with the Los Angeles Rams. That's where he experienced his greatest high and his most crushing low, both occurring on the same day, in no less a game than Super Bowl LVI.

In the first half, Beckham caught a 17-yard pass from quarterback Matthew Stafford to score the Rams' first touchdown against the Cincinnati Bengals. He added a 35-yard gain shortly after and was targeted for a third completion when he suddenly grabbed his knee – again, the left one - and dropped to the turf.

The Rams' medical staff assessed the damage as a torn ACL. The only thing Beckham could do in the second half was cheer for his teammates. The 24-10 win gave Beckham his first NFL championship and another rehabilitation for those who would doubt his future.

"There was a moment I was in the back room and they told me I was done, I couldn't play," Beckham told CBS after the game. "I had to come back out there (on the L.A. sideline) and be a part of this because this is so much bigger than myself. And these boys pulled through."

Beckham built a reputation for making the right play at the right time after being drafted out of Louisiana State University by the Giants. In a Sunday night game against Dallas, Beckham put the NFL on notice with one play, a backward-leaping, gravity-defying, three-fingered touchdown catch while being interfered with by Cowboys' cornerback Brandon Carr. It was a reception with an unbelievably high degree of difficulty, a very big deal. And it prompted the "catch-it-like Beckham" catch phrase that had rival defensive backs cringing.

Beckham didn't stop there. He had circus grabs against the Atlanta Falcons, Carolina Panthers, New York Jets, San Francisco 49ers. He set a Giants' rookie record by catching 91 passes for 1,305 yards and 12 touchdowns — and he did it in 12 games. The Pro Football Writers Association voted him the Rookie of the Year, and the NFL awarded him Offensive Rookie of the Year. The NFL also dubbed Beckham's iconic catch the 2014 Offensive Play of the Year.

Normally Beckham has vice grips for hands, but in 2015 he botched a sure touchdown pass against Carolina and its top cornerback Josh Norman. That set the tone for the rest of the afternoon. A hot-headed Beckham

Odell Beckham Jr. reaches to grab the ball in a November 2018 game versus the San Francisco 49ers.

threw punches at Norman, who was equally angry and punched back. They took turns battering one another with Beckham delivering a nasty helmet-to-helmet head shot. The NFL suspended Beckham for one game and fined Norman. Beckham was forced to sit out a one-sided defeat against the Minnesota Vikings and was not allowed to enter the Giants' practice facility when he came to gather some of his belongings. "All you can do is learn from it," he said. "You can't go back."

The Giants signed Beckham to a five-year, $95 million contract extension and announced they didn't do that to trade him. A year later, they did just that, dispatching him to Cleveland, where he had next to no on-field chemistry with quarterback Baker Mayfield. The one highlight was an 89-yard catch and run against the New York Jets in his return to MetLife Stadium, where the Giants also play their home games. The rest of the time was like the six-game stretch OBJ muddled through in 2021 when he averaged 2.8 receptions and 38.7 yards per outing. Piddling stuff.

With a knee that has now failed him twice in three years, it's a distinct possibility Beckham will never again be as good as he once was. The cautionary note worth mentioning is that every time he has been felled by injury, he has willed his way back. A different player, for sure. But one you can't afford to ignore. ◼

College: Louisiana State University
Drafted: 2014, New York Giants, 12th overall
Years active: 2014–present
Top honors: NFL AP Offensive Rookie of the Year (2014), NFL All-Rookie Team (2014), Super Bowl champion (2022)
Hall of Fame induction: N/A

TERRY
BRADSHAW QB

G	Att	Comp	Yds	TD	Int
168	3,901	2,025	27,989	212	210

DON'T LET THAT FOLKSY CHARM AND THE GOOD-OL'-BOY demeanor con you for an instant. The Smokey and the Bandit schtick that he has transformed almost into an art form on Fox NFL Sunday broadcasts is part Terry, surely.

But the kid from Shreveport, Louisiana, was — and is — nobody's fool.

In his day, his Pittsburgh Steelers had it all. They had the rampaging Mean Joe Greene, the snarling Jack Lambert and the unassailable Steel Curtain defense. They had the Mikhail Baryshnikov of wide receivers in Lynn Swann. They had a workhorse tailback in Franco Harris carrying the overland mail, and they had coach Chuck Noll pulling the strategic strings along the sidelines.

But most of all, they had a director fully equipped to draw the very best out of his ensemble cast.

"Imagine yourself sitting on top of a great thorough-bred horse," Terry Bradshaw would later say in describing the experience. "You sit up there and you feel the power. That's what it was like, playing quarterback on that team. It was a great ride."

At 6-foot-3 and 215 pounds, Bradshaw would never be confused with a jockey. But no one could argue that he wasn't the man in the saddle, driving the big, fast, unbeatable stallion relentlessly forward.

Today, he is one of the most amiable sports personalities in America. Funny. Self-deprecating. As at home in a TV booth at Lambeau Field as he is guesting on *Jimmy Kimmel Live!* Football fans love him for his wit, his candor and, naturally, for the four Super Bowl championships he directed in only six years.

What many conveniently forget now is that the Terry Bradshaw legend was painfully slow in developing.

In the formative years of his career (and after), Bradshaw was derided as a bumpkin, a rube. Every time he opened his mouth, it seemed, he stuck a cleat in it. His sound bites were peppered with phrases such as: "We had 10 turnovers in one game, seven fumbles and four interceptions." Or, "I may be dumb but I'm not stupid." His critics lapped it up.

Bradshaw arrived in Steeltown from Louisiana Tech as the first player selected in the 1970 draft. In his first five seasons, he threw 48 touchdown passes — and 81 interceptions.

In his second autobiography, *No Easy Game*, he recounted how much he had to endure to win over a city, establish a reputation and find his feet in the pro ranks. "I always wanted everyone to like me," he wrote. "I wanted the city of Pittsburgh to be proud of me. But my first few seasons, I could count the number of people on my bandwagon on one finger.

"I had people call me a dummy and a hick. I had a lady stop me outside the stadium and tell me I stunk. I heard the people cheer when I got hurt. Rub up against enough briar patches and your hide will get pretty tough. Mine did."

Bradshaw even lost the starting quarterbacking spot to Joe Gilliam in 1974 for a short time. But by the end of that season, he had regained control of the offense and the Steelers were on their way to Super Bowl IX, a 16–6 verdict over the snake-bitten Minnesota Vikings.

It would be the first bold step in an unparalleled march to greatness.

Terry Bradshaw gets set to throw a pass in a 1974 game.

The next year, Bradshaw and Co. were back at the Big Dance again for Super Bowl X. The man at the helm threw for 209 yards, including the now legendary 64-yard toss to Swann late in the fourth quarter, to ice a 21–17 win over the Dallas Cowboys.

As proficient as he was in directing his offense, utilizing its assets to the fullest measure, there was a streak of the riverboat gambler about him, too. One of the characteristics that made him such a perfect fit for this nearly perfect team was his unshakable confidence.

"My nature," he said once, "was attack. Throw it deep. Anybody can throw wide. Let's go deep." The air-out to Swann remains the most memorable example of that go-for-broke mindset.

Three seasons later, in 1978, the Steelers were once again back in the title hunt. Bradshaw produced his finest regular season and was named NFL AP MVP for 2,915 passing yards and 28 touchdowns. There wasn't much more he could

do professionally to convince people. Still, the snide remarks would not die.

Before Super Bowl XIII, mouthy Dallas linebacker Thomas "Hollywood" Henderson famously ratcheted up the rivalry between America's Team and the NFL's best team by saying of Terry Bradshaw, "He couldn't spell 'cat' if you spotted him the 'c' and the 't'."

Bradshaw didn't much care about spelling bees, but he certainly knew how to spell W-I-N. His 318 yards and four touchdown tosses earned him the Super Bowl MVP as Pittsburgh claimed its third championship in five years, 35–31.

Hollywood Henderson offered only a lame rebuttal.

No one knew it at the time, of course, but the 1979 season would be the swan song of that legendary Pittsburgh run. Another Super Bowl, this time a 31–19 shutdown of the Los Angeles Rams, and another MVP for the guy behind center.

Terry Bradshaw would soldier on for another four seasons, through injury and disappointment, finally

retiring in 1983. He was a first-ballot Hall of Famer, naturally. And although the Steelers do not make a habit of retiring numbers, no one in his right mind would be daft enough to ask for No. 12. So consider it unofficially retired.

Over 14 seasons, he threw for 27,989 yards, and his touchdown-to-interception ratio is only 212-to-210 — hardly impressive by conventional "great quarterback" standards. But then, Terry Bradshaw was never a conventional quarterback. Merely a great one. He just won, long before the Nike ads coined the phrase "Just do it." ◼

College: Louisiana Tech University
Drafted: 1970, Pittsburgh Steelers, 1st overall
Years active: 1970–1983
Top honors: NFL AP MVP (1978), Super Bowl Champion (1974, 1975, 1978, 1979), Super Bowl MVP (1978, 1979), First Team All-Pro (1978)
Hall of Fame induction: 1989

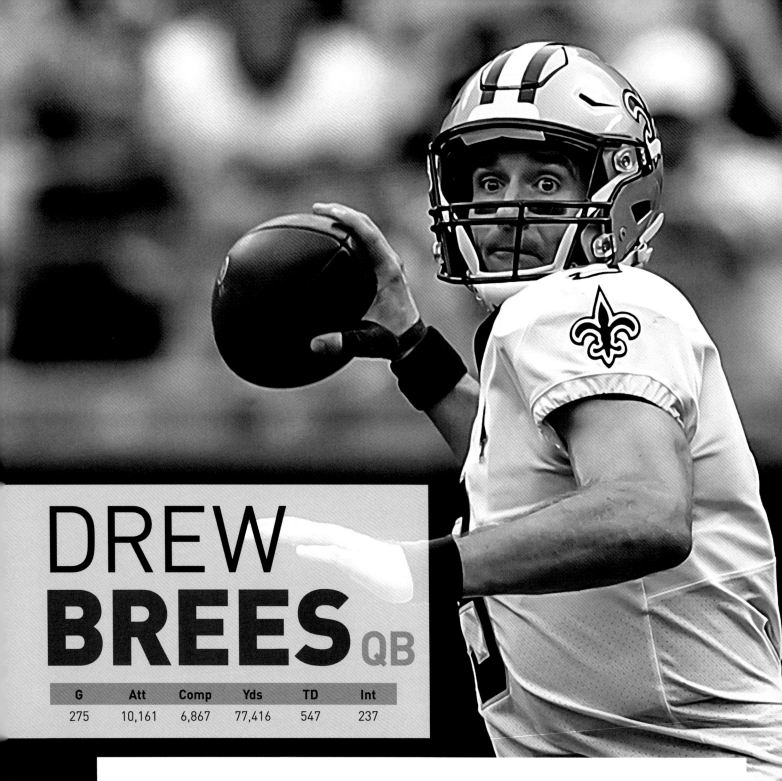

DREW
BREES QB

G	Att	Comp	Yds	TD	Int
275	10,161	6,867	77,416	547	237

THE BIG EASY, AS EVERYONE KNOWS, HAS WRAPPED its arms around Drew Brees and welcomed him into the family as its adopted son.

The Texas-born graduate, like many in the big state who toiled under those famous Friday night lights, is now as much a part of Bayou lore as Louis Armstrong, the French Quarter and those delectable powdered-sugar doughnuts locals call beignets.

Yet when the sure-fire first-ballot future Hall of Famer first signed on in New Orleans, more than a

smattering of fans and media pundits were skeptical, to put it mildly. After all, $60 million over six years buys a lot of boiled crawfish.

When Brees arrived in 2006, only six months after the devastation wrought by Hurricane Katrina, the Saints were a 3-13 mess. What many thought the team needed was a can't-miss pivot, and Brees — however dynamic and already accomplished — was a quarterback endeavoring to rebound from surgery to repair a torn rotator cuff and damaged right

He's taken a shredder to the NFL record book — leaving legends like Dan Marino and Dan Fouts in his wake.

labrum to his throwing wing.

Despite five impressive seasons in San Diego, the Chargers were skeptical, which is why they only offered an incentive-laden contract and let Brees leave for New Orleans in free agency. One opinion holder, however — Lorean Tomlinson, mom of the Chargers' superstar tailback, LaDainian Tomlinson — had an immediate inkling of how the Saints had made out like bandits.

"The San Diego Chargers have lost their mind," said Lorean flatly.

Time has proven LaDainian's mom an astute judge of sanity. Since San Diego decided to let Brees go, the once-damaged quarterback has not only won a championship, he's taken a shredder to the NFL record book — leaving legends like Dan Marino and Dan Fouts in his wake.

For his air and for his care, the Who Dat Nation has bestowed divinity status upon him. Breesus they call him, reverentially.

"For me, I looked at [going to New Orleans] as an opportunity -- an opportunity to be part of a rebuilding process," said Brees. "How many people in their life get to be a part of something like that? They had as much confidence in me returning from my shoulder injury that year as I had in myself. And that meant a lot to me."

The Saints' 31–17 Super Bowl victory over Peyton Manning and the Indianapolis Colts in 2009 continues to resonate among the

most emotional championships ever claimed, symbolizing as it did a shattered city's indomitable spirit and brave resurgence in the wake of profound natural devastation.

Leading the charge, Brees went 32 of 39 passes — tying an NFL completion record set by Tom Brady — for 288 yards and two touchdowns that day in Miami. Brees took home MVP honors, and the victory touched off a celebration that thrust the fabled bacchanalia of Mardi Gras into the shade.

"He is the perfect person for an imperfect situation," said Saints GM Mickey Loomis at the time.

For any situation, as it turns out.

Brees is tops in most 300-plus yard passing games in a season, with 13, and his 5,476 yards passing in 2011 are just 1 yard shy of Peyton Manning's single-season record. He's also tops in career passing yards per game (281.5) and is the third-fastest player in league history to reach 40,000 yards.

"At 211 degrees, water is just scalding hot. But at 212, it boils. It's the significance of one degree," said Saints coach Sean Payton. "Everything about Drew Brees's preparation is about that one extra degree."

That one degree, and what he could wring from it, has become the stuff of greatness. And the kid from Austin, Texas, has continued to shine — even if that second Super Bowl championship has proven elusive for the Saints.

In Week 5 of a troubled beginning to the 2012 season, one which included the fallout from the Saints'

infamous bounty-hunting sanctions, there was more Brees history to lift tattered spirits. In the first quarter, Brees delivered a 40-yard touchdown pass to Devery Henderson against his old team, the Chargers. The pass pushed Brees past Johnny Unitas, the slope-shouldered, crewcut deity who owned the NFL's consecutive-games touchdown streak record, then at 48 games. That record had only stood for over half a century. To put the feat in perspective, 10 different men have occupied the White House since Unitas set it.

"You watch guys like Johnny U on some of the highlight film, and watching the way he threw the ball in that era was pretty unbelievable," said Brees while savoring the moment. "He really revolutionized the game and the quarterback position ... Certainly, his accomplishments speak for themselves. His Baltimore Colts teams, I think that was the heyday and paved the way for what we have now."

Just as the heyday of Drew Brees is paving the way for the next generation of rocket-armed QBs who might someday eclipse his records. ■

College: Purdue University
Drafted: 2001, San Diego Chargers, 32nd overall
Years active: 2001–present
Top honors: NFL AP Comeback Player of the Year (2004), NFL Walter Payton Man of the Year (2006), First Team All-Pro (2006), NFL AP Offensive Player of the Year (2008, 2011), Super Bowl Champion (2009), Super Bowl MVP (2009)
Hall of Fame induction: N/A

EARL
CAMPBELL RB

G	Att	Yds	Avg	TD
115	2,187	9,407	4.3	74

THE KID WAS BIG IN HIGH SCHOOL — AND BY BIG, WE'RE talking about his status as a football star who carried his school to the Texas 4A state championship in a pigskin-crazy, football-mad state. Even his nickname radiated cool: Earl Campbell, from John Tyler High, better known as the Tyler Rose.

Campbell got even bigger when he enrolled at the University of Texas. He led the entire NCAA in rushing and was awarded the Heisman Trophy as the best player in U.S. college football. Next came the 1978 NFL Draft. Then things got really crazy.

When the Houston Oilers announced their first pick overall, the Texas faithful cut loose and cheered. Squat and muscular with power-packed legs, Campbell was a tough load to topple. His approach to running was straight on, straight at you. He liked to run into tacklers instead of avoiding them. That was his trademark — that, and the fact it usually took two or three players to wrestle him to the ground.

"I always thought if I let one or two guys tackle me, I wasn't doing something right," said Campbell. "I mean, I didn't think I was part of a game unless I had the ball in my hands 20 or 30 times. I had to get lathered up, you know? And right when the game was over was when I felt like really gettin' it on, not that I didn't get it on in the middle, but I always thought if there was a fifth quarter, I could really show 'em something, you know?"

Campbell showed plenty during his first few years in the NFL. In a *Monday Night Football* game against the Miami Dolphins, he led the Oilers to a 35–30 victory by gaining 199 yards and scoring four touchdowns. He was named Offensive Rookie of the Year after having

rushed for 1,450 yards. In his second season Campbell was named league MVP, and he followed that up in 1980 with 1,934 yards rushing — then the highest since O.J. Simpson's 2,003 in 1973 — including four games where he topped the 200-yard mark in rushing.

In all three seasons, Campbell was hailed as the Offensive Player of the Year and a First Team All-Pro. Marshall Faulk is the only other player to pull off that feat (1999–2001), but Campbell did it while also leading the NFL in both rushing yards and rushing yards per game.

By the time Campbell said farewell to football in the summer of 1986, he had totaled 9,407 yards rushing and 74 touchdowns in eight seasons and appeared in five Pro Bowls. In 1991 he was inducted into the Hall of Fame, where fans and former players alike regaled others with stories of how Campbell would purposely look for the largest collection of defenders, then charge headlong into them. As Oilers coach Bum Phillips liked to say of his 232-pound battering ram, "He may not be in a class by himself, but whatever class he's in, it doesn't take long to call roll."

Campbell's success had NFL coaches searching for bigger, bolder runners — "beefy, big-butted backs who could both bowl over and blow past the opposition," as *Sports Illustrated* described them. Consider the likes of Jerome Bettis, Eddie George, Jamal Anderson and Craig "Ironhead" Heyward, as those whose styles were allowed to rumble down a path blazed by Campbell.

"One time I asked Earl, 'Why don't you let one man bring you down sometimes?'" recalled former Dallas Cowboys running back Tony Dorsett. "He said, 'I got to get them. They're talking that noise.'"

Earl Campbell picks up yardage in the second quarter of an October 1984 game versus the Dallas Cowboys.

Soon after he retired, Campbell insisted all the pounding had been worth it. Born the sixth of 11 children in a working-class family, one of his early wishes as a pro football player was to earn enough money to buy his mother a new house, which he did. Sadly, though, all those on-field collisions and noisemakers wreaked havoc on Campbell.

Now into his mid-60s, Campbell has trouble walking. Sometimes the pain is so bad he has to get around in a wheelchair. He underwent back surgery to remove the bone spurs from his spinal column that had prevented him from sleeping in a bed. Instead, he would sleep in a recliner to ease the discomfort.

"Earl was the biggest, baddest player in the game," said Dorsett. "But no matter how big or strong you are, the game ultimately wins."

If you ever want to get a sense of what Campbell was like as a young, powerful football player, go to the southwest entrance of Darrell K Royal–Texas Memorial Stadium in Austin and look for the statue of Campbell, wearing his Longhorns jersey No. 20. Made of bronze, the statue stands nine feet tall.

Ask a lot of those 175-pound NFL defensive backs Campbell plowed through, and they'll probably tell you his statue would be easier to bring down. ■

College: University of Texas
Drafted: 1978, Houston Oilers, 1st overall
Years active: 1978–1985
Top honors: NFL AP Offensive Rookie of the Year (1978), NFL All-Rookie Team (1978), First Team All-Pro (1978–80), NFL AP Offensive Player of the Year (1978–80), NFL AP MVP (1979)
Hall of Fame induction: 1991

ERIC
DICKERSON RB

G	Att	Yds	Avg	TD
146	2,996	13,259	4.4	90

Jim Brown's running style came straight out of demolition derby. Gale Sayers was speed with panache. Bo Jackson was speed with power, while Walter Payton earned himself the best of all nicknames: Sweetness.

And then there was Eric Dickerson, the angular one, with the posture of a butler. He stood 6-foot-3 and didn't do a lot of bending at the waist to drop a shoulder into oncoming tacklers. Instead he kept his head up and turned on the speed.

Before the 1983 NFL Draft, Dickerson's style so mystified NFL general managers and scouts that they wondered: how can he run like that? He's so rigid, so straight up-and-down he looks like an exclamation mark. One big hit and he'll be carried off the field on two stretchers.

It just never happened that way.

The Los Angeles Rams bet on Dickerson's unorthodox style and took him second overall. Turned out that being tall and keeping his head up gave Dickerson a better view of where to run. His speed was tough to match, and with his long stride he didn't get caught from behind often. His first season with the Los Angeles Rams underlined that point.

In a 16-game schedule Dickerson started poorly, fumbling six times in his first three games. In his fourth outing he snapped off an 85-yard touchdown run and got himself on track. Overall, he set three rookie rushing records, with 390 carries, 1,808 yards and 18 touchdowns (plus he added two more TDs via receiving). For all that, he was named a First Team All-Pro, chosen for the Pro Bowl and awarded Offensive Rookie of the Year.

For his follow-up act, in 1984, Dickerson set single-season NFL records for most 100-yard games (12) and yards rushing (2,105), both of which had been held by O.J. Simpson since 1973. Statisticians and fans noted Simpson hit his numbers in 14 games, while Dickerson broke them both in Game 15.

No matter, really. Two years into his pro career, there wasn't a defense that could corral Dickerson. He continued to star for the Rams, leading the league in rushing attempts (404), yards rushing (1,821) and rushing yards per game (113.8) in 1986 to take home Offensive Player of the Year honors.

If there were criticisms of Dickerson — and there were several — they had to do with his attitude. He was a star player who needed

"If you were blind, he could run right by you, and you wouldn't know it unless you felt the wind. He was the smoothest runner I've seen." — Rams head coach John Robinson

to be treated like one. Instead he was sneered at for wearing every piece of protective gear he could find: elbow pads, sometimes gloves, a neck collar, even goggles that he wore to correct his myopia.

"Some of the things I've done, I've been wrong in doing," said Dickerson. "I've been hasty. You lose your cool and say things you don't really mean. I think mine was out of frustration. It's not fun losing a lot of games."

By 1987, after two years of contract disputes, holdouts and suspensions, the Rams chose to trade Dickerson to the Indianapolis Colts. It was a three-way transaction also involving the Buffalo Bills. When the players and draft picks were tallied, the three teams all insisted they got what they wanted.

With the Colts, Dickerson was reunited with Ron Meyer, who had coached him in college. In 1987 Dickerson played in just nine games with Indianapolis, but still gained 1,011 yards. Two years after that, he became the first player to gain more than 1,000 yards in seven straight seasons. He was also the fastest to reach the 10,000-yard mark, needing just 91 games.

Dickerson finished his career with cameos as a Los Angeles Raider and an Atlanta Falcon. He retired after the 1993 season and was enshrined in Canton in 1999. His rookie records and his marks

for most 100-yard games and yards rushing in a single season still stand, more than 25 years after he set them.

When asked which would be the toughest to surpass, Dickerson said, "I think the one record I look at most and means the most to me is my rookie rushing record. You get one shot at that. You don't get several. You don't get 10. You get one."

In 11 seasons, Dickerson's final rushing count was 13,259 yards. Eight players have run for more yards, but none had his combination of speed and grace and sense of Sweetness, too.

"If you were blind, he could run right by you, and you wouldn't know it unless you felt the wind," said Rams head coach John Robinson. "He was the smoothest runner I've seen." ▪

College: Southern Methodist University
Drafted: 1983, Los Angeles Rams, 2nd overall
Years active: 1983–1993
Top honors: NFL AP Offensive Rookie of the Year (1983), NFL All-Rookie Team (1983), First Team All-Pro (1983, 1984, 1986–88), NFL AP Offensive Player of the Year (1986)
Hall of Fame induction: 1999

TONY
DORSETT RB

G	Att	Yds	Avg	TD
173	2,936	12,739	4.3	77

WHEN TONY DORSETT WAS YOUNG, HE DREADED THE night and going to sleep. Sleeping meant dreaming, and dreaming meant going to the dark places he wanted to avoid. The worst ones were about living inside the darkest, soot-covered confines of a Pittsburgh steel mill, the kind his father endured for 30 years so he could support a wife and seven children.

Wes Dorsett was a hard-working man. Sometimes he came home so dirty his family couldn't recognize him. He always told his children they should concentrate on getting an education and finding a job they loved. Tony Dorsett took those words to heart. He would become a football player. Somehow he would go to university, get his degree, then play professionally. It would be his ticket out.

From star running back to superstar running back, from college hero to NFL All-Pro, Tony Dorsett made good on his promise. He won an NCAA national championship at the University of Pittsburgh one season (1976), then a Super Bowl with the Dallas Cowboys the next. He was a Heisman Trophy–winning standout, a sought-after first-round draft pick and the NFL's Offensive Rookie of the Year, with just over 1,000 yards rushing and 12 touchdowns. He exceeded everyone's expectations, even his own.

"Coming out of college, everyone said I would be too small to play professional football at 188 pounds," Dorsett recalled. "To be honest with you, I figured maybe I would play four or five years [in the NFL] and that would be it. I never dreamed I would play 12 seasons."

In those dozen seasons, Dorsett ran for 12,739 yards and 77 touchdowns and gave tacklers third-degree burns with his searing speed. His 99-yard scoring run against the Minnesota Vikings on January 3, 1983, is an NFL staple. He became the league's first player to surpass the 1,000-yard mark in each of his first five seasons. In 1981, he rambled for 1,646 yards, narrowly missing out on that season's rushing title — all remarkable feats considering how things could have turned out.

Having convinced himself that football was the key to his future, Dorsett almost quit after agreeing to attend Pittsburgh. He was shy and lonely, and the school's preseason practices were taking their toll. At one point Dorsett called his mother, Myrtle, and talked about coming home. His mom told him to stay strong, that things would get better. Things would work out.

They did.

As a 155-pound freshman, Dorsett led the NCAA in rushing with 1,586 yards and carried Pittsburgh to the 1973 Fiesta Bowl. He added 30 pounds of muscle and two more 1,000-yard seasons before his senior year, which began with a 181-yard performance in an easy win over Notre Dame.

When his college days ended, Dorsett had become the first player to rush for more than 6,000 yards in four seasons. The NFL beckoned — and that's when things once again worked in Dorsett's favor, as if fate had taken a liking to the young man with the big dreams.

Tex Schramm played the pivotal role this time. The Dallas general manager wanted Dorsett's speed and pass-catching skills in the Cowboys' multiple-formation offense. Unfortunately for Dallas, the Seattle Seahawks had the second pick overall in the 1977 draft and were keen to select the Pittsburgh prize. So Schramm

Tony Dorsett runs down field during a 1986 game.

made a deal. He packaged the Cowboys' first-round pick with three second-round choices and exchanged them for Seattle's No. 2 pick, which Schramm used to take Dorsett.

Had he gone to Seattle, would Dorsett have been as prominent a player in the NFL? Not likely. The Seahawks had just completed their debut season and were very much a work in progress. Dorsett would have played behind so-so blockers in an offense that had quarterback Jim Zorn, receiver Steve Largent and little else.

Dallas was the right fit for Dorsett and Dorsett was right for Dallas. Granted, the Cowboys could have given him the ball more, but how they used Dorsett proved to be as effective as how often they used him.

"If I wanted to risk Tony, I think he could gain as many yards as [Walter] Payton and [Earl] Campbell," Dallas coach Tom Landry once said. "But Tony is much different from Earl, who is so big. Payton is probably the strongest little man I've ever seen. Then there is Wilbert Montgomery, who did get used a lot and got hurt. I don't want that to happen to Tony."

Eventually the injuries came, and Dorsett had to retire. At his induction to the Pro Football Hall of Fame in 1994, he talked of his father and the desires forged by a working man's life.

"He taught me an awful lot about common sense, about street sense," said Dorsett. "He never forced me to do anything. He always told me, 'Son, if you're going to accomplish anything in life, do it yourself.'"

Tony Dorsett did, and he rarely had trouble sleeping again. ■

College: University of Pittsburgh
Drafted: 1977, Dallas Cowboys, 2nd overall
Years active: 1977–1988
Top honors: NFL AP Offensive Rookie of the Year (1977), NFL All-Rookie Team (1977), Super Bowl Champion (1977), First Team All-Pro (1981)
Hall of Fame induction: 1994

EZEKIEL
ELLIOTT RB

G	Att	Yds	Avg	TD
88	1,650	7,386	4.5	68

T HE NFL HAS AN ALL-TIME TEAM ROSTER, AND ON IT
are 12 of the league's finest running backs, including
Emmitt Smith, the all-time leading rusher with 18,355
yards. He is the only ball carrier to win the NFL's rushing title, the NFL MVP award, the Super Bowl and the
Super Bowl MVP all in one year.

That makes him Ground Hero.

And then there's this other Dallas Cowboy, the one
with the first name of the biblical prophet who fore-
saw the destruction of Jerusalem and the restoration
of Israel. In 2016, Ezekiel Elliott became the second
Cowboy to gain more than 1,000 yards in his rookie
season. Tony Dorsett was the first in 1977 with 1,007
yards in 14 games; Elliott's total was 1,631 yards in 15
games, which led the NFL. He also became the third
running back in league history to surpass the 1,000-yard
mark in just nine games. (Eric Dickerson and Adrian
Peterson were the previous two.)

He was genuinely thrilled when the Cowboys stopped
their game against the Baltimore Ravens to recognize
his setting a franchise record for most yards rushing by
a rookie back.

"It means a lot with the pedigree of this position, playing for the Dallas Cowboys," he said. "It's one step more
to where we want to be. One step more to greatness."

His first year as a pro also saw Elliott score 16 touchdowns (15 rushing, 1 receiving) and run for 125 yards
in his first playoff game, a 34–31 loss to the Green Bay
Packers. That tied Elliott with Duane Thomas, who was
the first to top 100 yards in a Dallas playoff game.

Elliott's immediate success had NFL observers
believing he was blessed with strong genetics. Stacy
Elliott, Zeke's father, played football at the University
of Missouri. Dawn Huff, his mom, was a high school
state champion in three sports and ran track at Missouri.
His maternal grandmother played basketball for Drake
University. That's a lot of sporting DNA to store in your
gym locker.

Following his highly publicized high school football
days, Elliott committed to Ohio State University, and in
2013, his freshman season, he ran 30 times for 262 yards
and two touchdowns. The following year he inherited
the starting running back spot when Carlos Hyde jumped
to the NFL. After that, the numbers started getting
bigger for Elliott — more starts, more carries, more
yards and more touchdowns. In 2015, he ran for more
than 100 yards in 10 straight games. In one, he rushed
for 274 yards, the second-highest total in school history.

That success continued with the Cowboys through his
rookie season up until August 11, 2017, when Elliott was
introduced to the one thing that could stop him in his
tracks — a six-game suspension for violating the NFL's
personal conduct policy. Elliott was accused of domestic violence, which the NFL had been investigating over
the course of a year. No criminal charges were filed at
that time.

Elliott served his full six-game suspension and was
back on the field for the Cowboys' crucial game against
the Seattle Seahawks. He gained 97 yards on 24 carries,
but Dallas lost 21–12 and was eliminated from the
playoffs.

The following season, Elliott was once again the NFL's
rushing leader, with 1,434 yards and 304 attempts, and
this helped propel the next Elliott drama — his contract.

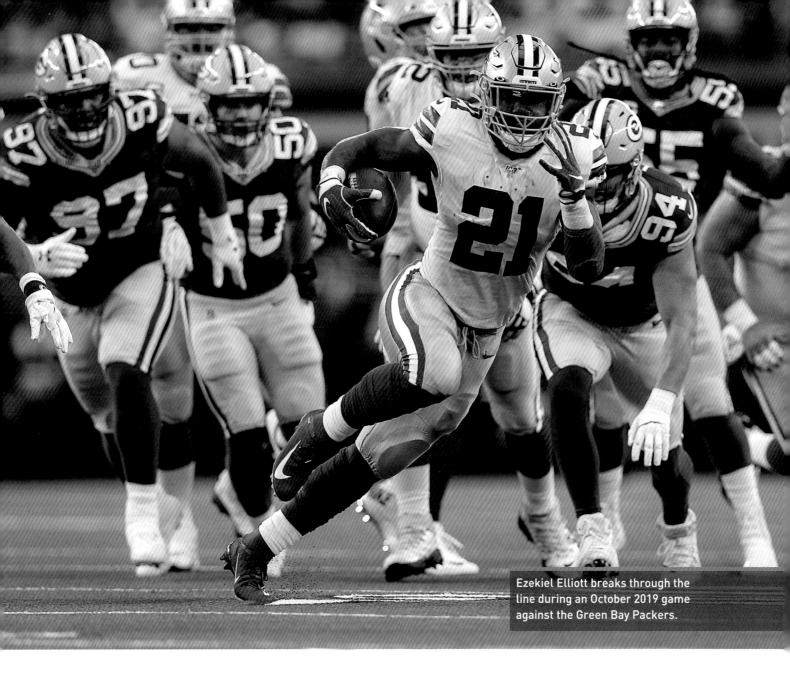

Ezekiel Elliott breaks through the line during an October 2019 game against the Green Bay Packers.

Wanting to be the highest-paid back in the NFL, he skipped the 2019 training camp and preseason games and threatened to continue his holdout into the regular season if he didn't get what he wanted. The morning of the team's first full workout before their home opener, Dallas and Elliott agreed on a contract extension worth $90 million over six years, with $50 million of it guaranteed.

Team owner Jerry Jones acknowledged the worth of someone with Elliott's skills: "Zeke has been arguably our best player. I'm not trying to be unfair to anybody else. But he's an incremental part to our success ... He's got a big heart. Now he's got a thick pocketbook, too."

All that money put an extra burden on Elliott. He was expected to lead the charge on every play of every possession. He got off to a sterling start, gaining 419 yards and five touchdowns in Weeks 2 to 5. Although he finished with just over 1,000 yards for the fourth time in six years, he suffered a torn posterior cruciate ligament and played the rest of the year on an injured knee. In the Cowboys' playoff loss to the San Francisco 49ers, Elliott looked sluggish in picking up a scant 31 yards on 12 carries.

He promised to be rested and ready for the 2022 season. ∎

College: Ohio State University
Drafted: 2016, Dallas Cowboys, 4th overall
Years active: 2016–present
Top honors: NFL All-Rookie Team (2016), First Team All-Pro (2016)
Hall of Fame induction: N/A

JOHN
ELWAY QB

G	Att	Comp	Yds	TD	INT
234	7,250	4,123	51,475	300	226

I F EVER THERE WAS A SENTIMENTAL FAVORITE, SOMEONE for the fence-sitters to root for, it had to be John Elway on the evening of January 25, 1998, at Qualcomm Stadium in San Diego. In 15 seasons, the toothy, bashful, matinee-idol Denver Broncos quarterback had accumulated everything a man could want in his chosen profession — wealth, fame, the devotion of a city and the respect of his peers. Everything, that is, but one thing.

That day, Elway shed the title of lovable loser. That day, he took the Mile High City higher than it had ever been before. That day, the demons were exorcised and the growing whispers of "all heart and no head" were forever banished.

The Broncos, after all, had a history of melting spectacularly in the Big One: three Super Bowl appearances for Elway, four for the Broncos; three losses for Elway, four for the Broncos.

Quarterback Brett Favre and the defending champions, the Green Bay Packers, were favored in Super Bowl XXXII. True to form, Favre marched the Pack for a touchdown on the game's opening drive. It seemed that fate would yet again spit derisively in the face of Elway and his compatriots.

But this time the script turned out differently. This time, Elway simply refused to roll over and play dead. In a back-and-forth contest, the old pro directed two second-half TD drives, including the winning touchdown with under two minutes to play, to give the Broncos a 31–24 win.

Running back Terrell Davis may have scooted for three touchdowns and gone home toting the MVP honors, but there was no doubt who had been the inspiration behind the renaissance. The fans in San Diego chanted him into the dressing room in tribute. The sound of "El-way! El-way!" reverberated around the stadium.

"John left it out on the field tonight," said Broncos linebacker Bill Romanowski. "He played his heart out. He left his soul on that field."

"This guy is almost 40 years old," added linebacker John Mobley. "And he is laying his life and body on the line."

For the man himself, a dream that for so long seemed tantalizingly out of reach had finally been realized.

"I've experienced the highest of highs and lowest of lows," said Elway. "I think to really appreciate anything, you have to be at both ends of the spectrum. I've always joked about Joe Montana not appreciating his Super Bowls nearly as much as I do because he never lost one. We lost three before we won one."

Elway was chosen first overall by the Baltimore Colts in 1983. He balked, convinced that the Colts offered him no chance to compete on a successful team, and used his baseball option as leverage. If Baltimore wouldn't trade him, he'd take his chances on the diamond. He held firm.

In this game of chicken, the Colts eventually relented, dealing Elway's rights to Denver in exchange for quarterback Mark Hermann, offensive lineman Chris Hint and a first-round draft choice in 1985.

Naturally, the Broncos were ecstatic. In sports parlance, this big, rawboned kid had all you could hope for from a competitive and a marketing standpoint: a gun for an arm, size, toughness, that Ultra Brite smile aligned with a boyish charm — everything an organization dreams of when looking to anchor a franchise.

John Elway passes from the end zone in a November 1992 game against the Los Angeles Raiders.

It would turn out to be one of the most lopsided trades in history.

Elway began to pay dividends almost immediately. He became not only one of the great quarterbacks of his era, but also the face of his franchise. For a decade and a half, he was Denver's favorite adopted son. Professionally, he had grown up in front of their eyes. They considered him one of their own.

After taking down the Packers in Super Bowl XXXII, it felt so damn good that the Broncos went out and did it again the next season. In what was to be Elway's swan song, he steered the only NFL team he'd ever played for to another title, throwing the ball for 336 yards and a touchdown while scoring one himself along the ground. Denver blew away the overmatched Atlanta Falcons 34–19, and Elway was named Super Bowl MVP.

When Elway retired, on top — a place many doubted he'd ever reach

— he ranked second of all time in passing yards (51,475), attempts (7,250) and completions (4,123). He had engineered 47 fourth-quarter game-winning or game-tying drives, the most celebrated being "the Drive," a 15-play, 98-yard march that tied the 1986 AFC Championship game at 20-20. In overtime, Elway fashioned a second drive that produced a 33-yard field goal and a trip to the Super Bowl. His record of 148-82-1 is one of the finest ever by a quarterback. He finished with nine Pro-Bowl selections, and among QBs only Tom Brady has played in more Super Bowls than Elway's five.

History would doubtlessly have looked slightly more ambiguously upon the Elway legacy had he not corralled those two late Super Bowl titles. Regardless, the statistics and the impact he made on the Broncos, and the league as a whole, stand on their own. With his induction to the Hall of Fame, Elway joined

the likes of Johnny Unitas and Bart Starr, Roger Staubach and Terry Bradshaw, Joe Montana and Dan Marino as a quarterback for the ages.

On the eve of what would turn out to be his first taste of Super Bowl glory, the man who had almost everything protested uneasily at being the people's choice: "I don't know if I like being the sentimental favorite."

By that time, John Elway had little choice. ■

College: Stanford University
Drafted: 1983, Baltimore Colts, 1st overall
Years active: 1983–1998
Top honors: NFL AP MVP (1987), NFL Walter Payton Man of the Year (1992), Super Bowl Champion (1997, 1998), Super Bowl MVP (1998)
Hall of Fame induction: 2004

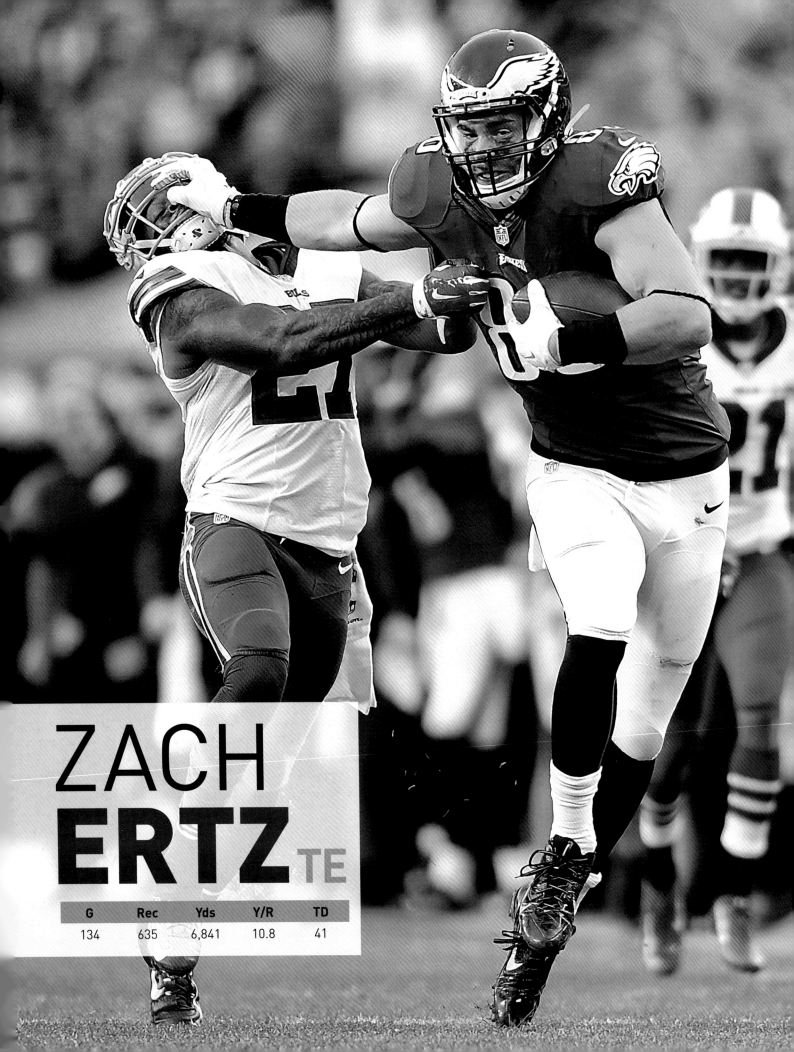

ZACH
ERTZ TE

G	Rec	Yds	Y/R	TD
134	635	6,841	10.8	41

NOT THAT ZACH ERTZ REQUIRED any formal introductions to those gathered at State Farm Stadium on the afternoon of Sunday, October 24, 2021.

But as a how-do-you-do/welcome, not a bad way to say hello.

A 47-yard catch and-run play for a touchdown — the longest of Ertz's 10-year pro career — from QB Kyler Murray that stretched the Arizona Cardinals' lead over the visiting Houston Texans to 24–5.

In his Arizona debut. Making him the first player in league history to have a TD catch in back-to-back games with two different teams. And on National Tight Ends Day.

"It was kind of surreal to see kind of the whole sideline come on the field for my first score," confessed Ertz, the longtime Philadelphia Eagle, after the game.

"It was awesome to see the defensive guys come up and celebrate with me. I think it just speaks to the culture of this team. I mean everyone wants to win so badly, everyone's happy for another man's success. And the best teams I've been a part of, that's the culture that it is.

"I would just say I'm jubilant right now to be here."

On October 21, six games into the 2021 season, the Eagles traded their 2017 Super Bowl star to Arizona in exchange for cornerback Tay Gowan and a 2022 fifth-round draft selection, despite Ertz's preference to remain in Philly.

"Zach Ertz built a special legacy in Philadelphia. Talented, tough, and passionate, he helped to establish our team's culture and played a vital role in our success over the years," said Eagles Chairman and CEO Jeffrey Lurie in a statement from the organization. "Zach created so many memories that will live on forever ... He will always be a member of the Eagles family."

In the decisive moment of that unforgettable 2017 Super Bowl game, with the Eagles on third-and-seven from the New England Patriots' 11-yard line, quarterback Nick Foles found his reliable collaborator running a slant. After connecting with the ball, Ertz launched himself toward the goal line.

He broke the plane, but the ball popped out on impact, contacting the ground.

As the wait for rubber stamping dragged on for the 67,612 souls crammed inside U.S. Bank Stadium and an estimated TV audience of 103 million in the United States alone, one person, the guy who'd caught the pass, harbored nary a shred of doubt.

"It seemed like an eternity over there," admitted Ertz an hour later.

"The city of Philly would've been hot if they'd overturned that."

When finally upheld, it gave Philly a shocking 38–33 lead.

The Eagles then held fast to record one of the more compelling upsets in Super Bowl lore, giving the City of Brotherly Love its first NFL title in 59 years.

Zach Ertz, already a star, had been transformed into a celebrity.

At 6-foot-5 and 250 pounds, the strapping tight end from Orange, California, is a load.

Ertz, fittingly, rhymes with hurts. He hits you, you feel it.

As a follow-up to his Super Bowl heroics, he only made history.

Ertz's 116-catch season in 2018 — good for 1,163 yards and eight TDs — represents the most ever for the position. On December 23, 2018, versus the Houston Texans, he broke the six-year-old record of 110 receptions set by Jason Witten of the Dallas Cowboys, part of a 12-catch afternoon. By then, Ertz had left wideout Brian Westbrook's franchise record of 89 catches in the proverbial dust.

Ertz married World Cup–winning U.S. national soccer team midfielder Julie Johnston in 2017. The two met at a baseball game at Stanford, where Ertz played four collegiate seasons for the Cardinals and in his final year earned All-American status.

Following his breakout junior year, he announced he'd be entering the NFL Draft and was subsequently selected by the Eagles.

By the time he left Philadelphia, Ertz was only 10 catches away from Hall of Famer Harold Carmichael's franchise-high career aggregate of 589.

In his first turn wearing Cardinals livery, he snared 56 passes for 574 yards and three touchdowns over 11 starts, but the season ended disappointedly with a wild-card playoff loss to the L.A. Rams.

Now 31 years old, Ertz's 6,841 yards in career receiving ranks 13th among tight ends all-time. And he's set to become an unrestricted free agent in March.

"I still feel like we have unfinished business as a team," he told reporters, postseason. "I would love to be a part of it." ∎

College: Stanford University
Drafted: 2013, Philadelphia Eagles, 35th overall
Years active: 2013–present
Top honors: Super Bowl Champion (2017)
Hall of Fame induction: N/A

BRETT
FAVRE QB

G	Att	Comp	Yds	TD	INT
302	10,169	6,300	71,838	508	336

I N AN ERA OF TRANSIENCE, OF QUICK FIXES AND FLEETING fads, he was a welcome constant. Game in and game out. Season in, season out.

In Green Bay he was the unofficial mayor of Titletown, USA. The Packers' version of the Pony Express. "Through wind and sleet and hail and dead of night ..." And those snow-cone frosty December afternoons at the legendary Lambeau Field.

"You're never guaranteed about next year," Brett Favre was famous for saying. "People ask you what you think of next season ... you have to seize the opportunities when they're in front of you."

When he finally retired at the age of 41 in 2011, Favre had done virtually all he could for the Packers and seized every opportunity as a New York Jet and Minnesota Viking before admitting it was time to leave — as hard as that was for him to do.

During his run with the Packers, it was impossible to think of a quarterback with a greater capacity for competition than No. 4 in green and gold. Favre loved the game. He embraced it like few others did. He was a man of action, a riverboat gambler, a throwback to the days of Slingin' Sammy Baugh.

Favre doesn't have the Super Bowl ring collection of Joe Montana or Terry Bradshaw or Tom Brady, but few in the history of the NFL have done more at the position. Look it up. The man played in 321 consecutive games, including playoffs, over 20 seasons. His 10,169 pass attempts, 6,300 completions for 71,838 yards and 508 touchdowns all set NFL records, the last of which was broken in 2014.

Not the 336 interceptions, however — though that statistic only serves to underline Favre's willingness to take chances. That earned him both love and infamy in Green Bay. As a Packer, his life was an open book. Fans lived through not only the wins and losses on the field, but also the death of Favre's father, the loss of his brother-in-law, his wife's breast cancer and the destruction of the Favre family home when Hurricane Katrina stormed through Mississippi.

For 16 years the Favre faithful followed his story. He was on television longer than *Bonanza*. The peak of his career came in 1996 — the season he led the Packers to a 13-3 record and playoff wins over the San Francisco 49ers and Carolina Panthers. In Super Bowl XXXI, Favre threw for 246 yards and two touchdowns as Green Bay blitzed the New England Patriots 35–21.

There would be another trip to the Big Dance and a slew of individual honors, but the one Super Bowl title would be all Favre would win. And that would have been fine for Green Bay fans.

But then Favre retired in 2008, only to say months later he wanted to come back. Packers management was ready to turn the page and go with a backup passer, some guy named Aaron Rodgers. Favre insisted on playing, and was traded to the Jets for a conditional fourth-round draft pick. He lasted one season in New York and then signed as a free agent with the Vikings, Green Bay's divisional rival.

That didn't sit well with Packer backers. They got to watch Favre add to his legacy by becoming the first quarterback in NFL history to defeat every one of the league's 32 franchises. They saw him set the league record for most games with four touchdown passes. They also got to see him take the hated Vikings to the

Brett Favre rolls out of the pocket against the Seattle Seahawks during the NFC divisional playoff game in January 2008.

2009 NFC Championship Game before losing to the New Orleans Saints.

Favre returned to the Vikings in 2010 and topped the 70,000-yard mark for his career, but the season didn't end well. A right shoulder injury ended his ironman streak, and a concussion ended his career. Unable to play in Minnesota's final regular-season game, Favre announced his retirement. This time it stuck.

"I think my stubbornness, hard-headedness and stupidity is what has allowed me to play for 20 years," said Favre.

A year later, when asked how he was faring away from the game, the old gunslinger stuck to his guns. There would be no comeback.

"I'd said in years past that I knew [I was done]," said Favre. "I really knew this time. I got beat up a little bit physically, but I still felt like I could do it. But I just felt like it was time. Mentally I was just burned out."

He needn't have concerned himself. Favre gave everything to football: over 18 and a half seasons of never missing a game, the most consecutive starts by any player in league history, three MVP nods, 11 Pro Bowl selections, no calculating how many hits absorbed.

Even Packers fans understood. No player ever earned the rest more. ◼

College: University of Southern Mississippi
Drafted: 1991, Atlanta Falcons, 33rd overall
Years active: 1991–2010
Top honors: NFL AP Offensive Player of the Year Award (1995), NFL AP MVP (1995–97), First-Team All-Pro (1995–97), Super Bowl Champion (1996)
Hall of Fame induction: 2016

LARRY
FITZGERALD WR

G	Rec	Yds	Y/R	TD
263	1,432	17,492	12.2	121

If a pass is anywhere near him, he's all over it with a butterfly net.

WHEN EVERYONE FIGURED HE had retired, Larry Fitzgerald's numbers did all the talking for him. He had eight seasons of 90 catches or more, an NFL record. In the 2008 postseason, he had 30 catches for 546 yards and seven touchdowns, all NFL records. His 17,492 receiving yards for his career wasn't a record, but it remains the closest anyone has come to the 22,895 yards Jerry Rice totaled to traumatize defensive backs.

What made Fitzgerald special wasn't his size, his quickness or his overall speed, which wasn't a strong suit when he reached his mid-30s. But his hands were supremely steady and sure, arguably the best to ever grab an NFL football.

"Larry Fitzgerald could catch a bee with chopsticks," gushed one television announcer.

Okay, so that was a stretch. And yet the Arizona Cardinals receiver had a knack for making every kind of catch — short, deep, improbable and "Did you see that?" If a pass was anywhere near him, he was all over it with a butterfly net. Defenders could be waving their arms, trying to position themselves in front of him, and Fitzgerald would reach over or around them and snag the ball. He made it look as easy as he described it.

"Just throw the ball up. I'm going to catch it," he said.

It had worked that way since his collegiate career at the University of Pittsburgh, where Fitzgerald racked up yardage and set an NCAA record by catching a touchdown pass in 18 consecutive games. It helped make him a Heisman Trophy runner-up and the third pick overall in the 2004 NFL Draft.

And it didn't take him long to show the Cardinals he would be just as valuable in the pros.

In his first season, at age 21, Fitzgerald became the youngest player in NFL history to catch two touchdown passes in the same game. He finished his rookie season with 58 receptions for 780 yards and eight touchdowns. The following season he was stunningly better: 103 catches, 1,409 yards and 10 touchdowns. Fitzgerald and teammate Anquan Boldin became only the third pair of NFL receivers to surpass 1,400 yards in the same season.

The best was yet to come.

In the 2008 NFL playoffs, Fitzgerald went from local star to national icon. His catapult to fame began against the Philadelphia Eagles. By halftime he had scored three times, setting an NFC Championship Game record for touchdown catches. That helped lift the Cardinals into a Super Bowl XLIII showdown with the Pittsburgh Steelers. Pittsburgh ended up winning the title, 27–23, despite Fitzgerald catching two touchdowns, both in the fourth quarter. Overall, Fitzgerald finished the postseason with 30 catches, 546 yards and seven touchdowns, each besting a Jerry Rice record.

A week after his Super Bowl loss, Fitzgerald competed in the Pro Bowl, where he caught two more touchdown passes and was named the game's most valuable player. He eventually fessed up and said he had played the entire postseason with a broken left thumb and torn cartilage in the same hand — a revelation that made his receiving numbers shine even brighter.

A year after Arizona's Super Bowl appearance, Boldin was traded to the Baltimore Ravens and quarterback Kurt Warner, the elder statesman of the club, retired. For two years, 2010 and 2011, the Cardinals posted a combined 13-19 record and failed to make the playoffs. Yet through it all, Fitzgerald worked on his timing with a carousel of quarterbacks.

In 2012 Fitzgerald topped the 10,000-yard mark for his career, making him only the second NFL receiver at the time to reach that number before his 30th birthday. (Calvin Johnson later joined Fitzgerald and Randy Moss on the elite list.) In 2013 Fitzgerald topped Moss as the youngest player in NFL history to reach 11,000 yards receiving.

As the years rolled on, Fitzgerald continued to excel. In both 2015 and 2017 he established career highs in seasonal receptions with 109. Then in 2020, he hit the wall, missing three games after testing positive for COVID-19 and producing just 409 yards and a single touchdown. He turned to free agency in 2021 and was given a pass of a different kind.

That won't be the case when it comes to the Pro Football Hall of Fame. ■

College: University of Pittsburgh
Drafted: 2004, Arizona Cardinals, 3rd overall
Years active: 2004–present
Top honors: First Team All-Pro (2008), NFL Walter Payton Man of the Year (2016)
Hall of Fame induction: N/A

DAN
FOUTS QB

G	Att	Comp	Yds	TD	Int
181	5,604	3,297	43,040	254	242

I T'S AN IMAGE THAT HUNG IN THE SAN DIEGO CHARGERS' offices for years. An image that encapsulated the man — his competitiveness, his mindset.

The nose, broken by a Ted Hendricks forearm, stuck out at an awkward angle with a swatch of tape holding it together, blood spattered on the front of his white jersey. His left shoulder, dislocated by another hit, hung limply, forcing him to take the snap with only his right hand.

"Darn fool, that guy," muttered Dan Fouts about himself years later.

In the Don "Air" Coryell years, when footballs filled the air in Jack Murphy Stadium like golf balls at a crowded driving range, one man, and one man only, led the San Diego Chargers. His word was sacrosanct.

"He's like E.F. Fouts," said Chargers teammate Kellen Winslow, in reference to the E.F. Hutton TV commercials of the day. "When he talks, people listen."

When Dan Fouts threw the ball — at any time, under any circumstance, on any down — defenses ran for cover, and Chargers fans ate it up.

"It was a real joy to be able to operate in that system," said Fouts. "I've been out of the game a long time now, but it's nice when people come up to you and say they really enjoyed the way we played the game in those years."

Daniel Francis Fouts was born to play pro. His father, Bob, called the San Francisco 49ers' games for years. Young Dan worked as a ball boy for the Bay Area team.

Fouts and the Chargers proved to be a fortuitous combination — a happy collaboration of man and moment.

Selected in the third round out of Oregon, Fouts struggled at first to find his identity in San Diego. The hiring of Coryell as head coach in 1978 changed all that.

When Dan Fouts threw the ball — at any time, under any circumstance, on any down — defenses ran for cover.

The Chargers surrounded their strong-armed, strong-willed, heavily bearded quarterback with a cast of exceptional pass-catching talents, from the likes of Charlie Joiner and All-Pro tight end Winslow to John Jefferson and Wes Chandler. The results were electrifying.

In 1980 and 1981 Fouts registered then-unheard-of numbers. He threw for a combined 9,517 yards (including a then-league record 4,802 in '81) and 66 touchdowns. Toss an interception? He couldn't have cared less. He knew where his strength lay. He'd be gunning again on the next series.

And mercy, the man was tough.

"Dan Fouts has a cool, steel-like nerve and courage," said a San Diego assistant coach in 1976. "He took a lot of beatings, a lot of pounding, but continued to play, hurt or otherwise. He played more physical football than anybody on his team, including the linebackers."

That man was Bill Walsh, who would, of course, go on to mentor Joe Montana in San Francisco.

Fouts remained a Charger his entire career. Perhaps his greatest moment came in the 1981 AFC divisional playoff game against the Miami Dolphins at the Orange Bowl. *Sports Illustrated* called it "A Game No One Should Have Lost," a wild 41–38 overtime victory for San Diego.

Dan Fouts in a game in 1984.

Fouts finished the afternoon that stretched into evening with 33 completions on 53 attempts for 433 yards and three touchdowns — all NFL postseason records at the time. He led the Chargers on a 74-yard drive to set up the decisive 29-yard Rolf Benirschke field goal.

The euphoria was short-lived, however. In bone-chilling cold at Riverfront Stadium, the pass-happy Chargers were beaten 27–7 by the Bengals in the AFC title tilt.

Fouts exited the NFL as a two-time First Team All-Pro with six Pro Bowl appearances. He was one of only three men at the time to throw for over 40,000 yards. His famous No. 14 is one of only four numbers retired by the Chargers.

The only thing missing? A ring.

"I'm over it," said Fouts on the day he was enshrined in Canton. "You strive to win a Super Bowl, and you do everything you can to get there. But being in the Hall of Fame, you never play for that honor. It's incredible."

On enshrinement day he joined the greatest quarterbacks of all time, including his choice to direct a late winning drive.

"Unitas," said Fouts. "But that's a tough call, choosing one quarterback. Some people would choose John Elway as their greatest quarterback. Some people would choose Marino. Some people would choose

Joe Montana. Some people would choose Fran Tarkenton. Some people would choose Joe Namath."

Others, of a later vintage, would likely choose Peyton Manning or Tom Brady.

And some people, it goes without saying, would choose Dan Fouts. ■

College: University of Oregon
Drafted: 1973, San Diego Chargers, 64th overall
Years active: 1973–1987
Top honors: First Team All-Pro (1979, 1982), NFL AP Offensive Player of the Year (1982)
Hall of Fame induction: 1993

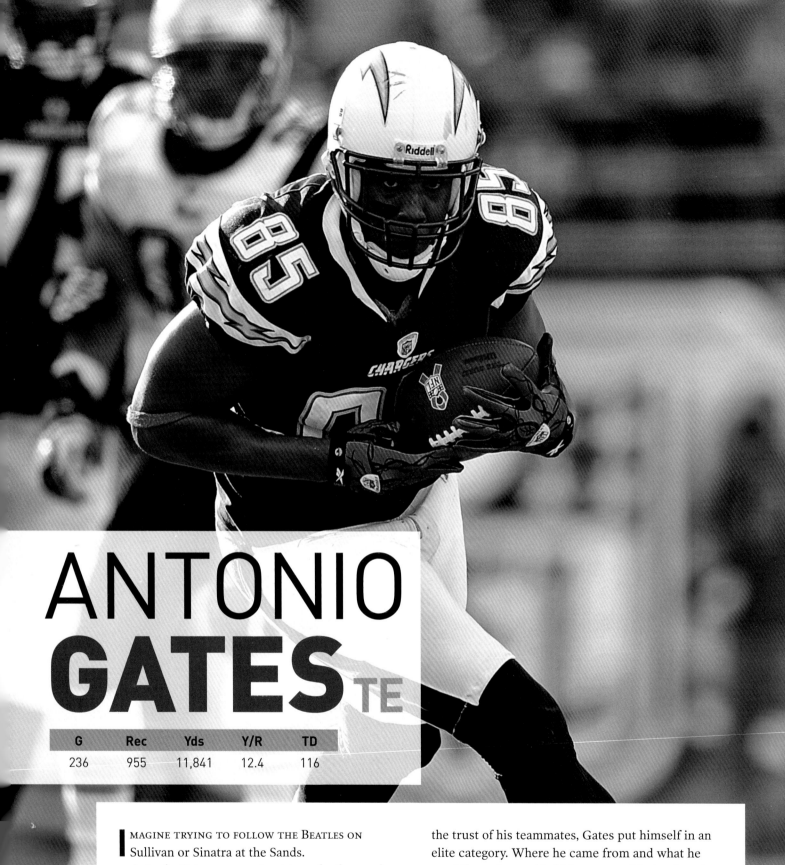

ANTONIO GATES TE

G	Rec	Yds	Y/R	TD
236	955	11,841	12.4	116

I MAGINE TRYING TO FOLLOW THE BEATLES ON Sullivan or Sinatra at the Sands.

Antonio Gates never set out to make the good people of San Diego forget Kellen Winslow. And, as it turned out, he couldn't. But to be held in the same rarified level of esteem is tribute enough.

By doing it his way, by making plays and gaining the trust of his teammates, Gates put himself in an elite category. Where he came from and what he went through provided his career with depth and resonance.

Winslow is revered in San Diego for those seasons spent playing pitch-and-catch with the pass-happy Dan Fouts in the Don "Air" Coryell era.

Gates emerged from Winslow's shadow to conjure up an even more pyrotechnic partnership with Philip Rivers.

From 2004 — his second season wearing the lightning bolt — though to the franchise's final year in San Diego before the move to Los Angeles in 2016, Gates averaged 67 catches per annum. That's what's called consistently excelling.

Sports writer Dan Pompei best caught the flavor of the thing when he noted of Gates, "He has the instincts to carve up a zone defense like an electric knife through a tender turkey breast."

The fact that Gates made it at all is what's most remarkable.

Gates grew up in inner-city Detroit, in a neighborhood teeming with drugs and other dangers. He credits his parents with steering him out of trouble and channeling his energies toward sports, which led him to star for Central High School in both football and basketball.

"You have to affiliate yourself [with] people that want to become something, that want to do something in life," said Gates in a documentary on his life, *Forging a New Path*. "I was trying a different path than a lot of my friends. You always want to hold onto that friendship and you still can. You just have to understand that your path is so different you can't do the same things. The first thing, for me, was that I had to surround myself with better people. Not that the people I was hanging with, my friends, were bad people, but I wanted to go to college, I wanted to become a professional athlete."

Gates yearned to become an NBA star. Truth be told, basketball was always his first love. In his senior year at Kent State, Gates became the Golden Flashes' top scorer (20.6 PPG) and rebounder (7.7 RPG) and was selected an AP Honorable Mention All-American. His great play propelled his school into the Elite Eight of the NCAA's March Madness tournament in 2002.

At 6-foot-4, however, Gates didn't quite have the height to convince NBA scouts, so he dropped his hoop dreams and decided to try football. He arranged a tryout for NFL bird-dogs, even though he hadn't played football in four years. Not a down in college.

It didn't matter. The Chargers took a look at his 255-pound frame, his competitiveness and quickness, and signed him to a contract in 2003.

A little faith can sometimes pay huge dividends.

Gates always had a first step — a separation step — in basketball, and it carried over into football. In his rookie season he rose from third on the depth chart to a starting spot, and he was at the forefront of a league-wide reemergence of the tight end position. With size, speed and hands as soft as a roll of Charmin, Gates became the prototype of a new era. His teammates were in awe.

"The best," said Chargers safety Eric Weddle. "You can't guard him."

After signing a hefty five-year, $36 million deal in the summer of 2010, Gates found himself slowed by nagging foot injuries. When healthy, however, he remained a force of nature, and the 2014 season proved that. Not only did he become the Chargers' franchise leader in receiving yards, surpassing Lance Alworth, Gates also became the fourth tight end in NFL history to gain more than 10,000 yards.

By the start of the 2019 campaign, however, after two seasons in a diminished role with the relocated Chargers, Gates found himself without an NFL home at age 39. He eventually retired the following January. He did so with the most touchdowns ever by a tight end.

No longer merely the heir apparent to a long-ago legend, Gates fulfilled the potential the Chargers saw in him and has now cast a rather large shadow of his own.

"I believe potential is a dangerous word, it can be used for anybody," said Gates early in his career. "I don't want people to always say, 'He has the potential to be good.' Or, 'He has a couple of years to go.' I want somebody to say, 'Damn, that's a good tight end.' Period."

One of the best ever. Period. ▪

> ## "He has the instincts to carve up a zone defense like an electric knife through a tender turkey breast."
> — Dan Pompei, Sports Illustrated

College: Kent State University
Drafted: undrafted
Years active: 2003–2018
Top honors: First Team All-Pro (2004–06)
Hall of Fame induction: N/A

ROB
GRONKOWSKI TE

G	Rec	Yds	Y/R	TD
143	621	9,286	15.0	92

SAVORING A UNIQUE MOMENT IN A UNIQUE CAREER, Rob Gronkowski stood back and allowed it to soak in.

All of it.

New team. New environment. New challenge.

Familiar result.

"What a start it was to the journey and what a finish!" he exulted following the Tampa Bay Buccaneers'

31–9 Super Bowl LV beatdown of the reigning champion Kansas City Chiefs on home (Bermuda grass) turf at Raymond James Stadium in Tampa Bay on February 7, 2021. "It's for real. It was the real deal.

"To come down here to Tampa, come to an organization that was ready to win ... Just unbelievable and it definitely ranks up there as one of my biggest accomplishments, ever.

"What a story it's been."

Yes, it was. Has been. May yet continue to be.

Rewind two years from that cameo-keepsake moment in Tampa, and Gronkowski had had enough of football, despite just winning a third Super Bowl on behalf of the New England Patriots.

Worn out mentally. Beaten up physically. Feeling like the ragged end of nowhere.

"I was not in a good place," he explained of his decision to retire in 2019. "Football was bringing me down, and I didn't like it. I was losing that joy in life…"

He spent a season away, but the combination of the Florida weather, the proximity to his mom two hours away from Tampa and, of course, a rekindling of the partnership with QB Tom Brady brought him back.

Together, Brady and Gronkowski have formed a partnership for the ages. Sort of a football equivalent of Woody and Buzz Lightyear or Han Solo and Chewbacca. Brains aligned with brawn.

"Gronk." Could there be a better nickname for a football player of his man-crushing abilities?

He is, after all, a demolition looking for a place to happen. He drags players — sometimes multiple players — who try to tackle him and knocks them flat. Sometimes he "Gronkowskies" them, leaving them looking like a pile of strewn rubble.

Gronk's amazing adventure began in Williamsville, New York, where he grew up the second youngest of five sports-mad brothers. Did the brothers fight? Always. Did Gronkowski get the worst of it? More often than not, but it did toughen him up and feed his anything-goes nature. He developed into an All-Pac-10 tight end at the University of Arizona, but back surgery affected his 2010 NFL Draft ranking, and it wasn't until the second round that the Patriots chose him with the 42nd pick overall.

Right from the start, most everything Gronkowski did with the Patriots was larger than life. He scored three touchdowns in one game as a rookie. And his second season dwarfed his first. He caught 90 passes for 18 TDs and 1,327 receiving yards — both single-season tight end records at the time (the TD number still stands).

That was only the start.

While John Mackey set the template for tight ends in the 60s, the 6-foot-6, 265-pound Gronkowski helped reimagine it into modern-day terms.

His 9,961 career yards receiving are fifth most by a TE, his 64.9 per game average trails only Travis Kelce, and his 92 TDs rank third highest.

And then there's a little matter of those four shiny rings.

Adding to Gronkowski's appeal was a sense of fun. Whether posing nude for *ESPN The Magazine*'s body issue or shirtless alongside an adult film actress who just happened to be wearing his New England jersey, dancing shirtless at a nightclub hours after the Patriots' loss to the New York Giants in Super Bowl XLVI, or winning the WWE 24/7 championship in his short-lived retirement, Gronk always seemed to be having himself a helluva time.

He's always been the big man for the big moment. In Super Bowl LIII against the L.A. Rams, as an example, he set career records for tight ends — 23 catches, good for 297 yards — as the Patriots prevailed 13–3, delivering him a third ring.

Weeks later, on March 24, 2019, a few months shy of his 30th birthday, he announced that decision to retire via a post on Instagram.

Only a year later, though, refreshed and gazing at new horizons, he joined Brady in Tampa and delivered, as always, catching those two touchdown passes versus the Chiefs to add an additional coat of luster to his legend.

The Bucs appeared primed for a repeat run in 2021, but the surprise-package L.A. Rams built up a 24-point lead and held on for a last-play-field-goal 30–27 upset in the NFC divisional playoff game.

Afterward, Brady hinted that, at 44, he might at last step away.

Gronkowski was also non-committal about what lay ahead.

"I love the action movies," Gronk once said. "I'd love to be part of those."

In a way, blowing up defensive backs and defenses in general and looking every bit the part of Sly, Jean-Claude or Bruce Willis, he already has.

And who knows, if he actually does decide to step away for good this time and is looking for a career change… ■

College: University of Arizona
Drafted: 2010, New England Patriots, 42nd overall
Years active: 2010–present
Top honors: NFL All-Rookie Team (2010), First Team All-Pro (2011, 2014, 2015, 2017), NFL AP Comeback Player of the Year (2014), Super Bowl Champion (2014, 2016, 2018, 2020)
Hall of Fame induction: N/A

FRANCO
HARRIS RB

G	Att	Yds	Avg	TD
173	2,949	12,120	4.1	91

THE EERIE LIFE-SIZE LIKENESS, SITUATED NEAR THE escalators leading to the baggage carousel at Pittsburgh International Airport, is in mighty good company.

There, leaning down to snatch the football maybe a foot from the ground, is the spitting image of Franco Harris, the famous No. 32 in Pittsburgh Steelers black. Directly beside him stands a statue of another fairly recognizable American hero: George Washington. That's how much Harris means to the city breastfed on pig iron. That's how much one play can linger in memory, decades later — the Immaculate Reception.

Even had Harris not rushed for 12,120 yards over 13 seasons, eight times for 1,000 or better; even if he had not played in nine Pro Bowls or piled up 14,622 all-purpose yards; even if he had not been part of four Super Bowl championship teams or been named MVP of Super Bowl IX or been enshrined among the immortals in Canton, Ohio — even then, Harris would have a starring role in the NFL's history for his part in arguably the league's most famous single play.

"I've played football since the second grade," said Steelers quarterback Terry Bradshaw in the aftermath. "And nothing like that ever happened. It'll never happen again."

The details are familiar to football fans across North America. On December 23, 1972, the hometown Steelers were trailing the Oakland Raiders 7–6 with just 22 seconds remaining in an AFC divisional playoff game. Bradshaw was flushed out of the pocket on fourth and 10 from his own 40-yard line, then pushed back inside. His desperation throw, too far for the intended

receiver, caromed off Steelers safety Jack Tatum and/or Pittsburgh wideout John "Frenchy" Fuqua.

There to pluck the ball off his shoe tops on the ricochet was Harris.

Forty-two yards later, he crossed the goal line, and the entire city of Pittsburgh went absolutely nuts.

"When I see the film, that's like proof that it happened," said Harris. "But it still seems like a dream."

If the ball did — as the Raiders insist — hit Fuqua at all, the play should've been ruled invalid, as it had touched two offensive players. If it only struck Tatum, the catch and the touchdown were legitimate. The debate rages on. Replays are inconclusive.

Steelers coach Chuck Noll praised his prize rookie's attitude in the controversial aftermath.

"Franco made that play because he never quit on the play," said Noll. "He kept running. He kept hustling. Good things happen to those who hustle."

Yet to remember one of the NFL's most versatile, durable backs for that piece of drama alone would be a disservice to the man — an injustice to his legacy.

Of course, Harris's Steelers all became a legendary lot. Bradshaw. The balletic Lynn Swann. The menacing Jack Lambert and Jack Ham at linebacker. Center Tom Webster. And, of course, the Steel Curtain defensive front of Mean Joe Greene, L.C. Greenwood, Dwight White and Ernie Holmes — the four horsemen of any quarterback's apocalypse.

"Halfway through the decade," recalled Harris, "we realized that we had a great team and could do great things, that we could probably have something here, that we believed had a chance to reach greatness."

Franco Harris eludes a tackle by Oakland Raiders cornerback Jimmy Warren before scoring the game-winning touchdown, in a play known as the Immaculate Reception.

In the 1970s Noll's Steelers reached greatness and then kept topping it. They had swagger. They had style. And they had the perfect complement to Bradshaw's aerial game.

At 6-foot-2 and 230 pounds, Harris had size enough to run over people and enough spring in his legs to slide past them. Besides his Hall of Fame career rushing totals, which include 100 or more yards on 47 occasions, the 13th overall pick in the 1972 NFL Draft also caught 307 passes for 2,287 yards and nine touchdowns. When he retired, his combined yardage of 14,622 was the third-highest total ever. Sparking the first of four title triumphs, Harris rushed 34 times for 158 yards

in Super Bowl IX, breaking Larry Csonka's record of the year before to earn MVP honors.

Harris spent his final year in Seattle as a Seahawk, but never looked right in anything other than vintage Steelers black.

During his dozen seasons in the Steel City, the man who inspired Franco's Italian Army in the stands at Three Rivers, who developed into one of the most dependable backs of his era, could run away from the most punishing, the most pursuant, of NFL defenses.

What he can never run away from is that incredible, improbable play, and Harris will never be able to shake that.

One play, forever frozen in time, beside the escalators leading down to the baggage carousel at Pittsburgh International Airport — right beside George Washington. ▪

College: Penn State University
Drafted: 1972, Pittsburgh Steelers, 13th overall
Years active: 1972–1984
Top honors: NFL AP Offensive Rookie of the Year (1972), Super Bowl Champion (1974, 1975, 1977, 1978) Super Bowl MVP (1974), NFL Walter Payton Man of the Year (1976), First Team All-Pro (1977)
Hall of Fame induction: 1990

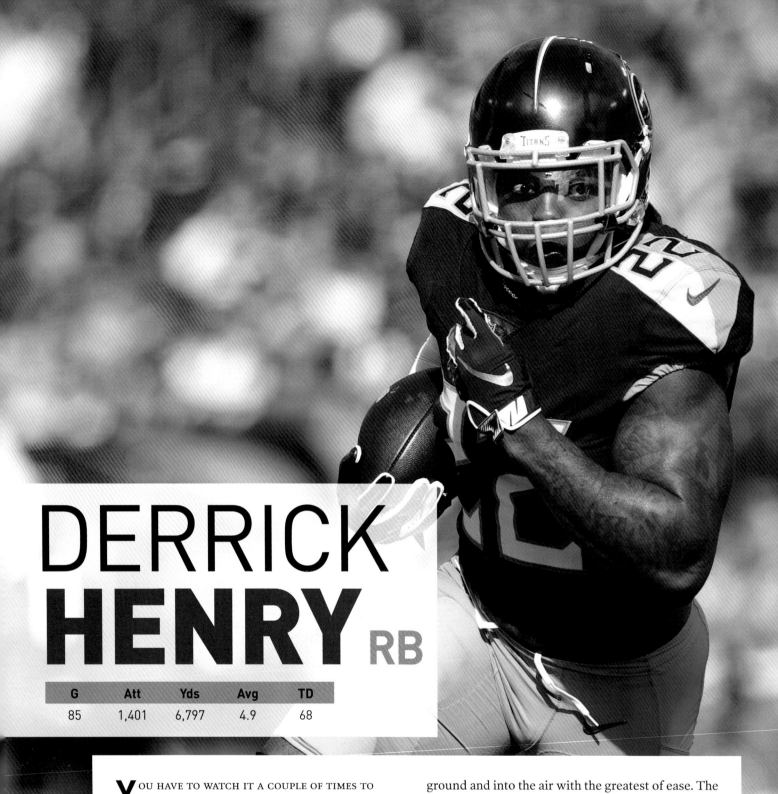

DERRICK
HENRY RB

G	Att	Yds	Avg	TD
85	1,401	6,797	4.9	68

YOU HAVE TO WATCH IT A COUPLE OF TIMES TO truly appreciate its enormity. Buffalo Bills defensive back Josh Norman was running to his right, locking on to a big target — the 247-pound demolition man Derrick Henry. The Tennessee Titans running back had the football and was heading upfield when Norman got in his way.

What happened next was a did-you-see-that moment. Henry stuck out his right arm and rammed into the 190-pound Norman, who was flung off the ground and into the air with the greatest of ease. The Tennessee sideline erupted in hoots and guffaws. The game's TV announcers marveled at the replays. The stiff-arm destroyer had struck again.

Many a large ball carrier has terrorized the NFL. Pittsburgh Steeler Jerome Bettis weighed 251 pounds when he rumbled through defenders for more than 13,000 career yards. That put him into the Pro Football Hall of Fame. And the feeling is King Henry, as he is known throughout the league, has the ability to do the same. No less an expert than Bettis believes that.

Prior to the 2020 season, Bettis said he expected "a big year" from Henry, who had topped the 1,500-yard mark the year before to win his first NFL rushing title. How clairvoyant was Bettis? Henry smashed his way to 2,027 yards, making him only the eighth player in NFL history to surpass the 2,000-yard barrier. He also became the fifth running back to rush for 145 yards or more, plus score a touchdown, in three consecutive games. Before that, he made NFL history as the first back to post a 200-yard rushing game in three consecutive seasons. Bettis said there has been a reason for that.

"I think people, especially the Tennessee Titans, they're starting to understand how you fully utilize a running back like Derrick Henry," explained Bettis. "You don't get his true ability with five, six, 10, 15 carries. He needs 25 carries, 30 carries for you to see his true effectiveness and how special he is as a running back."

The Titans came to that conclusion in 2019 when they handed Henry the ball 303 times. That number went up to 378 in 2020, giving Henry enough chances to show what kind of destruction he could unleash with his trademark stiff-arm.

Henry first began unloading on tacklers before they unloaded on him while playing high school football in Yulee, Florida. With the Yulee Hornets, he scored 26 touchdowns — his first year. He followed up by scoring 38, 34 and 55 times over the next three seasons for a total of 153 touchdowns. His final yardage count was 12,124 and

included a state-record 510 yards in a single game. Please note that aside from football he played basketball and ran track. He clocked a personal best 11.11 seconds in the 100-meter dash as a 15-year-old.

After committing to the University of Alabama, where he polished his stiff-arm tactics, Henry led the Crimson Tide to the 2015 College Football Playoff National Championship. In a 45–40 win against Clemson, he rushed for 158 yards and three touchdowns. He won the Heisman Trophy as the top college player that season but was not a first-round selection in the NFL Draft. Instead, Tennessee used the 45th pick overall to make Henry a Titan.

NFL scouts gave Henry high marks for his size and power but were concerned about his running style, saying it was too upright. Apparently, that was going to make him easier to bring down. Then came the one-arm assaults.

Against the Indianapolis Colts, Henry shoved 315-pound defensive lineman Grover Stewart aside as if he were a 98-pound weakling. Detroit Lions defensive back Alex Myres had been warned not to play into Henry's strength. Myres came in on the wrong approach and surrendered his leverage. The next thing Myres knew, he was dropped in his tracks. His defensive coordinator said Myres deserved the lesson in tackling. It was Myres' first game in the NFL.

The Jacksonville Jaguars have been mistreated by Henry more than once. On one play, he broke loose and then twice stiff-armed the same defender, Jarrod Wilson, to score on a 74-yard run. Then came Henry's signature effort. He

burst outside the Jaguars' defensive line before sending cornerback A.J. Bouye to the turf and then doing the same to linebacker Leon Jacobs, then shoving linebacker Myles Jack out of the play to cap a 99-yard touchdown that tied Tony Dorsett for the longest run from scrimmage in NFL history.

Tennessee quarterback Ryan Tannehill spoke for everyone when he said of Henry's performance, "I screamed, 'Holy crap!' That was unbelievable."

"I just look at how a defender is going to approach," said Henry of his thought process. "Usually, they'll start high, then go low real quick, so I'm not able to get my hand to be able to stiff arm … I just waited and timed it, and it worked."

Everything was working nicely for Henry and his teammates until Week 8 of the 2021 season. Not only did Tennessee lose to Indianapolis in overtime, but the Titans were stunned when Henry suffered a fractured bone in his right foot and needed season-ending surgery. At that point, Henry was leading the NFL with 937 rushing yards on 219 carries. It put a gigantic hole in the Titans' offense. He ran for a touchdown and just 62 yards in a playoff loss to the Cincinnati Bengals.

Tennessee fans are anxious for the King's return in 2022. ◾

College: University of Alabama
Drafted: 2016, Tennessee Titans, 45th overall
Years active: 2016–present
Top honors: All-Pro First Team (2020), NFL AP Offensive Player of the Year (2020)
Hall of Fame induction: N/A

TYREEK HILL WR

G	Rec	Yds	Y/R	TD
91	479	6,630	13.8	56

THE TOP SPEED OF A CHEETAH HAS BEEN RECORDED at around 68 to 75 miles per hour.

Okay, so maybe Tyreek Hill isn't quite *that* fast … But his explosiveness sure does remind people of the big cat species that roams the plains of Africa.

"He's one of the fastest human beings I've ever seen line up in a pair of cleats," marveled Kansas City Chiefs offensive coordinator Eric Bieniemy to ESPN. "There's only been a few [players] that

I've looked back and said, 'Wow!' One being Deion Sanders. Rocket Ismail.

"When you have a player that has that unique gift to take the top off everything, yes, it does lighten the load for a lot of different people."

Remember that Muhammad Ali signature line "I'm so fast, I can turn off the lights and be in bed before the room gets dark"?

Tyreek Hill can relate.

> *"He's one of the fastest human beings I've ever seen line up in a pair of cleats."*
> *— Kansas City Chiefs offensive coordinator Eric Bieniemy*

In 2021, he broke teammate Travis Kelce's franchise record for receptions in a season (105), finishing with 111. A season earlier, he'd tied Dwayne Bowe's K.C. single-season standard of 15 touchdown catches, and in 2018 he compiled the most seasonal pass-catching yards in K.C. annals, 1,479.

Hill has been on the fast track since high school.

In 2012, representing Coffee High School in Douglas, Georgia, he collected two medals: a gold in the 4-by-100-meter relay and a bronze in the 200-meter race at the world junior track and field Championships in Barcelona, Spain.

Naturally, he began to generate national attention at Garden City community College before enrolling at Oklahoma State. However, on December 11, 2014, one year after arriving, the Cowboys dismissed Hill from their football and track teams for a domestic violence charge.

He subsequently enrolled at West Alabama.

The talent level was indisputable, but the off-field issues made NFL organizations uncomfortable. The Chiefs eventually wound up choosing Hill in the fifth round, the 165th player taken in the 2016 NFL Draft.

Despite being fourth on the WR depth chart to open his rookie campaign and starting just one game, Hill caught 61 passes and racked up 12 total touchdowns, three on returns.

In 2017, he made 75 catches. And the acceleration has only continued.

The Chiefs, energized by the head-turning MVP performance of QB Patrick Mahomes, went 12-4 on the regular season and then advanced all the way to the AFC Championship Game against the dynastic New England Patriots.

The New England defense did a masterful job of muffling Hill, limiting him to one catch. The Pats advanced after a compelling 37–31 OT victory. Nevertheless, Hill was named both a Pro Bowl and a First Team All-Pro selection, and he signed a three-year, $54 million contract extension in September 2019.

With the pain of losing to New England fresh in their collective psyche, Hill and his mates made championship amends in 2019, finishing 12-4 on the regular season before mounting a pair of jaw-dropping playoff comebacks — first against the Houston Texans and then the Tennessee Titans — to reach Super Bowl LIV against the San Francisco 49ers.

At Miami's Hard Rock Stadium on February 2, 2020, Mahomes and Co. pulled another rabbit out of another hat, scoring 21 straight points in the final 6:13 of the fourth to win 31–20, ending a half-century title drought for the franchise.

Hill snared nine passes for a game-high 105 yards, two of those on the pivotal drive that resulted in Kansas City's 24–20 lead, including one catch for 44 yards.

"We're something special," exulted Hill. "If I can continue to play on this team for the rest of my career, I would love that, because the band of brothers, the way we believe, the way we play for each other, is crazy."

Since that dizzying high, a Super Bowl mauling by Tampa and a heartbreaking overtime AFC Championship loss to Cincinnati in consecutive years have managed to slow the Kansas City express.

And although no one knew it, that band of brothers Hill had spoken of was on borrowed time. On March 23, 2022, the Chiefs, unable to make headway in contract terms, in a shock move, dealt Hill to the Miami Dolphins in exchange for five draft picks.

"I love Tyreek Hill," said coach Andy Reid following the trade. "There's no rift between Tyreek Hill and myself.

"We came in aggressive (with an offer), and after we got to a point, we just said, 'Listen, in this day and age, you have issues you have to deal with the cap.' So we felt like it was better to allow him to go ahead and be traded. ... You can go different routes with a player. You can play hardball or you can go about it the way I did, or we did."

Hill immediately signed a four-year extension worth $120 million, making him the league's highest-paid receiver.

The Cheetah was primed and ready to run in southeast Florida. ■

College: University of West Alabama
Drafted: 2016, Kansas City Chiefs, 165th overall
Years active: 2016–present
Top honors: NFL All-Rookie Team (2016), First Team All-Pro (2016, 2018), Super Bowl Champion (2019)
Hall of Fame induction: N/A

DeANDRE HOPKINS WR

G	Rec	Yds	Y/R	TD
136	789	10,581	13.4	68

DeANDRE HOPKINS RECKONS HIMSELF SOMETHING OF A Venus flytrap among receivers.

"This is something I haven't told many people, because it's embarrassing," the Arizona Cardinals' star wideout once confessed. "We always used to catch flies with our hands. I was the only one who could catch 'em. One-handed, two-handed.

"I actually studied flies. I'd watch 'em. How do you catch flies? They fly up.

'If I can catch that, I can catch anything."

Yes, he can.

Ball's in the air, and ... Snap! The prey is in his clutches.

Hopkins, first and foremost, is an athlete driven by the example set by one very special person.

His mom, Sabrina Greenlee, was left to raise four children as a single mom following the death of her husband, Harris Steve Hopkins, in a car crash at age 25. DeAndre was five months old.

When DeAndre was about 10 years old, his mother was blinded when a jealous woman, who was also dating Greenlee's boyfriend at the time (unbeknownst to Greenlee), threw a boiling mixture of lye and bleach in her face. The attack cost Greenlee all sight in her right eye and 40 percent in her left. She subsequently lost all vision.

DeAndre watched his mother endure these crippling hardships with determination and grace, and her day-to-day example of courage and resilience couldn't help but have a profound effect on the young Hopkins as he grew up in Central, South Carolina.

Hopkins spent three seasons at Clemson University, just a hop, skip and a jump (or 9 miles) away from home.

With his mother nearby, he recorded 206 catches for 3,020 yards for the Tigers. His junior season thrust him into the vanguard of collegiate receivers; he made 82 catches for 1,405 yards and a school-record 18 touchdowns. Hopkins decided to forgo his senior season and was selected 27th overall at the 2013 NFL Draft by the Houston Texans.

An instant starter after signing a four-year, $7.62 million deal with the Texans, Hopkins corralled 52 passes for 802 yards as a rookie — enough for him to be named to the All-Rookie Team. The next season he conquered the 1,000-yard barrier, piling up 1,210 yards off of 76 catches. A year after that, his catch total had risen to 111 for 1,521 yards. In 2017 he made a career-high 13 touchdown receptions, top among all receivers, and was named a First Team All-Pro for the first time.

The progression continued at a startling pace in 2018. Hopkins finished second in the league in yards receiving (1,572) and third in catches (115) en route to another All-Pro selection.

"If I drop a ball, I'm going to beat myself up," said Hopkins. "Or if I go out and a rep isn't perfect, I feel like I've got to do it again ... Repetition makes perfect."

Does it ever. In 2018 the analytics website Pro Football Focus tracked Hopkins and announced he had made 105 catchable passes without a drop.

Whenever he feels tired, out of sorts or on the verge of maybe cutting a corner, Hopkins has only to close his eyes and think of the magnificent lady who raised him.

"I'm always picturing her, whenever I make a catch, her reaction. And sometimes, when I drop a ball, I'm like, 'Darn it. I let my mama down.'"

DeAndre Hopkins runs through traffic in an October 2019 game against the Oakland Raiders.

The powerful tale of mother and son was featured on an *ESPN The Magazine* cover story. Then, in late April 2019, plans were announced for a motion picture based on Greenlee's life, entitled *Sabrina* (Hopkins nominated Oprah Winfrey for the role).

The Hopkins–Texans partnership, though, came to a surprising end on March 20, 2020, when Houston dealt its star receiver to the Arizona Cardinals along with a draft selection in exchange for tailback David Johnson and a pair of picks.

The consensus: an absolute steal for Arizona.

Hopkins quickly signed a two-year, $54.5 million contract with the Cardinals.

In his Arizona debut on September 13, 2020, Hopkins grabbed a career-high 14 passes for 151 yards versus the 49ers. He finished the season with 115 catches, good for 1,407 yards and six TDs. On November 19, he became the youngest player to join the 700-catch club, supplanting then-teammate Larry Fitzgerald atop the list.

But 2021 proved a struggle. A hamstring issue cost Hopkins three games before an MCL injury in Week 14 ruled him out for the remainder of the regular schedule and a 31–14 wild-card playoff loss to the L.A. Rams.

As Arizona looks to retool and take a serious run at a championship, they'll be counting on a healthy DeAndre Hopkins to act as a catalyst.

At 29, he's just entering his prime. And that drive, instilled by mama Sabrina, will continue to fuel him.

He makes it look easy.

As easy, really, as catching flies. ■

College: Clemson University
Drafted: 2013, Houston Texans, 27th overall
Years active: 2013–present
Top honors: NFL All-Rookie Team (2013), First Team All-Pro (2017–19)
Hall of Fame induction: N/A

DON
HUTSON E DB DE

G	Yds	TD
116	7,991	99

YOU NEVER GET A SECOND CHANCE TO MAKE A GOOD first impression. Well, Don Hutson only ever made good impressions.

His initial catch as a pro, one of the 488 he'd accumulate on behalf of the Green Bay Packers, was quite the introduction: an 83-yard touchdown hookup with quarterback Arnie Herber against the archrival Chicago Bears. First play of the game from scrimmage, no less, second fixture of the 1935 NFL season.

Years later, he would recall with customarily quiet satisfaction some unexpected pregame motivation he received listening to a popular radio sports pundit.

"[He] took 15 or 30 minutes ... before the game started every Sunday to discuss Mr. [Curly] Lambeau and the Packers," reminisced Hutson. "To say the least, he was highly critical.

"The 15 minutes before this first game, he devoted entirely to how dumb Lambeau had been to sign me to play with Green Bay. It was a very discouraging 15 minutes, because we always listened to it to hear what the guy had to say. Well, everybody was shaking their heads, looking at me.

"They kicked off to us and brought the ball out to the 20-yard-line. And on the first play, Herber threw me an 80-yard pass, and the game ended 7-0."

Before the glitz and glamour of the NFL's TV and big-money era, Hutson is often regarded as the game's first modern receiver, credited with refining route running.

Consider that in 1939, he *averaged* 24.9 yards a snare. In 1942, Hutson caught 74 passes for a career-high 1,211 yards — the first man ever to top the 1,000 mark — and 17 touchdowns.

In seven of his 11 NFL seasons, all as a Packer, he led the league in receiving yardage. In eight, he topped the passes-caught list. In nine, he was first in touchdown receptions.

On October 7, 1945, Hutson, during what would be his final NFL campaign, scored 29 points in *one quarter*, still an NFL record 76 years later, with touchdown catches of 56, 46, 17 and 6 yards, along with five kicking points.

"I asked him to sum up the game and he gave it to me about as succinctly as you can," Lee Remmel told the *Milwaukee Sentinel-Journal* decades later. "He said: 'I'll give it to you in three words: Too much Hutson.'"

Through the course of his pro career, the willowy 6-foot-1, 183-pound Hutson would help steer the Pack to three NFL titles and be selected league MVP twice. He lined up on defense too, at safety. In his final six seasons, he swiped 30 opposing quarterbacks' passes and led the league with six picks in 1940.

Add his place-kicking prowess to the mix, and Hutson could be considered a legitimate triple threat.

But it was as a home-run-hitting receiver that he gained lasting fame. In six of his 11 seasons, Hutson posted at least one catch of 70 yards or more. Agile, graceful, intelligent and durable (he never missed a game), he was a human highlight reel long before NBAer Dominique Wilkins got the tag.

Beneath the spectacular, though, lay a foundation.

"For every pass I caught in a game," Hutson once said, "I caught a thousand in practice."

Donald Montgomery Hutson was born on January 31, 1913, in Pine Bluff, Arkansas. His father, Roy, worked as a railroad conductor.

Hutson, a natural, developed into a star high school athlete. In 1931, a buddy, Bob Seawall, was recruited by the Alabama football program, and Hutson tagged along. He impressed enough to be offered a baseball scholarship as a center fielder, ran sprints in track and wound up as a football team walk-on.

In 1934, the Crimson Tide went undefeated. A year later, Hutson produced six catches for 165 yards, including two touchdowns of 54 and 59 yards, in the Rose Bowl game against Stanford.

Hutson actually came close to not joining the pass-prone Packers postcollege, signing NFL contracts with both Green Bay and the Brooklyn Dodgers.

League president Joe Carr ruled that the contract with the earliest postmark would be the one to be honored. Turned out, the Packers' contract had been postmarked 8:30 a.m., 17 minutes earlier than the Dodgers' offer.

Don Hutson was off to Wisconsin. And it is there that his legacy lives on. A once-and-always Packer, just the way they like 'em in Titletown.

Hutson's 14 was the first number retired by the organization, in 1951. A street in the Packerland Industrial Park in Green Bay is named for him. And in 1994, the team christened its new indoor practice facility the Don Hutson Center.

In his ability to lead the way in expanding the limits of the passing game, Hudson was definitely a player for his time.

Paul Hornung, another Golden Boy of Packers fame, considered Hutson a player for any time.

"You know what Hutson would do in this league today?" Horning once

Don Hutson catches a pass during an NFL game.

quipped. "The same things he did when he played."

When Don Hutson stepped away from the game in 1945, his 99 career touchdown receptions stood as the most ever.

That record held fast for more than four decades. ▬

College: University of Alabama
Drafted: N/A
Years active: 1935–1945
Top honors: NFL Champion (1936, 1939, 1944), NFL MVP (1941, 1942), First Team All-Pro (1938-1945)
Hall of Fame induction: 1963

BO
JACKSON RB

G	Att	Yds	Avg	TD
38	515	2,782	5.4	16

THE SENTIMENT ENCAPSULATED THE MAN'S uncompromising style.

"If my mother put on a helmet and shoulder pads and a uniform that wasn't the same as the one I was wearing," Bo Jackson famously confessed, "I'd run over her if she was in my way.

"And I love my mother."

That is only part of why we all loved Bo.

Born the eighth of 10 children, Vincent Edward "Bo" Jackson hailed from Bessemer, Alabama (selected the state's Worst City to Live In by website 24/7 Wall St. in 2019). He was named after his mom's favorite actor, Vince Edwards, star of the popular medical TV series *Ben Casey*.

Blessed with size, strength, lickety-split speed and an appetite for you-versus-me competition, he'd go on to become the most famous multisport athlete of his age — arguably of any age.

The kid who grew up dreaming of being an airline pilot took flight at Auburn University, excelling at any sport that caught his fancy. Over four seasons, as the workhorse running back for the Tigers, he amassed more than 4,300 yards and scored 36 touchdowns on his way to winning the Heisman Trophy in 1985.

Jackson was selected first overall at the 1986 NFL Draft by Tampa Bay, but refused to play for the Buccaneers, citing an all-expenses-paid visit to Tampa he received that was supposedly allowable under NCAA rules. In actuality it wasn't, and it cost him the final stages of his collegiate baseball career.

Bo knew loyalty, too, and so on principle he spurned a $7.6 million, five-year contract from the Bucs in favor of a $1.07 million three-year contract with the MLB's Kansas City Royals.

Jackson was redrafted the next year, this time by the Los Angeles Raiders. And so began four astounding years in which he played in both the MLB *and* the NFL — a stretch that made Jackson's versatility and athletic portfolio, quite simply, unrivaled.

"I was the type of guy," said Jackson, "that used to get up in the morning and go out and just outrun everybody on the field without stretching or warming up or anything."

Bo could drop a shoulder and flatline a 230-pound linebacker. Bo could hit a 100-mph fastball into the bank of lights beyond the deepest part of center field. Bo could run track in college, good enough to qualify for an NCAA 100-meter final. Bo could be named a Second Team All-Pro in the NFL and play in the MLB All-Star Game.

Bo could inspire the athlete ad craze with his "Bo Knows" campaign for Nike, a series of commercials for his cross-training shoe that had him taking a whirl at a number of other sports and even trading riffs with blues music legend Bo Diddley, who told him, from one Bo to another: "You don't know Diddley!"

Bo could write an autobiography called *Bo Knows Bo*. Bo could dabble (somewhat unconvincingly) in the thespian arts, guest-starring on, among other hit TV shows of the era, *The Fresh Prince of Bel-Air*, *Lois & Clark: The New Adventures of Superman* and *Married... with Children*.

Bo, as a generation understood, could do just about anything.

He could become a two-sport phenomenon — playing football at the highest level while starring in the outfield for the Royals.

In only his fifth career NFL start, on November 30, 1987, Jackson utterly dismantled the Seattle Seahawks for 221 yards rushing. That total remains a record for a *Monday Night Football* telecast. Included in that carnage was a 91-yard touchdown romp that Jackson actually let up on around the Seattle 30-yard-line and put in cruise control the rest of the way. In fact, he didn't stop running until he hit the tunnel in the dressing room, and then tossed the Pete Rozelle-autographed ball into the air and swung at it with a make-believe bat. Just for emphasis.

During Jackson's long-distance commute, color broadcaster Dan Dierdorf delightedly exclaimed, "He

Bo, as a generation understood, could do just about anything.

might not stop 'til Tacoma!" His hit of the night came when he slammed into Seattle linebacker Brian "The Bos" Bosworth and carried him 2 yards into the end zone. So much for Bosworth's pregame chatter about how he was going to stop Bo cold.

Bo would play only 38 games over four abbreviated seasons for the Raiders, forced out of football by a fractured hip. He sustained the injury in his final NFL game when he was tackled by Kevin Walker in a postseason loss to the Cincinnati Bengals.

During his NFL pitstop in L.A., Jackson piled up 2,782 yards and 16 touchdowns.

"Before I injured my hip, I thought going to the gym was for wimps," said Jackson.

He returned to baseball, doing a lot of pinch-hitting for the Chicago White Sox and California Angels before retiring to private life in 1995.

So, yes, Bo's gridiron sample size was small. Yet nearly three decades have passed since Jackson last strapped on the shoulder pads, and Bo's signature No. 34 still remains at the Raiders' team merchandise store. ▮

College: Auburn University
Drafted: 1987, Los Angeles Raiders, 183rd overall
Years active: 1987–1990
Top honors: NFL All-Rookie Team (1987)
Hall of Fame induction: N/A

JULIO JONES WR

G	Rec	Yds	Y/R	TD
145	879	12,330	15.2	61

THE SPLIT WAS PRETTY MUCH ANNOUNCED ON AIR, cold call, coast to coast, via cell phone.

"Right now, I want to win," confessed Julio Jones to cohost Shannon Sharpe during a segment of Fox Sports' *Undisputed* program in June of 2021.

"I'm out of there, man."

Mere weeks later, he was.

After 10 spectacularly productive seasons in Atlanta, where Jones had developed a wonderful symmetry with QB Matt Ryan that helped him establish 18 franchise career receiving records, including yards (12,896) and receptions (848). Where he'd reached a Super Bowl in 2016 only to lose in soul-crushing fashion.

Where he'd often been described as "a Falcon for life" by team owner Arthur Blank.

The organization, in the throes a of rebuild, was facing salary-cap issues. Jones was 32 and coming

He has fame, riches and security, but the lessons learned watching his mom raise her family alone continue to fuel his competitive juices.

off a season bedeviled by hamstring issues.

The personal challenge was no longer to establish himself as one of the game's elite. Or to tally up the number of catches he made week to week.

But to finally rise to the collective challenge of helping to win a Super Bowl.

And challenges are something Quintorris Lopez Jones Jr. had been taught to face head on.

He was born and raised not far from the Gulf Coast in Foley, Alabama, the hometown of legendary Hall of Fame QB and Hall of Fame party animal Ken "Snake" Stabler.

When Jones was just five years old, his father left his young family, so Jones and his brother were raised by their mom. Queen Marvin logged nine-hour shifts at a local fried chicken restaurant just to make ends meet. She gave her boys everything. She even gave Quintorris the nickname he's known by now, when he was in seventh grade.

Julio Jones would go on to fame, riches (in September of 2015, he signed a three-year, $66 million extension, becoming the highest-paid wide receiver in the league) and security, but the lessons learned watching his mom raise her family alone continue to fuel his competitive juices.

"I'll tell you, he was out there playing one day, and he said, 'Mom, one day, when I get old enough, I'm going to play pro football, and I'm going to buy you a car and a new house,'" recalled Queen Marvin. "I said, 'OK, I appreciate that.'"

Promised it. Meant it. Did it.

After starring at Foley High School, Jones was highly recruited, eventually committing to the University of Alabama in 2008, where he starred. In 2009, then a sophomore, he and the Crimson Tide ran the table, a 14-0 season culminating in a 37–21 dusting of the Texas Longhorns in the national championship game.

Opting to forgo his senior season, Jones was selected sixth overall in the 2011 draft. The Falcons were so stone-cold sure of what they were getting that they traded five draft picks to the Cleveland Browns to move up and snare him.

A bold decision. But one that paid off, handsomely.

In seven of his 10 seasons as a Falcon, Jones went over 1,000 yards. The 136 passes he latched on to for 1,871 yards in 2015 still represent the third-highest single-season total in NFL annals, trailing only Calvin Johnson's 1,964 in 2012 and Cooper Kupp's 1,947 in 2021. He reached the summit of 10,000 career receiving yards faster than any man, ever.

The Falcons entered the 2016 playoffs with weighty expectations and, after subduing both Seattle and Green Bay, reached Super Bowl LI in Houston. Jones made four receptions

for 87 yards that day, including a tiptoe sideline beauty, but somehow, in some way, the Falcons managed to squander a 28–3 lead versus the New England Patriots and fell in heart-busting style, 34–28 in overtime.

A playoff berth the next season was followed by three disappointing postseason misses for Atlanta.

When the Titans added Jones to a potent offense that already boasted tailback Derrick Henry and wideout A.J. Brown, all seemed in readiness.

Although another hamstring issue limited Jones to 10 games and 31 catches his first year at Nissan Stadium, the Titans still finished 12-5 to secure top seed in the AFC and marched into the divisional round against Cincinnati in an expansive mood.

"I'm in a great place right now," Jones told SI.com pre-kickoff. "We gonna go out there and put on a show. That's what a week of preparation [will do] — coming out here, working each and every day, not taking it for granted and understanding what we have in front of us."

Once again, however, what Julio Jones had in front of him was heartache.

He caught a team-high six passes, for 62 yards, but the homesteading Titans were stunned by a 52-yard walk-off field goal, falling 19–16 to the Bengals.

The quest continues. ▪

College: University of Alabama
Drafted: 2011, Atlanta Falcons, 6th overall
Years active: 2011–present
Top honors: NFL All-Rookie Team (2011), First Team All-Pro (2015, 2016)
Hall of Fame induction: N/A

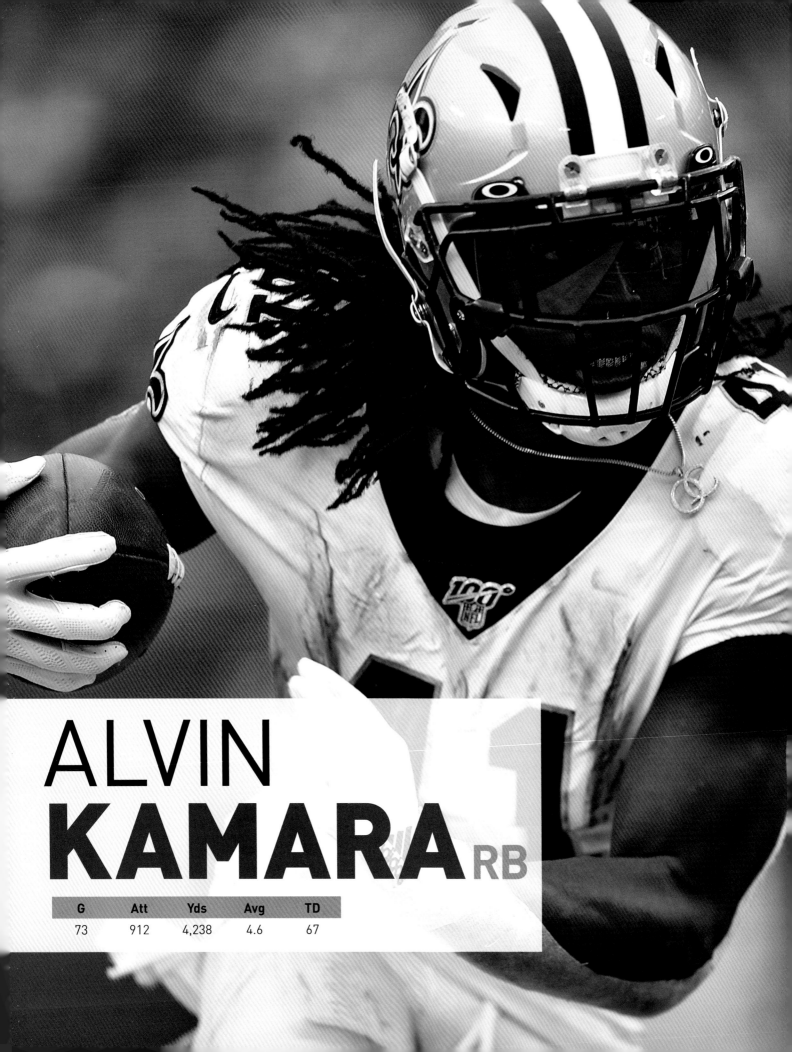

ALVIN
KAMARA RB

G	Att	Yds	Avg	TD
73	912	4,238	4.6	67

HIS FIRST TOUCHDOWN, ON Christmas Day 2020, was beautiful. Powerful and explosive, Alvin Kamara put it all out there on a 40-yard run through the Minnesota Vikings' defense.

His next five touchdowns covered less ground but proved every bit as important. It was his sixth and final trip to the end zone that secured a 52–33 win for the New Orleans Saints. It earned Kamara a slice of NFL history, too.

Only one other player — Ernie Nevers of the 1929 Chicago Cardinals — has scored six rushing touchdowns in a single game. For Kamara, it would run his touchdown count to 21 for the season, 16 on the ground, five through the air, making him a scoring threat no matter how he gets his hands on the ball. Or how many tacklers he faces.

"[His] balance is insane," said San Francisco linebacker Fred Warner. "It's always going to take more than one guy to bring him down."

Kamara has game and flair to spare. He comes equipped with gold teeth, a nose ring and dreadlocks aplenty. He's been Q&A-ed by *GQ*, featured in *Sports Illustrated* and feted up and down Bourbon Street. The man even had a beer brewed in his honor, with just a hint of Airheads — Kamara's favorite taffy. Then again, virtually everything about the jack-of-all-trades tailback is sweet.

There's no sugarcoating Kamara's path, however.

In 2013, after Kamara received Georgia Mr. Football honors from the *Atlanta Journal-Constitution* in his senior year, the Crimson Tide were desperate to land him. In fact, coach Nick Saban wanted Kamara so badly he reportedly penned

105 recruiting letters to entice the Norcross, Alabama, high school star.

The ploy worked, but Kamara's Alabama adventure imploded quickly following surgery for a knee injury late in the preseason. He was later banned by Saban from practicing with the team because of "behavioral issues," and then suspended for the Tide's bowl game against Oklahoma.

In 2014 Kamara enrolled at Hutchinson Community College in Kansas but transferred to the University of Tennessee after one season. In two years, he started eight of 24 games and compiled 1,294 yards rushing and 683 receiving, good for 23 touchdowns.

Forgoing his redshirt senior season, Kamara entered the 2017 NFL Draft, where the Saints grabbed him in the third round. The selection was one of those happy strokes of luck.

As a rookie, Kamara caught — and held — the attention of the football world, as New Orleans posted an 11-5 record to capture the NFC South. Starting only three games, Kamara split totes in the backfield with Mark Ingram, another high-octane runner. The pair became the first running back duo in NFL history to each accumulate over 1,500 yards from scrimmage in the same season. Kamara was named to the All-Rookie Team and waltzed off with Offensive Rookie of the Year honors after becoming the first Saint, and just the third rookie in NFL history, to eclipse 700 yards in both rushing (728) and receiving (826).

A star had been born.

"Aw, man, that dude is slippery," said former Saints center Max Unger. "You just have to get him

free, have him break a couple of tackles."

Year 2 proved every bit the equal of its predecessor as Kamara again toppled the 1,500-yard rushing/receiving mark, with 883 along the ground and 709 via the skies. His 18 touchdowns tied a franchise record.

The Saints entered the post-season with legitimate title-topping hopes, yet they were denied in heartbreaking fashion on the final play: a 57-yard field goal in front of 73,028 stunned fans inside the Mercedes-Benz Superdome that sent the Los Angeles Rams to the Super Bowl. Kamara had 96 yards receiving, 15 rushing.

In 2020, he put down a career-best 932 yards rushing and scored a combined 21 touchdowns. Those numbers slipped in 2021 due to a knee injury. In his first game back in the starting lineup, Kamara throttled the New York Jets with 120 yards on the ground. He finished the season with a 146-yard effort against the Atlanta Falcons. It wasn't enough to lift New Orleans into the playoffs but it proved again just how valuable Kamara is to the Saints.

"He does so much for this team, just being there," said teammate Taysom Hill. ▪

College: University of Tennessee
Drafted: 2017, New Orleans Saints, 67th overall
Years active: 2017–present
Top honors: NFL All-Rookie Team (2017), NFL AP Offensive Rookie of the Year (2017)
Hall of Fame induction: N/A

TRAVIS
KELCE TE

G	Rec	Yds	Y/R	TD
127	704	9,006	12.8	57

I F PATRICK MAHOMES IS THE UNDISPUTED BRAINS OF the operation, Kelce represents the brawn. If the Lamborghini-sleek, lickety-split Tyreek Hill is the limitless sky, Kelce represents mother earth.

In this renaissance age for tight ends, Travis Kelce, at 32, may be in the process of separating himself from a pretty impressive pack.

At 6-foot-5 and 260 pounds, he's simply a beast to bring down for overmatched DBs. Then there are those dependable hands of his, as soft as the green felt on a billiard table or as pancake-syrup sticky, when need be.

"He's just a competitor, man," praised his Kansas City Chiefs pitch-and-catch partner, Mahomes. "Obviously he's super talented and everybody knows that. The routes he runs, how big and athletic he is, everything like that, but he's the guy you want to go to battle with.

"He'll fight to the very end. That's the type of dude he is."

That fight has transformed him into one of the best, ever.

Kelce's current run of six consecutive seasons of 1,000-plus yards receiving has never been done before by anyone at the position. Not by Casper or Mackey, Newsome or Winslow, Gronk or Gates or Gonzalez.

He does it all. Blocks. Sheds blockers with ease. Quotes Beastie Boys lyrics in media conferences. And the man is absolute money, as they say, when the stakes are highest. Over 15 postseason appearances, Kelce has made 106 catches — one of only three men to ever crack the 100 mark, joining Jerry Rice and Julian Edelman — for 1,291 yards and 12 touchdowns.

During the Chiefs' pulsating AFC divisional overtime win over the Buffalo Bills in 2021, Kelce also proved he'll make a pretty astute offensive coordinator somewhere down the line. Trailing by three points with only 13 seconds to work with in the fourth quarter and scrimmaging from the K.C. 25-yard line, Kelce suggested to Hill what route to run, and the All Pro wideout promptly wriggled open for a 19-yard gain. Then Kelce instructed Mahomes that given Buffalo's defensive setup, he'd be free on a seam route on the next snap. That netted another 25 yards.

NFL Films caught the conversations on a live microphone for posterity.

Bingo! Two plays. Forty-four yards. To set up the tying field goal. Followed by an overtime win,

Mahomes' touchdown pass going to Kelce, naturally.

Why, the one-time Cleveland Heights High School signal-caller even has a playoff TD pass on his accomplishments sheet, a 2-yarder to Byron Pringle a week earlier, during K.C.'s 2021 opening-playoff-round stomping of the Pittsburgh Steelers.

In the doing, he made history, becoming the first NFL player to throw a touchdown, catch a touchdown and have more than 100 receiving yards in a playoff game.

"As a kid, I always dreamt of being an NFL quarterback," confessed Kelce afterward. "I remember being 10 years old and saying: 'Mom... I'm gonna throw a football in the NFL, and it's going to be a touchdown, and everybody's gonna love it.'"

Everybody, at least throughout the state of Kansas, certainly did.

The hiring of Andy Reid as head coach at Arrowhead Stadium paved the way for Kelce's arrival in K.C. Reid had worked with Kelce's older, All-Pro O-lineman brother, Jason, at Philadelphia and knew the family, and so the Chiefs selected Kelce the Younger in the third round, with the 63rd pick, in the 2013 draft, out of the University of Cincinnati.

By his third full pro season, Kelce led all NFL tight ends in receiving yards (1,125), the next year in catches (83) and in 2020 set a record for most yards ever at the position in a single season (1,416).

"I'm technically the utility guy on the field," said Kelce, with undue modesty. "Whether you need a plumber or an electrician, man, I'm here for you."

All the stars came into alignment, of course, at Hard Rock Stadium in Miami Gardens, Florida, on

February 2, 2022. The 12-4 Chiefs had eliminated both Houston and Tennessee to set up a title bout against the San Francisco 49ers.

In Super Bowl LIV, Kelce had, for him, a relatively quiet afternoon, latching on to six passes for 43 yards. Among his catches, though, was a 1-yard touchdown from Mahomes six minutes into the fourth quarter to cut the 49ers' lead to 20-17.

K.C. would go on to prevail 31–20 and collect their first championship since 1970.

A subsequent heavy Super Bowl loss to Tampa-directed Tom Brady and a shock AFC Championship ouster by the Cincinnati Bengals has stalled what many thought might become a dynasty.

But those setbacks, it's understood, can only serve to further stoke Travis Kelce's competitive embers.

"My passion for this game is never going to change," he once said. "You're always going to see me have that fieriness.

"That's just the only way I know how to play this game and I love it for that because I get to release that energy and that passion; that anger that I have."

Chiefs kingdom wouldn't have him any other way. ∎

College: University of Cincinnati
Drafted: 2013, Kansas City Chiefs, 63rd overall
Years active: 2013–present
Top honors: Super Bowl Champion (2019), First Team All-Pro (2016, 2018, 2020)
Hall of Fame induction: N/A

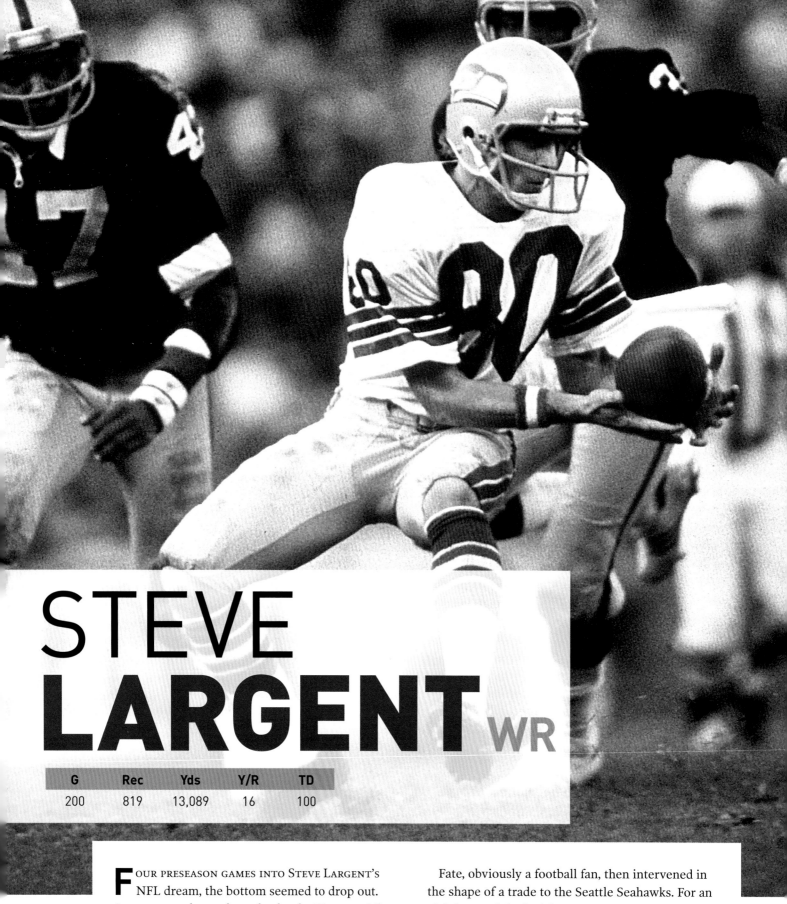

STEVE
LARGENT WR

G	Rec	Yds	Y/R	TD
200	819	13,089	16	100

FOUR PRESEASON GAMES INTO STEVE LARGENT'S NFL dream, the bottom seemed to drop out. Largent was deemed surplus by the Houston Oilers — and it seemed like it was over before it had even had the chance to begin.

Fate, obviously a football fan, then intervened in the shape of a trade to the Seattle Seahawks. For an eighth-round draft pick, yet.

Seems absurd now, to be traded for an eighth-round pick — especially since for the next

14 years, Largent caught more footballs than anyone who had gone before him. But because of the mediocre teams he played on during his years in Seattle, Steve Largent has been largely overlooked by the casual fan when listing the greatest receivers in NFL history. But he rates. He definitely rates.

From the perspective of the defensive backs assigned to cover him, the clean-cut, religious kid out of Tulsa wasn't super-fast like a Bob Hayes. Or built as if he'd been chiseled from a block of Carrara marble like a Kellen Winslow. He was ... just — just fast enough. Just slippery enough. Just tough enough. Just flat-out good enough to beat you just about every time he wanted to.

We're all so quick to measure things when judging an athlete: height and weight, speed in the 40, how much weight someone is able to bench press. What remains elusive — what cannot ever be measured or quantified — is heart. There has never been, and will never be, an instrument capable of calibrating that.

The No. 80 in blue and silver, who would go on to the Hall of Fame, is further proof of that.

Seems amazing now, but pro scouts weren't all that impressed with Largent, despite the All-American status at the University of Tulsa and leading the nation in touchdown catches his final two seasons. He wasn't selected until the fourth round of the 1976 draft, 117th overall.

How good was Largent?

So good that Jerry Rice, who would eventually shatter all of Largent's receiving records, admitted to studying the way Largent ran pass routes, picking up pointers to incorporate into his own game. Sort of comparable to Orson Welles watching John Ford's iconic western *Stagecoach* over a hundred times in preparation for *Citizen Kane*.

So good that when he retired, the guy who wasn't big enough, strong enough or fast enough — who only missed four games due to injury in his first 13 NFL seasons — had latched onto every major receiving record available: receptions (819), yards (13,089), TD catches (100) and games with a reception (177).

He caught 50 or more passes for 10 seasons. He caught 70 or more in six seasons. A tireless worker for community and charity, he was voted the NFL's Walter Payton Man of the Year in 1988.

Not bad for a guy that the Houston Oilers, in all their wisdom, were convinced didn't have the right stuff to be in the NFL.

He might've been only 5-foot-11 and 187 pounds, but Seahawk fans still recall with relish the afternoon he chased down Denver Bronco defensive back Mike Harden on the return of an intercepted pass thrown by Seahawk quarterback Dave Kreig. Largent not only tracked him down but leveled his prey, knocking the ball loose and then recovering the fumble.

Sweet justice, in that Harden had almost ended Largent's career earlier in the season, hitting him with such viciousness that the Seahawks' All-Pro, as legend has it, lost two teeth and wound up with a dented helmet.

A quiet, humble person and exemplary pro, Largent wouldn't crow about his payback — a play that has now entered franchise lore. Well, not much, anyway. "It wasn't meant to be a vindictive thing," he is quoted on the Spirit of the Seahawks website as saying, "but it sure felt good."

His final two years represented a significant drop-off in production. But nothing could diminish the glories of what had gone before.

In his post-football life, Largent entered politics, serving in the U.S. House of Representatives for Oklahoma from 1994 to 2002 as a Republican. He was once asked which press corps was tougher: beat writers who cover the NFL or the political writers who cover Capitol Hill. Largent laughed and replied: "Let's put it this way. On Capitol Hill, I still need a helmet."

Largent later moved to the business world, serving as president and CEO of the CTIA Wireless Association, after losing in a three-way dogfight for the governorship of his home state.

Perhaps his mistake was in where he decided to run. Maybe he should've just shifted over to the State of Washington. In Seattle, as one of a handful of athletes who has attained iconic status, it goes without saying that he could've gotten elected to anything he wanted. Anything at all. ■

College: University of Tulsa
Drafted: 1976, Houston Oilers, 117th overall
Years active: 1976–1989
Top honors: NFL All-Rookie Team (1976), First Team All-Pro (1985), NFL Walter Payton Man of the Year (1988)
Hall of Fame induction: 1995

BOBBY LAYNE

G	Att	Comp	Yds	TD	Int
175	3,700	1,814	26,768	196	243

I N LUBBOCK, IT WAS WRITTEN OF BOBBY LAYNE THAT HE was the ultimate West Texas good ol' boy — "a superb athlete, a world-class party animal, a shrewd business-man and a family man in his spare time."

He could also curse like no one else, only we're not talking about swearing. When the Detroit Lions traded him two games into the 1958 season, the NFL quarter-back who helped his team win three league champion-ships made it a point of saying Detroit wouldn't win another title for 50 years.

The Lions reached that gloomy landmark in 2008. That makes it the longest-running jinx in major profes-sional sports.

On the football field, Layne was undeniably force-ful, a steely-nerved winner who helped Detroit claim the NFL crown in 1952 and 1953 and put the team in position to win in 1957. In his illustrious pro career, he thrived under pressure, engineering 18 game-winning drives as the master of the hurry-up offense. His career passing statistics include 26,768 yards, 196 touchdowns and 243 interceptions, all of which were NFL records upon his retirement in 1962. He was twice named a First Team All-Pro; four times he was chosen a Second Team All-Pro. His accomplishments earned him a spot on the 1950s All-Decade Team.

By most measures, Layne was a true football star. He won big games in high drama playing for the University of Texas Longhorns. His All-American status convinced the Pittsburgh Steelers to draft him third overall. He responded by saying he didn't want to play for the Steelers, who then traded him to the Chicago Bears. As soon as he found himself the third-stringer behind

quarterbacks Sid Luckman and Johnny Lujack, he pushed the Bears into another trade.

That sent him to the New York Bulldogs, who listed singer Kate Smith as one of their owners. "Every time Kate got a sore throat, we got worried about getting paid," said Layne. "If she couldn't sing 'God Bless America' there wouldn't have been any cheques."

As part of his rough and tumble image, Layne refused to wear even a single-bar facemask on his helmet and often came to the stadium on game day reeking of alco-hol. Baltimore Colts defensive lineman Art Donovan recalled the time he made a second-half tackle on Layne, who smelled like a wet bar towel. "You must have had a hell of a time last night," said Donovan. Layne replied, "I may have had a few [drinks] at halftime."

Layne's drinking added to his mystique. So, too, did his vexing of the Lions. Teammates and fans alike were willing to believe in the veracity of Layne's curse because it sounded exactly like something he would do. It was in 1957 that Layne's time with the Lions began to run out. Before the season started, he was charged with driving under the influence. He was cruising on the wrong side of the road with his headlights off when he was pulled over by the police.

He badgered the police officer enough to get himself arrested. As part of his defense, Layne said he'd consumed "only six" cocktails and that his speech wasn't slurred, as the police officer had claimed. Rather, it was just Bobby's good ol' West Texas drawl. A judge listened to Layne's explanation and acquitted him.

Late in the 1957 season, Layne didn't get off so easily in a game against the Cleveland Browns. When two defenders tackled him for a loss, they left him with a broken ankle. Done for the remainder of the regular season and playoffs, Layne could only watch his team carry on without him. The Lions had been rotating Layne with Tobin Rote and would name their Sunday starter based on which man had the better week of practices. With Layne sidelined, Rote beat Cleveland by 45 points in the NFL Championship Game, securing his future with Detroit while clouding Layne's at the age of 31.

After more drinking incidents and questions about Layne's durability, Detroit head coach George Wilson traded his veteran quarterback to Pittsburgh on October 6, 1958, for younger QB Earl Morrall and a pair of draft picks. Layne was crushed by the trade, then furious. His curse was never reported at the time because he never said it to the media. He did, however, say it to a select few family members and friends. And as time rolled on, Layne's curse grew in stature until it was the talk of the city, the state and the entire NFL.

Layne's nine seasons in Detroit were his high-water mark, although his first year with the Steelers offered a small taste of retribution. Layne was reunited with former Lions head coach Buddy Parker and went 7-2-1. He made the Pro Bowl in both 1958 and 1959. And when Pittsburgh struggled offensively, Layne did his best to keep things interesting. One well-told story had to do with a play Layne created and dubbed "What's going on?" It went like this: The Lions were positioned deep inside the opposition's territory. Instead of lining up behind the center, Layne walked toward his receivers and began yelling

Bobby Layne of the Pittsburgh Steelers throws upfield.

instructions at them. Running back John Henry Johnson then shouted, "What's going on?" and took a direct snap from center. The play was so perfectly executed, Johnson scored on an easy touchdown run.

That was one of the last highlights of the great Bobby Layne. The Lions followed his curse to the letter, still without a championship after all these many years. But for the quarterback who believed winning was all that mattered, there was a disappointment he too had to withstand. Once out of Detroit, he never again made the playoffs.

He retired in 1962 and was inducted into the Pro Football Hall of Fame five years later. He was only 59 when his body broke down and he passed away. ▪

College: University of Texas
Drafted: 1948, Chicago Bears, 3rd overall
Years active: 1948–1962
Top honors: NFL Champion (1952, 1953, 1957), First Team All-Pro (1952, 1956)
Hall of Fame induction: 1967

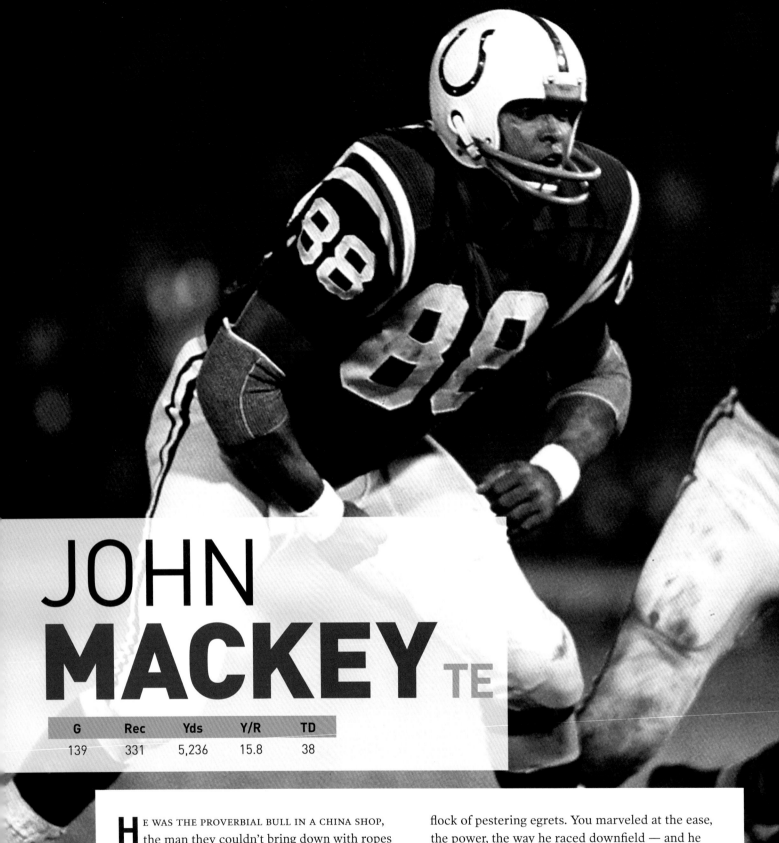

JOHN
MACKEY TE

G	Rec	Yds	Y/R	TD
139	331	5,236	15.8	38

H E WAS THE PROVERBIAL BULL IN A CHINA SHOP, the man they couldn't bring down with ropes or a tranquilizer gun. He did more than reinvent the tight end position — he made football fans forget anyone had ever played it before he came along.

Watching John Mackey catch a pass and shrug off tacklers was like watching a rhinoceros shake off a flock of pestering egrets. You marveled at the ease, the power, the way he raced downfield — and he could run.

In 1966, his fourth season with the Baltimore Colts, Mackey caught nine touchdown passes, six of which were 50 yards or more. That was unheard-of at the time. Tight ends were supposed to be accomplished run blockers, extra offensive tackles that could occasionally slip out of their yokes to catch a pass or two. Never for 50 yards, though — that was a wide receiver's job.

But there was no controlling Mackey. In college, at Syracuse, he was a running back and learned how to challenge tacklers. When he got to the Colts, head coach Don Shula wasn't sure where to play the 6-foot-2, 224-pound Mackey. Shula watched him overpower smaller defensive backs and out-maneuver linebackers in practice, and decided, "Tight end it will be."

Mackey started every game in his rookie year (he also ran back kickoffs for a 30.1-yard average) and became a fixture for the Colts in the 1960s, playing in five Pro Bowls. Twice he averaged more than 20 yards per catch in a season, and after 10 years in the league his career average was 15.8. When the NFL voted on the Pro Football Hall of Fame's All-1960s team, Mackey was picked at tight end by a landslide.

Mackey played in two Super Bowls. The first was Baltimore's stunning loss to the New York Jets in Super Bowl III. In that game, the Colts were supposed to leave their hoofprints all over the Jets. They didn't.

Two years later the Colts beat the Dallas Cowboys in Super Bowl V on Jim O'Brien's late field goal. The game was a Marx Brothers movie of goofs, gaffes and comedic blunders, including a Johnny Unitas pass for Eddie Hinton that was off the mark. The ball deflected off Hinton's hands, off the hands of Dallas defensive back Mel Renfro and into the hands of

Mackey, who ran untouched for a 75-yard touchdown. The Cowboys complained, noting that a ball can't be tipped from one receiver to another. But Renfro had touched the ball in between the two Colts (which the replays show), so the touchdown stood.

Mackey left the Colts in 1972 and signed with the San Diego Chargers, but a knee injury eventually forced him to retire after just one season.

As soon as he was out of the game, Mackey was back in the thick of things. He had been named president of the NFL Players Association and now sued the NFL for the owners' restrictive policies regarding free agency.

"They gave us what they wanted to give us, made us smile and say 'thank you,'" said Mackey. "But from that day forward we decided to build a legitimate union."

Mackey saw to it that the NFLPA hired its first executive director, attorney Ed Garvey. Together they fought the NFL's free-agency policy. Today's players, who can move at will when their contracts expire, owe a debt of gratitude to Mackey's tenacity.

"John revolutionized the tight end position," said Shula. "[But] as much as he made an impact on the field, he did the same off the field. He was a leader of men of all colors at a time when that was not an easy thing to do."

Mackey wasn't the first true tight end to be inducted into the Hall of Fame. Mike Ditka was, and even he asked, "Why wasn't John in first?" Eventually the petty politics that branded Mackey a militant union man were put aside, and in 1992 he finally joined the Hall. In 2000

the NCAA commissioned the John Mackey Award to be presented to the best tight end in college football.

The following year, Mackey received something else — something unwanted. He was told he was suffering from frontotemporal dementia. Ultimately his conditioned worsened, to the point where he required full-time care. His plight prompted the 88 Plan, named in honor of his jersey number. It guaranteed $88,000 annually in nursing home care for afflicted former NFL players.

On July 6, 2011, Mackey died at the age of 69. Researchers at Boston University determined he had chronic traumatic encephalopathy (CTE), brain damage symptomatic of dementia, believed to be caused by repeated hits to the head. Mackey's case added more fuel to the debate over player safety in the NFL.

Even in death, the former Colt couldn't help but lead the way. ∎

> *Watching John Mackey catch a pass and shrug off tacklers was like watching a rhinoceros shake off a flock of pestering egrets.*

College: Syracuse University
Drafted: 1963, Baltimore Colts, 19th overall
Years active: 1963–1972
Top honors: First Team All-Pro (1966–68), Super Bowl Champion (1970)
Hall of Fame induction: 1992

PATRICK
MAHOMES QB

G	Att	Comp	Yds	TD	Int
63	2,345	1,550	18,991	151	37

IN THE QUEST FOR PROFESSIONAL GREATNESS, AS IN personal growth, there are always dead ends to deal with, painful setbacks to be surmounted.

Patrick Mahomes has only piggybacked his Kansas City Chiefs to the AFC Championship four of his years as a starting quarterback. Won one Super Bowl. Reached another.

Been named MVP of the league, as well as in the big game with the roman numerals that everyone watches.

That'd be more than enough for a career for most people.

In his first season as a No. 1, remember, Mahomes became one of only two men (joining Peyton Manning) in history to throw for 50 TDs and 5,000 yards in a season. When improvising in the pocket, he's as hard to pin down as a shadow in sunshine.

He's turned 13 seconds into a "thing," completing two passes in that tight time window for 44 yards to set up a game-tying field goal that set the stage for the Chiefs' one-for-the-ages 42–36 overtime victory over the Buffalo Bills and a spot in the most recent AFC Championship tilt.

"When it's grim," K.C. head coach Andy Reid instructed Mahomes, "be the Grim Reaper."

Beware the Reaper.

Why, only the week before, with the AFC wild-card playoffs as a backdrop, he'd torched the Pittsburgh Steelers for five TD passes in a span of 11 minutes and 31 seconds.

Mahomes has captured the imagination of the football world and beyond since arriving from Texas Tech, flashing more swash and more buckle than Errol Flynn in green tights brandishing a sword in Sherwood Forest.

Evolving his game, he's gone from predominantly a

swing-for-the-fences home-run hitter to someone willing to take what's on offer and make the most of it.

Every bit as important, he's shown a willingness to accept responsibility in those moments.

"They just had a spy on me, for the most part, and I've usually done a good job getting around that guy, but they had a good game plan," said Mahomes, in the ashes of a 27-24 overtime loss to the Cincinnati Bengals in that 2021 AFC Championship Game, a game in which Kansas City once led by 18 points. "They were doing a lot of similar stuff in the first half, we were just executing at a higher level. They stayed with it.

"I mean, I gotta be better.

"When you're up 21-3 at one point in the game, you can't lose it, and I put that on myself."

Accountability is what real leaders do.

It isn't so long ago since February 2, 2020, Super Bowl Sunday, when, facing the San Francisco 49ers, Mahomes rallied the Chiefs from a 10-point deficit, shaking off two interceptions to direct 21 late unanswered points and propel his franchise to its first title in a half century.

"It's Magic Mahomes," said Kansas City tight end Travis Kelce. "It's Showtime Mahomes. He's going to be himself no matter what the scenario is, and you know what? I love him. I love him."

Born in Tyler, Texas, into a sporting family — his dad, Pat, had been a pitcher for six Major League Baseball franchises — the young Mahomes turned into a three-sport (including baseball) star at Whitehouse High School.

Signs of approaching greatness were readily apparent during his college football career at Texas Tech. On October 22, 2016, versus the Oklahoma Sooners,

Patrick Mahomes passes against the Houston Texans on January 12, 2019. The Chiefs advanced to the AFC Championship after beating the Texans 51–31.

Mahomes went, well, absolutely bonkers, tying the NCAA record of 734 yards passing on 88 throws in a 66–59 loss. He'd go on to lead the nation in passing yards per game (421) and total passing yards (5,052).

Unsurprisingly, he skipped his senior year of college eligibility to enter the 2017 NFL Draft and was chosen 10th overall by the Chiefs, who dealt their No. 27 overall pick, a third-round selection, and a 2018 first-round selection to the Bills to move up.

Mahomes began his NFL odyssey as backup to Alex Smith, but that lasted only a season.

Now, with Big Ben Roethlisberger officially retired and Tom Brady turning 45 and Aaron Rodgers 39, Mahomes, although only 26, has become the comparable for the younger generation.

"I don't know if you can pick up anything from him," marveled QB Taylor Heinicke to the Washington Commanders website. "He's one of those … I'm going to say a wildcard. He's just an unbelievable athlete/quarterback. I kind of go back to when I was training kids when I wasn't playing and they're trying to do Mahomes-type stuff. I'm like, 'listen, you're not Mahomes. That's something that he can do. We can't.'"

Every year since he took the wheel, Mahomes and the Chiefs have been knocking on the title door with the persistence of a fed-up landlord toting an eviction notice.

On his personal Twitter account after the Cincinnati heartbreak, he vowed: *Love y'all #ChiefsKingdom. This one hurts but we will be back! See y'all next year!*

Heed his words.

Because even if Patrick Mahomes doesn't — at this particular moment in time, anyway — seem to have the football world wholly at his feet, the possibility (some would say probability, but nothing is certain in this world) is still there, clear as day, directly in view. ∎

College: Texas Tech University
Drafted: 2017, Kansas City Chiefs, 10th overall
Years active: 2017–present
Top honors: NFL AP MVP (2018), NFL AP Offensive Player of the Year (2018), First Team All-Pro (2018), Super Bowl Champion (2019), Super Bowl MVP (2019)
Hall of Fame induction: N/A

PEYTON
MANNING QB

G	Att	Comp	Yds	TD	Int
266	9,380	6,125	71,940	539	251

INSIDE THE DENVER BRONCOS' OFFICES ON MARCH 7, 2016, the air was thick with emotion, with nostalgia.

Peyton Manning was saying goodbye.

"There's something about 18 years," said the man who made that double-digit his own. "Eighteen is a good number.

"I fought a good fight. I finished my football race and after 18 years, it's time. God bless you and God bless football."

There was nothing remotely heaven-sent about Manning's gifts. His miracles were performed not via divine intervention but through preparation and flop-sweat. Yet if there is such a thing as a football deity, then Peyton Williams Manning is it.

Whether an Indianapolis Colt or a Denver Bronco, the approach never altered. "Pressure is something you feel when you don't know what the hell you're doing," he has said.

With a football in his hands, Manning always knew what needed to be done. It had been that way since he was old enough to watch his dad play quarterback in the NFL, since he started at the University of Tennessee as an 18-year-old freshman and since he joined Indianapolis as the first pick overall in the 1998 NFL Draft.

And when the Colts released him in March 2012, after he had spent a year on the shelf recovering from neck surgery, it didn't take long for Manning to show his new Denver teammates there was still plenty of game left in a right arm that was supposedly spent and a body that some feared might no longer hold up to the rigors of NFL football.

In the Broncos' 2012 season opener, Manning passed for two touchdowns in a 31–19 win over the Pittsburgh Steelers. His first scoring toss was the 400th of his career, putting him in an elite group with Dan Marino and Brett Favre.

"When you take a year off from football, you come back for all the enjoyable moments," he said then. "When you're not playing, you miss out on all the highs, but you also miss these disappointments. But I would rather be in the arena to be excited or be disappointed than not have a chance at all. That's football. That's why everybody plays it."

The following campaign, he threw for the single-season NFL record of 55 touchdowns and earned his fifth MVP award; early in 2014 he tossed his 509th career touchdown pass to put him in sole possession of first place for career TD passes.

Through every stage of his career, Manning has known how to win. But being impervious to pressure didn't come easily. Imagine what it must have been like always being Archie Manning's son, the one with the bloodlines and newspaper headlines. Some people are born great, the expression goes. Some have greatness thrust upon them.

Peyton Manning had both.

Because his father was a Hall of Fame quarterback, Peyton was supposed to be something special. When he played well, it was due to lineage. When he played poorly, it was because he couldn't handle the stress.

Manning was expected to step into the Colts' offense in 1998 and perform spontaneous miracles. He did amazingly well, passing for 3,739 yards and 26

Peyton Manning throws a pass against the New England Patriots in the AFC Championship Game on January 24, 2016.

touchdowns while setting five NFL rookie records. The problem was the Colts' inexperience coupled with a hole-in-the-wall defense. At season's end, Indianapolis had won just 3 of 16 games.

In 1999 Manning lifted the Colts to a 13-3 record. But when the team lost 19–16 to the Tennessee Titans in the playoffs, people began to openly wonder if the prodigy could win the big ones.

He shed those doubts forever eight years later by throwing for 247 yards in a 27–19 Super Bowl dismissal of the Chicago Bears. Along with a ring, he was named game MVP.

Manning never saw his heritage as a burden. He grew up not just with a celebrity dad, but also with two brothers, Connor and Eli, who competed at everything. Their most infamous battles were on the basketball court. The loser had to drag the family garbage cans from the house and down a long, bumpy dirt path to the road, often having to stop to pick up the smelly scraps that fell out.

Younger brother Eli would be the first pick overall in the 2004 NFL Draft and go on to be a two-time Super Bowl champion and two-time Super Bowl MVP. Big Bro would finally collect his second title ring at Super Bowl 50 as a Bronco, avenging a 48–3 drubbing by the Seattle Seahawks two years prior. That Sunday in Santa Clara, California, Manning's stat line was modest, especially by his standards: 13-for-23, 141 yards, one interception, two fumbles and he was sacked five times.

He couldn't have cared less. He knew games are always about the W.

Taking it as a whole, the 14 Pro Bowl appearances, the seven First Team All-Pro selections, those 71,940 yards passing and those 539 touchdown tosses were all reasons why the room at Broncos' headquarters was so charged with emotion and nostalgia on March 7, 2016.

"You don't have to wonder if I'll miss it," Peyton Manning confessed quietly. "Of course I will."

The feeling is entirely mutual. ◼

College: University of Tennessee
Drafted: 1998, Indianapolis Colts, 1st overall
Years active: 1998–2015
Top honors: NFL All-Rookie Team (1998), NFL AP MVP (2003, 2004, 2008, 2009, 2013), First Team All-Pro (2003–2005, 2008, 2009, 2012, 2013), NFL AP Offensive Player of the Year (2004, 2013), Walter Payton Man of the Year (2005), Super Bowl Champion (2006, 2015), Super Bowl MVP (2006), NFL AP Comeback Player of the Year (2012)
Hall of Fame induction: N/A

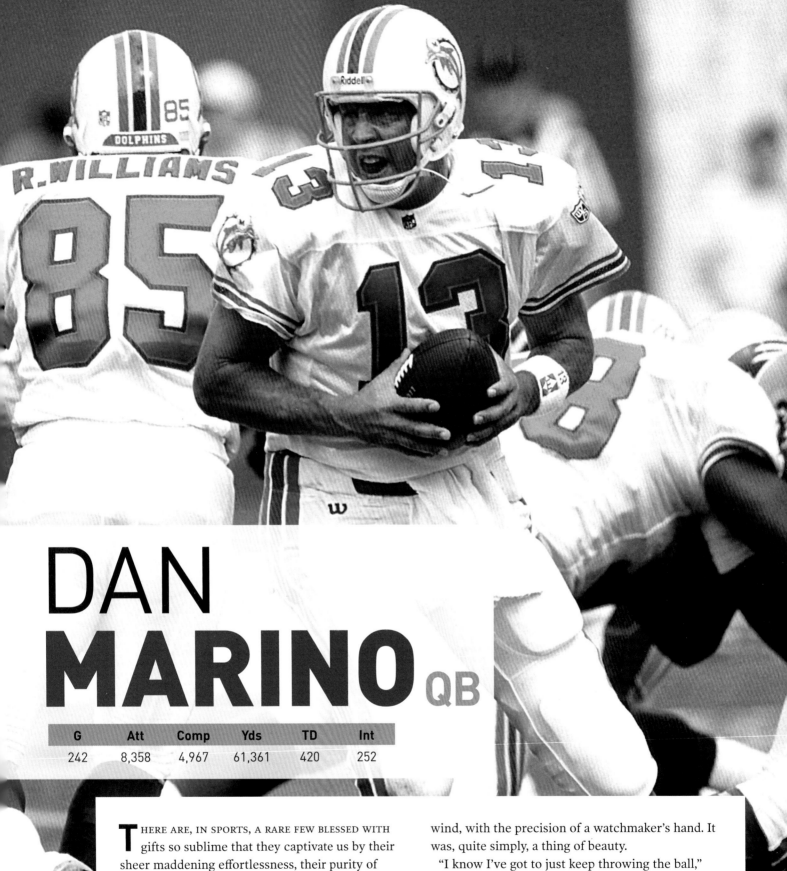

DAN
MARINO QB

G	Att	Comp	Yds	TD	Int
242	8,358	4,967	61,361	420	252

THERE ARE, IN SPORTS, A RARE FEW BLESSED WITH gifts so sublime that they captivate us by their sheer maddening effortlessness, their purity of line. For close to two decades of unrivaled passing opulence in Miami, there was Dan Marino's release — quick and accurate. He delivered the ball crisply, like the snap of a wet towel being cracked in the wind, with the precision of a watchmaker's hand. It was, quite simply, a thing of beauty.

"I know I've got to just keep throwing the ball," said Marino. "That's what I do best."

Better, arguably, than anyone before or since.

Nurtured by the ideal coach in Don Shula, and blessed with an array of gamebreakers at receiver that included Mark Duper and Mark Clayton, Marino didn't merely play quarterback — he redefined the position.

"Sure, luck means a lot in football," said Shula. "Not having a good quarterback is bad luck."

If so, Shula was the luckiest man in the NFL.

Other quarterbacks have left their legacies: Brett Favre is legendary for his toughness, Joe Montana for dramatics, Johnny Unitas for his reading of a game, Joe Namath for his swagger, Tom Brady for his unrivaled acumen in the ultimate moments. But throwing the ball? That was Marino's domain. Interceptions didn't faze him. He never shied away from a mistake. Caution is for losers.

Remember the movie *The Matrix*? Keanu Reeves's character, Neo, discovers he is mentally able to slow everything around him down to a standstill and catch bullets. Marino seemed to do the same thing when he was throwing a football.

"There are times on the field when I feel like I can't miss, when I'm in complete control and everything just clicks," he wrote in his autobiography. "The ball is always on time, it's always catchable, and I'm making the right decisions on who to throw to."

Marino's rise to the NFL began in a working-class neighborhood in Pittsburgh, where his father would get up at 2 a.m. to deliver bulk copies of the *Pittsburgh Post-Gazette*. There Marino learned the value of hard work; he carried that work ethic with him all the way up to the pros, where he let his skills do the talking. In an age of nonconformity, where others would generate headlines with their mouths and their antics, Marino

> ## "There are times on the field when I feel like I can't miss, when I'm in complete control and everything just clicks. The ball is always on time, it's always catchable, and I'm making the right decisions on who to throw to."
> ## — Dan Marino

took the high road and worked hard for everything he earned.

The hard work paid off immediately in the NFL, when he became the first rookie ever to start in a Pro Bowl, and it continued to pay off in 1984, his second year after replacing David Woodley as Miami's starter. Marino was close to unstoppable as he put together one of the greatest individual seasons in history, on the way to being named league MVP. He broke six passing records that year, including touchdown tosses (48) and yards passing (5,084).

The Dolphins finished the regular season 14-2 and reached Super Bowl XIX against Joe Montana and the San Francisco 49ers. Marino went 29 out of 50 for 318 yards, one touchdown and two interceptions, as the Dolphins lost 38–16. It would be his only Super Bowl appearance.

Over 17 seasons Marino adjusted his game, alternating between long-ball thrower, precision midrange passer and proven leader. When talk surfaced near the end of the road that he might consider joining another organization to prolong his playing career, the possibility was met with disbelief. The Pope is Catholic, Dan Marino is a Dolphin. End of story.

Marino retired prior to the 2000 season. On September 17 of that year, at the halftime of a home game against the Baltimore Ravens,

Marino's signature No. 13 was the second jersey number ever retired by the Dolphins. A life-sized bronze statue of him was erected at Pro Player (now Hard Rock) Stadium.

The lack of a Super Bowl ring remains the one sticking point in the vast Marino legacy. But he doesn't need one, at least not to validate his brilliance as a quarterback.

"I am extremely proud of the fact that I was able to play 17 years for the Miami Dolphins," said Marino in retirement. "And I'm going to miss it. I'm going to miss everything about it. I'm going to miss the relationships with the players, I'm going to miss the fans, I'm going to miss the great friends that I have made over this time. I am going to miss all the good times that we've had together. But most of all, I'm going to miss Sunday afternoons."

All these years later, Sunday afternoons still miss Marino, too. ▮

College: University of Pittsburgh
Drafted: 1983, Miami Dolphins, 27th overall
Years active: 1983–1999
Top honors: NFL All-Rookie Team (1983), NFL AP Offensive Player of the Year (1984), NFL AP MVP (1984), First Team All-Pro (1984–86), NFL Walter Payton Man of the Year (1998)
Hall of Fame induction: 2005

BRUCE MATTHEWS C

G	FR
296	10

THIS IS HOW YOU DEFINE VERSATILITY, AT LEAST IN football.

If you have a great player at this spot, a position where every offensive play begins with the ball in his hands, it's a true luxury. This is the guy who breaks the huddle and scans how the other team is lining up on defense. Are they in a three-man front or four? Are the linebackers readying them-selves for a blitz? Are special blocking assignments needed?

It was a mental exercise that took Bruce Matthews to the line of scrimmage, where he would shout out instructions. Then the quarterback's call would commence. Matthews would snap on command, and it would all come together. Organized bedlam.

Being in the middle of it gave Matthews a greater sense of responsibility, and he thrived on that. In many ways he was more than just the center for the Houston Oilers/Tennessee Titans. He was an offensive line unto himself. He would start at one

In many ways he was more than just the center for the Houston Oilers/Tennessee Titans. He was an offensive line unto himself.

position and be listed as the backup for the other four.

This is how the Oilers/Titans franchise tracked Matthews's career: 17 games at left tackle, 99 at left guard, 67 at right guard and 22 at right tackle. He also had 87 starts at center and was the long snapper for every point after a touchdown, every field goal and every punt. This went on season after season, award after award.

As proof of what that versatility and accountability means in football terms, Matthews was a seven-time First Team All-Pro. He had his jersey, No. 74, retired by the Titans in 2002 and was named to the Pro Football Hall of Fame in 2007. He was also named to the Pro Bowl 14 times, a record shared with four other players, including Tom Brady.

But this is where Matthews's Pro Bowl experiences rise a notch above his fellow record holders: he made those appearances at two different offensive line positions.

In recognition of his ability to take the inside heat at guard and then face those speeding linebackers at offensive tackle, Matthews was named to the NFL's 100 All-Time Team.

"As someone who grew up a fan of the game," said Matthews, "I can't tell you how humbling an honor it is to be named to this team."

It was an overwhelming tribute to a man who grew up in a football family in Arcadia, California. His father, Clay Matthews Sr., was an All-American at two positions (offensive tackle and defensive end) with Georgia Tech and played four seasons with the San Francisco 49ers in the 1950s. Clay Matthews Jr. (Bruce's brother) spent 19 years and 278 games in the NFL as a linebacker with the Cleveland Browns and Atlanta Falcons.

When Matthews Jr. retired in 1996, the proud father stood on the 50-yard line at the Georgia Dome with his two sons and soaked up the adulation of the crowd.

"I had a set of rules I could use on all of my kids," said Matthews Sr. "I told them all you can do whatever you want to. You can go and play any sport you want to ... But there are two rules you can't ignore. One of them is, 'I don't care if you're on the last string and sitting on the bench all of the time and are the worst guy out there, you can't quit.' And No. 2 is, 'If I ever see you play or practice and you're not giving 120 percent, I'll yank you out of there myself.' I think they all pretty much got the message."

Bruce settled on football and enrolled at the University of Southern California, where he played every position along the offensive line and made the All-America team in his senior year. He was drafted by Houston in the first round in 1983 and was soon blocking for Earl Campbell, the bone-crushing running back who laid waste to tacklers.

After having established himself as a player and team leader, Matthews came out with a revelation that surprised friends and family — even as a pro, and a successful one at that, he was most motivated by fear.

"That's the thing that drives me," said Matthews, while still calling the shots at the line of scrimmage. "It's not so much throwing a great block that springs a guy for a touchdown. It's more, don't get beat for a sack. Don't be the guy who causes the running back to get blown up. Don't be the guy who makes the mental mistake that causes Steve [McNair] to be blindsided."

Matthews established himself not just through his skills but through his resilience. He played 296 games, more than any other full-time positional player in league history at the time, was in the lineup for 232 consecutive games and made 229 straight starts — all franchise records.

Late in his career Matthews got to experience a Super Bowl, even if it meant coming up 1 yard short of the end zone in the Titans' 23–16 defeat to the St. Louis Rams in Super Bowl XXXIV.

Others may have been crushed by the loss, but Matthews refused to let it define his life's work. He took the ball in his hands and kept showing up for work. ▪

College: University of Southern California
Drafted: 1983, Houston Oilers, 9th overall
Years active: 1983–2001
Top honors: NFL All-Rookie Team (1983), First Team All-Pro (1988–90, 1992, 1998–2000)
Hall of Fame induction: 2007

WARREN
MOON QB

G	Att	Comp	Yds	TD	Int
208	6,823	3,988	49,325	291	233

WHEN HE WAS 10 YEARS OLD AND HAD SIGNED UP TO play Pop Warner football at the Baldwin Hills Community Park in Los Angeles, Warren Moon wanted to be a quarterback. The coaches made him a linebacker. The kid playing defensive end in front of him? James Lofton, future NFL receiver.

Throughout high school and college — even after his Rose Bowl MVP showing for the University of Washington — it had become painfully clear to Moon that no one wanted to invest in his potential as a black quarterback. The NFL didn't invite him to its predraft evaluation camp. No one called to arrange an individual workout to see what Moon had to offer as a passer and a runner. He probably had a better chance of making the NFL as a linebacker, his old Pop Warner position.

But Moon was not about to give up: "As a young, stubborn and confident player, I was going to play quarterback."

And play it he did.

Now, with the benefit of 20/20 hindsight, it looks like the no-brainer to end all no-brainers. Moon didn't just man the position, he opened its parameters by proving that black quarterbacks can lead a team, call their own plays and be every bit as successful as their white peers. Moon delivered serious numbers for the Houston Oilers (now the Tennessee Titans) and the Minnesota Vikings, and he had short stops with the Seattle Seahawks and the Kansas City Chiefs until his retirement at age 44. By the end of his NFL career, his figures totaled 49,325 yards, 291 touchdowns and 233 interceptions.

When informed he was being inducted into the Pro Football Hall of Fame, Moon had several people to thank for helping him change the NFL's opinion of black quarterbacks. When it came to who had the biggest supporting role in his quest for a quarterbacking job, he thanked an entire country — Canada.

Moon set foot in the Canadian Football League in 1978, to much fanfare. The Edmonton Eskimos signed him and made sure he spent plenty of time with Tom Wilkinson, the starting quarterback, who knew the differences and subtleties between the three- and four-down games.

The long-term plan called for Wilkinson to work his experience while Moon watched from the sideline. When Wilkinson sputtered, head coach Hugh Campbell sent in Moon, whose powerhouse passing arm and ability to run provided a change in pace that had the opposition scrambling to stay close.

The 1978 season ended with the Eskimos defeating the Montreal Alouettes for the Grey Cup. By 1982 the Eskimos were in a position to win a fifth-consecutive league championship. After giving up some early points to the Toronto Argonauts in the final, Moon went on the attack, completing 21 of 33 passes for 319 yards and two touchdowns. He was named the Grey Cup's most outstanding player.

Campbell left the Eskimos to coach the Los Angeles Express of the fledgling USFL for its 1983 season. Moon spent one last year with the Eskimos before signing with the Houston Oilers in 1984. To ensure Moon got the right coaching for his NFL debut, the Oilers hired Campbell away from the Express. The Moon-Campbell duo was being counted on to deliver as best as it could, as fast as possible. Being a black quarterback meant being held to a different set of expectations. There had

Warren Moon looks to pass during a 1985 game.

to be winning results in both the regular season and playoffs, and those wins had to come quickly.

The first two seasons in Houston were significant disappointments, so much so that Campbell was fired during the 1985 season. Fortunately, Moon made big strides while the team around him got better. In 1990 and 1991 he led the league in passing yards (4,689 and 4,690, respectively), becoming the third quarterback in NFL history to post back-to-back 4,000-yard seasons. He also broke NFL records in 1991 for pass attempts (655) and completions (404) in a season.

But the following year came the playoff game that may have convinced Oilers' management that Moon couldn't win in the playoffs.

The Oilers built a 35–3 lead against Buffalo, then slowly watched it slip away as the Bills came back to take a 38–35 advantage. Houston sent the game into overtime with a late field goal, but Buffalo retaliated with a game-winning field goal in OT to send the Oilers home broken and stunned. It was the largest comeback victory in NFL history.

In 1993, his last season in Houston, Moon led the Oilers to one win in their opening five games. After that, the team went 11-0 before losing in the divisional round of the playoffs. Moon was then traded to Minnesota. In his second season with the Vikings, he threw 33 touchdown passes, matching a personal best first set in Houston.

Having already been inducted into the Canadian Football Hall of Fame, Moon was named to the Pro Football Hall of Fame in 2006 — both the first African-American quarterback and the first undrafted quarterback to be enshrined in Canton. Years later, when asked how far the NFL had come in its acceptance of black quarterbacks, Moon recounted how one game he was surrounded by police officers on the sidelines in Cleveland because someone had threatened to shoot him for beating the Browns.

Moon defused the situation with composure and showed the strength of his character.

"Some guy had said I was going to be shot. I kind of chuckled, 'Someone wants to kill me over a football game?' I just couldn't believe it," Moon recalled. It was a lesson in perseverance for other black quarterbacks to follow — never let the lunatics, and definitely not the naysayers, force you out of a position you fought so hard to earn. ∎

College: University of Washington
Drafted: undrafted
Years active: 1984–2000
Top honors: NFL All-Rookie Team (1989), Walter Payton Man of the Year (1989), NFL AP Offensive Player of the Year (1990)
Hall of Fame induction: 2006

RANDY
MOSS WR

G	Rec	Yds	Y/R	TD
218	982	15,292	15.6	156

THAT FIRST SEASON WITH THE Minnesota Vikings, Randy Moss was out-of-his-mind good. He made the hardest catches look ridiculously easy. On 69 receptions, he gained 1,313 yards — an average of 19 yards per grab — and scored 17 touchdowns, a number that remains the touchstone for rookie receivers in the NFL.

That first season with the New England Patriots, his 10th in the NFL, Moss was nearly unstoppable. Off 98 catches, he gained 1,493 yards and scored 23 touchdowns, a number that remains the touchstone for receivers across the NFL.

Those two seasons were like no others for Moss. Not only were they statistically top-shelf, they came with the pain of unfulfillment. In 1998 the Vikings had the NFL's best regular-season showing, 15-1, and set all kinds of offensive records — only to lose to the Atlanta Falcons in the NFC Championship Game. Margin of defeat? Three points. In overtime.

If failing to get to the Super Bowl was a soul-crushing experience, getting there and losing was worse. That happened at Super Bowl XLII, with Moss receiving for the Patriots, who were looking to crown an undefeated season by toppling the New York Giants.

The 1972 Miami Dolphins were the only post–World War II team to go undefeated through the regular season and playoffs. Under the current format, New England had to win two more games than the Dolphins did. The last one was the Super Bowl.

You probably remember how that one went: Moss put the Patriots ahead 14–10 after scoring on a 6-yard touchdown catch with less than three minutes remaining in regulation. The Giants answered back in a highly unexpected way: Their quarterback Eli Manning ran around, avoiding Patriot tacklers, then let fly a pass to receiver David Tyree, who made the catch by pinning the ball against his helmet. That set up New York's game-winning touchdown and a 17–14 upset of the Pats.

There was one more Super Bowl appearance for Moss. In 2012 he came out of retirement and signed on with the San Francisco 49ers. That season he added three more touchdowns to his career run of 156 majors. In Super Bowl XLVII, the 49ers faced the Baltimore Ravens and lost 34–31 to define Moss's career as one of the game's greatest receivers to never win an NFL title.

At 6-foot-4 and 210 pounds, Moss was dubbed "The Freak" for his ability to go up and over, around and under defensive backs. He could cover a lot of ground and always seemed to run fast enough to get the job done.

While his talent was beyond reproach, his temperament left him open to critics and cynics alike. The showboating always drew a response. Of note was the Green Bay incident, where, after he scored a touchdown against one of the Vikings' archrivals, he pretended to drop his pants at Lambeau Field and moon the crowd. There were other incidents involving Moss: once, angry with a referee's call, he used a water bottle from the Minnesota bench to squirt the official. But whenever the Vikings played the Dallas Cowboys, Moss wasn't thinking of simple pranks. He wanted revenge.

Moss, who was born in Rand, West Virginia, was a Dallas fan growing up. As his draft day drew nearer, team owner Jerry Jones had told Moss he would be selected by the Cowboys. Evidently that didn't happen. In fact, the Cowboys had discussed Moss and whether he could keep his cool both on and away from the field, then passed on him.

Drafted by Minnesota, Moss made it his mission to turn up the heat on Dallas every chance he got. In his first game against the Cowboys in November 1998, he had just three catches — as in, three catches for 163 yards and three touchdowns for the win. He was pretty sure the message was sent and received. His teammates never ceased to be amazed by Moss's abilities.

"I have never seen a guy that big or that fast," said Vikings receiver Cris Carter.

To underscore his maturation, Moss used his 2018 induction speech at the Pro Football Hall of Fame ceremony to say he'd learned from his youthful miscues and had become the man God wanted him to be. ▨

College: Marshall University
Drafted: 1998, Minnesota Vikings, 21st overall
Years active: 1998–2012
Top honors: NFL AP Offensive Rookie of the Year (1998), NFL All-Rookie Team (1998), First Team All-Pro (1998, 2000, 2003, 2007)
Hall of Fame induction: 2018

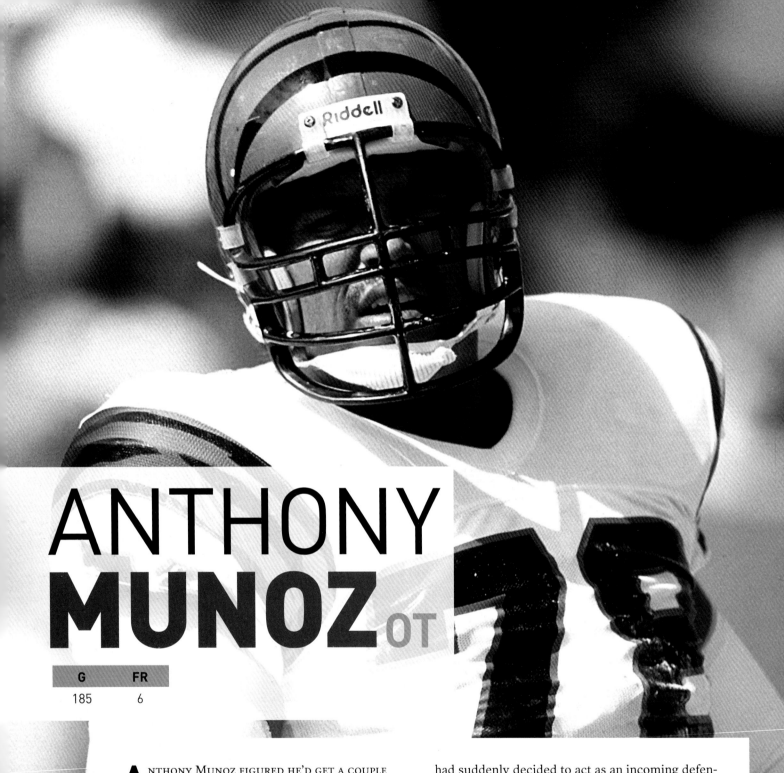

ANTHONY MUNOZ OT

G	FR
185	6

Anthony Munoz figured he'd get a couple platitudes to make him feel better. "You move pretty well for a big man," the coach would say. Then there would be the "we're-going-in-a-different-direction" bit, followed by the farewell handshake. It would all be code for, "Face it, Flounder — you are done."

It sure seemed that way to Munoz, fresh out of college. One minute he was showcasing himself and doing drills for the Cincinnati Bengals; the next he was facing their head coach, Forrest Gregg, who

had suddenly decided to act as an incoming defensive lineman. Gregg gave it his best inside-outside move until Munoz slipped into auto-response and dropped him like a sack of wet laundry.

Now, a lot was wrong with that exchange. First off, Munoz was 6-foot-6, 278 pounds and just 22 years old when he faced Gregg, who, although 6-foot-4 and 250 pounds, was 25 years Munoz's senior. Munoz also had a longer reach and used it well. Gregg's lone advantage was that he had been taught by Green Bay Packers legend Vince Lombardi, who said Gregg was the greatest football player he had ever coached. And Munoz plunked him without hesitation.

"He put me through some drills and I moved along and all of [a] sudden he decided to pass rush me," said Munoz. "I reacted like any offensive lineman would. Just as he made [his moves], I stuck both hands right into his chest and jammed him to the ground.

"You better believe I was scared. I extended a hand, I apologized, and he said, 'No problem.' He smiled; he goes, 'That's okay.'"

It was better than okay. It was everything Gregg needed to experience up close. He had come to Los Angeles to see Munoz's athleticism — how fast he could move off the line, how well he could change directions. The goal was to determine how high Munoz might go in the 1980 NFL Draft and, if he was still available, whether the Bengals should take him with the third-overall pick. If he wasn't taken by then, it would be a signal that teams were leery of Munoz because of his three knee operations in four years at the University of Southern California. What Gregg needed was a clear indication that Munoz was ready to jam anyone who challenged him — even the head coach of an interested team.

On draft day, Billy Sims of the Detroit Lions and Johnny "Lam" Jones of the New York Jets went first and second overall. The Bengals took Munoz with the third pick, and all was right with the NFL universe.

Nothing about his road to the NFL was easy. Munoz never knew his father, who bolted and left Esther Munoz to raise five children on her own. Munoz's neighborhood in Ontario, California, was poor and laced with gangs, drugs and hostility. The Munoz family had no car, so Anthony had to use his bicycle if he wanted to go anywhere.

Munoz played flag football because he was too big for the Pop Warner kids' football program. He also played a lot of baseball and liked to pitch. When he earned a scholarship to USC, Munoz pitched for the Trojans' 1978 national championship baseball team before settling on football. That same year, he was named All-American at tackle.

In his final season at USC, Munoz vowed to recover from his third knee operation and play in the 1980 Rose Bowl against Ohio State. He made that pledge while still wearing a cast. He told his coach, John Robinson, that he'd be back for the Rose Bowl. Robinson said sure, he'd put Munoz in for a play or two at wide receiver, just to reward his senior lineman.

Munoz wanted no such pity. He wanted to play, and he did, helping USC to a 17–16 win for the national championship while winning the Lombardi Trophy as college football's best lineman.

"[Munoz] is one of the greatest players at any position I ever saw," Robinson said later.

After being drafted by Cincinnati, Munoz would become the dominant offensive lineman his supporters believed he would be, and his impact was immediate. The Bengals had allowed 63 quarterback sacks the year before he was drafted. In his first season, 1980, Munoz helped his blocking mates cut that number to

> ## "[Munoz] is one of the greatest players at any position I ever saw." — former USC coach John Robinson

37. The next year it was down to 35.

And those injury problems he had at USC? Munoz missed only three games in 13 NFL seasons because of injury. In nine of those seasons, he was named a First Team All-Pro. He played in the Pro Bowl for 11 consecutive seasons.

"There has never been a lineman as great as Anthony Munoz," said former Bengals offensive line coach Jim McNally. "And I doubt we will see his equal ever."

Cincinnati head coach Sam Wyche would say much the same after coaching Munoz in the NFL, noting how much better the Bengals were as a team when Munoz stepped into the starting lineup. They won a pair of AFC Championships and went to the Super Bowl twice, losing both times to the San Francisco 49ers by a total of nine points.

After he retired, Munoz was inducted into the Hall of Fame. And it all began by knocking down his head coach. ∎

College: University of Southern California
Drafted: 1980, Cincinnati Bengals, 3rd overall
Years active: 1980–1992
Top honors: NFL All-Rookie Team (1980), First Team All-Pro (1981–1983, 1985–1990), NFL Walter Payton Man of the Year (1991)
Hall of Fame induction: 1998

BRONKO
NAGURSKI FB

G	Int/Yds	TD
97	9/2,778	25

THE IMPACT CARRIED THE BRUTE FORCE OF JACK Dempsey delivering a right cross to the heart.

A 6-foot-2, 235-pound battering ram of a man. That was Bronislau Nagurski.

"When you hit Bronk," recalled Chicago Bears teammate Red Grange, the Galloping Ghost, "it was like getting an electric shock."

So much about Bronko Nagurski has gone down into lore since he first donned the livery of the Bears in 1930: The fact that he never earned more than $5,000 a season from the notoriously thrifty George Halas, for starters. His more lucrative post-football foray into professional wrestling, for another. Those three NFL championships. The signature No. 3, retired by Chicago. Induction into the College Football Hall of Fame in 1951. His 1963 charter membership into the Pro Football of Fame, along with the fact that he is the only player honor-listed both in the offensive backfield and as a defensive lineman.

Mostly, though, what continues to resonate, archived from the memories, the recollections, is an intangible: power. The bone-breaking, soul-shattering certainty of it. Bronko was no scenic-route kinda guy.

N.Y. Giants coach Steve Owen once said famously: "The only way to stop him is to shoot him before he leaves the clubhouse."

New York linebacker Mel Hein, himself nicknamed Old Indestructible, added admiringly: "If you hit him low, he'd run over you. If you hit him high, he'd knock you down and run over you."

The stories — true and embellished — are, naturally, legion.

On one occasion, seems an overflow crowd at the back of the end zone was being kept at bay by a phalanx of mounted policemen. With the Bears near pay dirt, Nagurski supposedly built up such a head of steam that he crossed the goal line, kept right on going and knocked over one of the horses and its rider.

On another TD run against the Redskins at Wrigley Field, onlookers swore that Nagurski pinballed two linebackers in opposite directions, trampled some poor defensive back and, as a coup de grâce, knocked his last remaining obstacle, Washington's safety, ass-over-teakettle before slamming into a goal post, and then — depending on the source — a brick wall beyond the end zone.

"The last guy," Bronko is reported to have told teammates, "hit me awfully hard."

Bronislau Nagurski was born in Rainy River, Ontario, on November 3, 1928, to Ukranian-immigrant parents. His father, a laborer, Bronko would note proudly in later years, helped build the Trans-Canada railroad.

The family moved to International Falls, Minnesota, when Bronislau was 3 years old. He claims to have received the famous nickname when his mother trekked him down to register for classes at Falls High School. Between her spotty English and the impatience of the teacher acting as registrar, he became, to one and all, Bronko.

Discovered and conscripted into football by University of Minnesota head coach Clarence Spears, the raw-boned Nagurski excelled at both defensive tackle and fullback in college. The Gophers went 18-4-2 during his time with them, winning the Big Ten Conference championship in 1927.

Legendary sportswriter Grantland Rice selected Bronk at two positions on his 1929 All-America Team. Rice's admiration for the Big Ukranian was boundless. "Who would you pick to win a football game — 11 Jim Thorpes, 11 Glen Davises, 11 Red Granges or 11 Bronko Nagurskis?" he asked readers. "The 11 Nagurskis would be a mop-up."

No coincidence, then, that the Bears' now-famous moniker, Monsters of the Midway, coincided with Nagurski's arrival in the City of Big Shoulders.

In 1932, the first of three straight seasons Bronko would be named All-Pro, the Bears bested the Portsmouth Spartans in a play-off title clash, highlighted by a Nagurski-to-Red-Grange option touchdown pass.

In 1935, having helped Chicago to another title in the interim, Nagurski retired to join the pro wrestling circuit, dissatisfied that he was unable to pry a raise up to $6,500 from the Bears. Not an out-of-line figure when you consider that Detroit owner Dick Richards once reportedly offered Nagurski, making $3,000 at the time, $10,000 just to step away from the game and stop beating the hell out of his Lions.

If right there, right then, had, indeed, been his football exit, the Bronk's legacy would've already been cemented.

His wrestling career flourished but in 1943, in the teeth of World War II and a shortage of players to go around, he rejoined the Bears, at 35 years old, scoring a go-ahead touchdown in Chicago's championship victory over the Redskins.

Nagurski then retired from football for a second time, for good, returning to wrestling as both a participant and, later, a referee.

Bronko Nagurski died of natural causes on Jan. 7, 1990, aged 81,

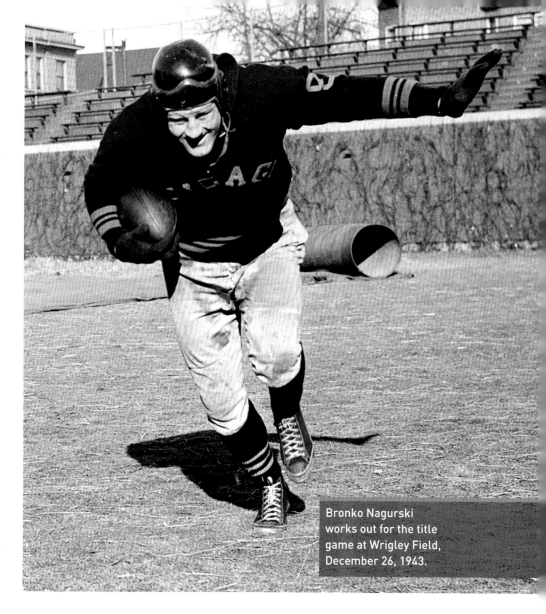

Bronko Nagurski works out for the title game at Wrigley Field, December 26, 1943.

living back in International Falls, where he'd returned post-wrestling to open a service station. One of his six children, Bronco Jr., played for seven seasons as an offensive tackle for Hamilton of the Canadian Football League, helping the Ti-Cats secure two Grey Cup titles.

"Never fancy, he just ran straight ahead, over and through the opposition," lauds the elder Nagurski's biography on the Pro Football Hall of Fame website. "Although he is best remembered for his bull-like running, he had no peer as a blocker and his tackling was as effective as any the game has seen."

A true standard-bearer, as well. A bruising player in a violent sport

who also happened, by all accounts, to be a gentle man.

"This country," Nagurski was quoted in *The Sports Immortals*, "was started by pioneers. And so was football. I think those people who missed out on the pioneer days missed out on a lot. I was a pioneer." ■

College: University of Minnesota
Drafted: Undrafted
Years active: 1930–1943
Top honors: NFL Champion (1932, 1933, 1943), First Team All-Pro (1932–1934, 1936)
Hall of Fame induction: 1963

JOE NAMATH QB

G	Att	Comp	Yds	TD	Int
140	3,762	1,886	27,663	173	220

At one time or another, every male in North America of a certain generation would've sold his soul to spend a week as Broadway Joe: the guy who'd called his shot before Super Bowl III — "We'll win, I guarantee it" — just like Babe; the guy who owned Manhattan's trendiest club, Bachelors III; the guy who could be spotted on the bench wearing a full-length mink coat.

"I like my Johnnie Walker red and my women blonde," he said.

Everyone lapped it up.

Joe Willie Namath, the slope-shoulder kid with the lopsided grin from Beaver Falls, Pennsylvania, did more over the years than become a great quarterback, arguably the finest pure passer in history. He came to symbolize a moment in time, the way author F. Scott Fitzgerald had back in the flapper era.

This guy could pitch pantyhose and get away with it. He didn't look ridiculous in a Fu Manchu mustache, which he later shaved in a Remington commercial for a fee of $10,000. He wore white cleats. If he wasn't autopsying defenses with chilling precision, he was off starring in a chopper flick and cozying up to Hollywood actresses like Ann Margaret.

Those knees may have been held in place by ruinous ligaments. But that pass release? Heaven-sent.

"He was like a cause," said teammate John Dockery. "It was like traveling with a rock star. He just was a magnet. Talk about energy and excitement. Wow!"

On November 28, 1964, the St. Louis Cardinals selected Namath 12th overall in the 1965 NFL Draft. That same day, the New York Jets drafted him first

When Joe Namath talked, people around him listened — and believed.

overall in the AFL Draft. Namath, of course, made the risky choice. It was a huge coup for the fledgling American Football League in its determination to rival the clout and star-wattage of the established NFL. The Jets promptly signed Namath for a reported $400,000 a season. Now he had to back up the hype.

The time was ripe for a rebel, and Namath fit the bill brilliantly. The 1960s were a decade of musical and political upheaval. The young believed in dissent, thumbed their noses at the status quo and sought out antiheroes. The Johnny Unitas crewcut and Bart Starr's Bible studies didn't wash anymore. But Joe Willie did.

Namath broke rules and ruffled the establishment. His hedonistic lifestyle drove the old guard crazy. Vince Lombardi, the ultimate establishment coach, couldn't hold back from venting his displeasure, even while in hospital battling the cancer that would claim his life. His widow, Marie, would later recall: "He talked once in his sleep about Namath. I just heard his end of the conversation. He was shouting at Namath, telling him to sit down and yelling about how he was a disgrace to football."

Lombardi might've hotly disagreed with the methods and the style, but no one could dispute Namath's gift.

Lost in the fact that Namath was a state of mind as much as a quarterback are the accomplishments.

Joe Namath looks to pass during a game in the 1974 season.

He is, never forget, the only man to throw for 4,000 yards in a 14-game season — his third year as a pro, first as a starter, in 1967. Three times he led the AFL/NFL in passing.

In addition to that sublime right arm and a great football intellect, he possessed a tremendous will to win. When Joe Namath talked, people around him listened — and believed.

"To be a leader, you have to make people want to follow you," said Namath. "And nobody wants to follow someone who doesn't know where he's going."

Where Namath planned on going was right to the top against Don Shula's seemingly unbeatable Baltimore Colts in Super Bowl III.

The lead-in surrounding "the guarantee" of victory is a bit hazy. Namath made his bold — some would claim insane — promise in response to a heckler at the Miami Touchdown Club dinner three days before the Jets were predicted to be wiped out by the NFL's monster truck from Baltimore. It made for headline-grabbing fodder.

Then Namath went out and backed up the talk, completing 17 of 28 passes for 206 yards to snare MVP honors, as the upstart AFL cemented its legitimacy in the neon glow of a 16-7 Jets victory. It may not be the most memorable Super Bowl ever, but it remains the most famous.

"When we won the league championship," quipped Namath, "all the married guys on the club had to thank their wives for putting up with all the stress and strain all season. I had to thank all the single broads in New York."

100-proof Joe.

Over his entire career, Namath threw more interceptions than touchdowns and had just a 50.1 percent completion rating. Yet to this day, he remains one of the game's most famous quarterbacks. The knee injuries that compromised his brilliance and cut short his career dated back to his senior year at Alabama. We are only left to ponder what he would've been like on two healthy pins.

What we saw, however, was more than enough. For his swagger and sass, boldness and daring, Broadway Joe remains timeless. ■

College: University of Alabama
Drafted: 1965 (AFL Draft), New York Jets, 1st overall
Years active: 1965–1977
Top honors: Super Bowl Champion (1968), Super Bowl MVP (1968), AFL First Team All-Pro (1968), AFL AP Player of the Year (1968, 1969)
Hall of Fame induction: 1985

TERRELL
OWENS WR

G	Rec	Yds	Y/R	TD
219	1,078	15,934	14.8	153

HE WAS ONCE THE MOST PUBLICIZED CHARACTER IN the NFL, and he had the game and the name to prove it. He was "Terrible" Terrell Owens, T.O. — the sure-fingered, tongue-flapping malcontent. A nonstop grumbler who would incite and ignite, then walk away as if he had nothing to do with it.

Consider these nuggets from the Terrible One's past: he insinuated that one of his quarterbacks (Jeff Garcia of the San Francisco 49ers) was gay and that another (Donovan McNabb of the Philadelphia Eagles) wasn't in shape. When Owens scored two touchdowns for the 49ers in a game against the Dallas Cowboys, he celebrated both majors by standing at midfield inside the Dallas star logo. That drew an angry response from the Cowboys, who went after Owens, and an angrier one from

San Francisco head coach Steve Mariucci.

Mariucci tore a strip off his players, but he specifically got after Owens for his showboat antics, saying, "We will never win like that." Owens couldn't stand the fact his coach embarrassed him in front of his teammates. "That fractured our relationship forever," admitted Mariucci, who suspended Owens for a week. Mariucci was fired before the 2003 season, and Owens left in 2004 after being caught in a three-way trade that ended with him in Philadelphia. There he signed a new contract, worth $49 million over seven years.

Things went well early on in the Owens-Eagles partnership. In his first season with the strong-armed McNabb, Owens was able to go deep and beat defensive backs with his speed. The situation unravelled when Owens came back to the huddle after being left uncovered. He told McNabb he was wide open. The quarterback responded with a, "Shut the f— up." That was the iceberg that sunk the Titanic.

In the off-season following the Eagles' heartbreaking 24–21 loss to the New England Patriots in Super Bowl XXXIX, Owens lashed out at McNabb, implying his QB was out of shape by saying he "wasn't the guy who got tired in the Super Bowl," in reference to media reports that McNabb was sick or tired during the game.

Added to this misstep was a fistfight with Hugh Douglas, a former Eagle who was working as a "goodwill ambassador" for the team. In November 2005 Douglas had made a comment in the Eagles locker room about players faking injuries; Owens took exception,

believing that to be a slight aimed at him. He and Douglas started swinging without a hint of goodwill.

With all that animosity bubbling around him, Owens was ordered by the Eagles' management to make a public apology. He did, but there was nothing directed specifically at McNabb. Terrible Owens was suspended for the balance of the regular season and playoffs. "It's tough to lose a guy of his caliber," McNabb said. "But I think we might be better off without him."

After all that, Owens was released by Philadelphia and claimed by Dallas — the team he took great pleasure in provoking. His first season with the Cowboys was a statistical success; his second was better. He had 81 catches for 1,355 yards and 15 touchdowns. True to form, he irked Dallas into the inevitable — after three seasons he had to pack up and leave town. Cowboys owner Jerry Jones talked about how Owens lacked the right attitude; better he went somewhere else to find a team that would accept his ways.

As amusing as some of his on-field antics were, they kept him out of the Pro Football Hall of Fame. Voters remembered him scoring a touchdown and then taking a Sharpie out of his sock and signing the football for his financial advisor. They remembered the time he grabbed a fan's box of popcorn and poured it through his facemask

for a quick snack. There were a lot of times, enough to cast him in an unfavorable light.

But in 2018 Owens's efforts were put in a different perspective. Thirty players and coaches came forward and insisted the Hall of Fame was about football — what a player did to make himself, his team and the game better.

That argument was best made by Garcia, who weathered his share of Owens's taunts. "He wore his emotions on his sleeve and some-times that was taken in a negative way from the fact he wanted to win badly," Garcia wrote. "No matter who his QB was or what team he played for, his production was consistent and raised the standard of the position from a performance aspect.

"The proof is in what he did on the field."

And with his catches and touchdowns, Owens should have been a Hall of Famer years ago. Absolutely. ■

> ## "No matter who his QB was or what team he played for, his production was consistent and raised the standard of the position from a performance aspect."
> — former teammate Jeff Garcia

College: University of Tennessee at Chattanooga
Drafted: 1996, San Francisco 49ers, 89th overall
Years active: 1996–2010
Top honors: First Team All-Pro (2000–02, 2004, 2007)
Hall of Fame induction: 2018

PHILIP
RIVERS QB

G	Att	Comp	Yds	TD	Int
244	8,134	5,277	63,400	421	209

THIS WAS THE GAME THAT PUT PHILIP RIVERS ON THE map: It was October 8 during the 2006 NFL season, and the defending Super Bowl champions, the Pittsburgh Steelers, were going to do everything they could to stop San Diego Chargers running back LaDainian Tomlinson. According to the Steelers, that would put all the pressure on Rivers.

Was he quarterback enough to get the job done?

As it turned out, Rivers turned in a stellar showing. He wasn't out-of-his-mind crazy, throwing for 500 yards and five touchdowns in a giddy upset of the Steelers. Not that passing for 242 yards and two touchdowns in a 23–10 win is a bad day at work.

But this was more about substance, about converting on third downs and defying Pittsburgh's untamed defense. What Rivers demonstrated in his fifth consecutive start was a level of gamesmanship that highlighted just how far he had come as a quarterback, and how much potential he had the more he played.

In March 2020, at age 38, Rivers decided his time with the Los Angeles Chargers had come to an end. He used his free-agent status to sign with the Indianapolis Colts, leaving behind a slew of records as the Chargers' all-time top quarterback — the leader in most games played (228), most wins (123), most passing yards (59,271) and most touchdowns (397). It was enough to fuel the debate over wonder Dan Fouts or the southern-born Rivers, whose ability to throw a football was something to behold.

"My coach told me [Rivers] doesn't throw passes, he throws hand-offs," said former defensive lineman Dan Williams. "Because his accuracy is always the same. The ball ends up in the hands of a receiver."

Rivers' fight to prove himself as a top-gun quarterback began soon after he finished his university career at North Carolina State. Some NFL scouts didn't like the way he threw the football in a semi-sidearm fashion. The Chargers, then based in San Diego, were prepared to take quarterback Eli Manning with the first overall pick in the 2004 Draft. That didn't sit well with Manning, who told the Chargers he wouldn't sign with them.

To resolve things, Manning was drafted by San Diego and then traded to the New York Giants for Rivers, who had been taken fourth overall. The deal also included two draft picks for San Diego. They were used to take linebacker Shawne Merriman and kicker Nate Kaeding. Both players became useful cogs in the Chargers' machinery.

If Rivers figured he would report to San Diego and be fast-tracked into the starter's position, he was woefully mistaken. At his first training camp, he was third on the depth chart behind Drew Brees and Doug Flutie. As the season unfolded, Rivers got precious little prime time given how well Brees was playing.

It took Flutie's release and a shoulder injury to Brees before Rivers got his first start on September 11, 2006, against the Oakland Raiders. The result was a 27–0 win for the Chargers, who followed that with a 40–7 win over the Tennessee Titans, which took them to the telltale Pittsburgh game where Rivers proved he could manage an offense about as well as anyone. San Diego compiled a 14-2 record for that season but lost to the New England Patriots in the divisional playoff game, 24–21.

From then on, every time Rivers took to the field, he was expected to produce results, and there were dozens of wins and some lingering disappointments along

Philip Rivers looks for a receiver during a December 2019 game against the Jacksonville Jaguars.

the way. The biggest regret was not being able to get the Chargers into a Super Bowl, where he could fling passes to Antonio Gates or let Tomlinson run over the opposition.

At his 2019 season-ending news conference — by then he had already moved his family to Florida in the hope of signing with an eastern-based franchise — Rivers spoke about how team unity was so imperative to success and how fortunate he was to have played with so many talented people. Then he summed up his 16 seasons in southern California, while choking back the emotions: "I think I can say I gave it everything I had."

Rivers wound up signing a one-year, $25 million deal with Indianapolis, in the market for a marquee QB following the surprise retirement of Andrew Luck. He helped the Colts to 11 wins and a playoff berth in 2020. Following a wild-card loss to Buffalo, though, Rivers decided to walk away at 39, after 17 seasons, and coach high-school football.

No, he may not have won a Super Bowl game, but only seven men, household names all — Brady, Manning, Favre, Roethlisberger, Elway and Marino — could claim more regular-season successes. ∎

College: North Carolina State University
Drafted: 2004, New York Giants, 4th overall
Years active: 2004–2020
Top honors: NFL AP Comeback Player of the Year (2013)
Hall of Fame induction: N/A

AARON
RODGERS QB

G	Att	Comp	Yds	TD	Int
213	7,118	4,651	55,360	449	93

O VER THE COURSE OF 17 LATE FALLS/FRIGID WINTERS on the job at the county seat of Brown County, Wisconsin, the passing acumen of the long-shot kid from Chico, California, has become an authentic piece of Green Bay Packers lore.

On par with Lombardi's fedora, Nitschke's maniacal toothless grin, Reggie White's laser-focus GPS to the quarterback, a Bart Starr sneak behind Jerry Kramer on a sheet of ice or a ceremonial Lambeau Leap into the end zone crowd following a green-and-gold touchdown.

Aaron Rodgers, of course, isn't merely among the best of his time at his chosen profession, but of any time.

On Green Bay's career passing yardage list, he nestles in behind leader Brett Favre and ahead of Bart Starr.

That's quite the company to be keeping.

The Aaron Rodgers list of individual accomplishments is, as everyone knows, extensive, capped by the 2015 Super Bowl title, a 31–25 taming of the Pittsburgh Steelers, to go along with game MVP at Cowboys Stadium in Arlington, Texas.

"I know I'm capable of reaching greatness," he had

predicted early on in his pro career. "And I'm expecting to reach that level."

Making the proof of that even sweeter is that he believed when few else did.

Coming out of high school, Rodgers was passed over by every single NCAA Division I program except one. The University of Illinois offered him a walk-on tryout, no scholarship. He declined.

His unlikely rise to stardom really began in the California Community College Athletic Association at Butte College, where Rodgers was asked to play quarterback by the only program that would have him. He did well enough in a single season to lead his school to a No. 2 national ranking. University of California, Berkeley head coach Jeff Tedford came to Butte to scout a prospect at tight end. He watched tape of the Butte offense and noticed Rodgers. Tedford, a former Canadian Football League quarterback, liked Rodgers' mechanics and offered him a Division I scholarship.

At Cal, Rodgers became the starting quarterback midway through his first season. He never looked back. In 2004 he took the Golden Bears to a 10-1 record and a No. 4 national ranking.

Rodgers decided to skip his senior year to enter the 2005 NFL Draft. His favorite team, the San Francisco 49ers, had the first pick overall but passed on him. Twenty-two other teams followed suit. Finally, with the 24th pick overall, Green Bay tagged Rodgers.

After three years of apprenticing under the legend, Favre, he took control of the Packers (Favre having retired, un-retired and then been dealt to the NY Jets to make way for his successor in the interim), and in only Year 2 of the Aaron Era, the sixth-seeded Pack beat the Eagles in Philadelphia, the Falcons in Atlanta and then the Bears in Chicago to reach Super Bowl XLV against the Steelers.

Rodgers commanded the spotlight and held it. He completed 24 of 39 passes for 304 yards and three touchdowns as Green Bay won its fourth Super Bowl championship. Rodgers was named game MVP.

The next season, he claimed his first league MVP, while posting an NFL-record 122.5 passer rating. A second MVP bauble arrived in 2014, and a third in 2021 that saw him hit on a career-high 70.9 completion percentage.

What continued to remain maddeningly elusive was a second Super Bowl ring.

After a very public push to leave Green Bay was solved, the 2021 season brought equal shares of further achievement and unfamiliar controversy. Rodgers' "misleading" assurances that he had been immunized against COVID-19 and subsequent violation of league protocols for unvaccinated players triggered a maelstrom of social media comment.

On the field — at least through the regular season — things proved far less problematic. Rodgers' TD-to-INT margin, 37 to just four, and 4,115 yards passing propelled the Packers to a 13-4 record and the No. 1 seeding in the NFC come playoff time, making him the odds-on favorite to claim a fourth MVP award.

But once again, his draft team of choice, the 49ers, spoiled the storyline, inflicting a fourth playoff loss on Rodgers and the Packers, this time by a 13–10 count on a frozen, snow-blown, windswept Lambeau, in the second round of postseason action.

Facing a salary-cap overload north of $40 million for the 2022 season, with Rodgers set to turn 39 years old and perhaps quietly looking for a new venue to reach a long-standing second title, his future seemed uncertain.

"Nothing," he declared, "is off the table."

Staying, leaving or, as far-fetched as it may seem, retiring.

Packer Backers everywhere were permitted a huge sigh of relief when the recently crowned back-to-back NFL MVP announced he would, indeed, return, and to Green Bay, eventually signing a deal on March 15, reported to be worth $150.815 million over three seasons.

Thereby further cementing the kid from Chico, California, among the authentic pieces of Packers lore.

Now and evermore. ∎

Yet here he is today, the undisputed franchise focal point of the Packers, who took over from the legendary Brett Favre and silenced his skeptics.

College: University of California, Berkeley
Drafted: 2005, Green Bay Packers, 24th overall
Years active: 2005–present
Top honors: Super Bowl Champion (2010), Super Bowl MVP (2010), NFL AP MVP (2011, 2014, 2020, 2021), First Team All-Pro (2011, 2014, 2020, 2021)
Hall of Fame induction: N/A

BEN
ROETHLISBERGER QB

G	Att	Comp	Yds	TD	Int
249	8,443	5,400	64,088	418	211

THE QUARTERBACK THEY CALLED BIG BEN WAS hunted by Jaguars, trampled by Broncos, pillaged by Vikings and beaten by Patriots. But it was a Chrysler New Yorker that almost did him in.

On the morning of June 12, 2006, Ben Roethlisberger, the Super Bowl–winning quarterback for the Pittsburgh Steelers, was cruising along atop a Suzuki motorcycle, not a care in the world,

when suddenly he and the New Yorker got into a nasty collision.

Those who saw the accident said the 6-foot-5, 240-pound Roethlisberger was sent flying off his bike and into the car's windshield, shattering it with his head and leaving him with a nine-inch gash and several broken facial bones. It took four surgeons seven hours to repair Roethlisberger's face. He later

At 23 he became the youngest quarterback to win the Vince Lombardi Trophy, which added his name to the list of Steelers superheroes.

recalled paramedics at the crash site telling him they had to stop the bleeding in his throat to save his life.

And just think — all that pain and suffering could have been lessened if only Big Ben had been wearing a helmet. The way he did whenever he stepped onto a football field. There, with his Pittsburgh teammates, he went about his business as arguably the most physical quarterback in the NFL. He took big hits and threw himself into oncoming tacklers. He had the size and fearlessness of a defensive end. It made him a wrecking ball, and there were many times when it was fun to watch.

But during the 2021 season it became clear it was time for a battered Roethlisberger to step out of the huddle and away from the game. Facing the Minnesota Vikings, Big Ben was sacked five times and Pittsburgh trailed 29–0 at the half.

In the third quarter, Roethlisberger rallied the offense with three touchdown passes and had a fourth dropped in the end zone, sealing a 36–28 defeat. Talk of his retiring grew to the point where Roethlisberger acknowledged the game against the Cleveland Browns would be his last at Heinz Field. It ended in a win.

Days after the Steelers were soundly beaten in the playoffs by the Kansas City Chiefs, Big Ben went on social media and confirmed he was cleaning out his locker and calling it a career.

The Steelers took on the New England Patriots in the 2004 playoffs and lost 41–27. The benefits from that beating came the following season, when Pittsburgh advanced to Super Bowl XL. Roethlisberger had a rough time passing that day but managed his team's plan of attack well enough to defeat the Seattle Seahawks 21–10. At 23, he became the youngest quarterback to win the Vince Lombardi Trophy, which added his name to the list of Steelers superheroes.

"It's backyard football," said Baltimore Ravens defensive lineman Brandon Williams of Roethlisberger's quarterbacking style. "Just run around then bombing downfield. That's what he does."

Then came the motorcycle accident that sent Roethlisberger to an emergency room. He would return to the ER for an appendectomy months later that kept him out of the 2006 season opener. Pittsburgh coach Bill Cowher said of his team and his quarterback's mentality, "Adversity is not what knocks you down, it's how you handle it."

The Steelers made good on their return to the Super Bowl on February 1, 2009. Trailing 23–20 with 2:37 remaining in the fourth quarter, Roethlisberger passed to Santonio Holmes, who took the ball 40 yards to the Arizona Cardinals' 6-yard line. The QB and receiver teamed up again for the touchdown that gave Pittsburgh a record sixth Super Bowl victory. (The Patriots tied Pittsburgh when they won their sixth in 2019.)

Roethlisberger served a four-game suspension in 2010 for violating the NFL's personal conduct policy, only to return and lead his team back to the Super Bowl — his third trip. The Steelers trailed the Green Bay Packers 31–25 with 2:07 remaining in the fourth quarter. Roethlisberger moved the ball 20 yards on two passes, then couldn't complete another as the Packers took over on downs and won the game.

The Steelers were unable to return to the Super Bowl despite strong performances from their star quarterback. For six straight seasons, between 2013 and 2018, he threw for over 3,800 passing yards and 28 touchdowns. He hit career highs in 2018, leading the league in several categories, including passing yards (5,129) and completions (452). His 34 touchdown passes that season set a franchise record.

At his home-field goodbye, Roethlisberger summed up his performance as he did his 18 years in yellow and black. "That's been the story of my career," he said. "Not always pretty, but we find a way." ▪

College: Miami University
Drafted: 2004, Pittsburgh Steelers, 11th overall
Years active: 2004–2021
Top honors: NFL AP Offensive Rookie of the Year (2004), NFL All-Rookie Team (2004), Super Bowl Champion (2005, 2008)
Hall of Fame induction: N/A

BARRY
SANDERS RB

G	Att	Yds	Avg	TD
153	3,062	15,269	5.0	99

IT WAS NEVER ENOUGH TO UNDERSTAND WHAT MADE Barry Sanders run. What people wanted to know was what made him quit. How could he walk away from the game just days after turning 31? What about the records, the fortune, the adulation?

Sanders wasn't hurting physically. Certainly he wasn't hurting for money, not with $20.9 million left on a four-year deal with the Detroit Lions. How could he retire without really explaining why? Where was his loyalty, his sense of responsibility?

"I tell you what I heard from Ol' Blue Eyes one time — Frank Sinatra," said Sanders, five years after his retirement. "He said the same question was put to him: 'What do you owe the fans?' And he said, 'First of all, I owe them a good performance.' I really listened to that and really took a hold of that.

"First and foremost, I owe people everything that I was as a football player when I stepped onto the field ... and I think I did that. Once I left the field, I've never been good or comfortable with all the other stuff, of what you owe everyone else as far as the media and fans and people like that, and I may have been clumsy with those things at times."

No NFL running back has been more exciting to watch and less understood than Sanders. He didn't just perform in shoulder pads, he conducted recitals. He didn't run, he accelerated and exhilarated.

Sanders was a uniquely built, stunningly gifted athlete. He stood 5-foot-8 and weighed 203 pounds. As fast as he was when running in a straight line, it was his ability to maneuver without losing top speed that allowed him to out-distance his adversaries.

Sanders set all kinds of records in college, where he produced five consecutive 200-yard games and scored at least two touchdowns in 11 consecutive games. The record-breaking continued in the NFL, where he rushed for at least 1,500 yards five times in his career and scored 15 touchdowns on runs of 50 yards or more.

It was impossible to keep tabs on Sanders's highlights. Picking out his best run was like trying to name your favorite Beatles song. There was that amazing recovery against the Buffalo Bills, the one where he was in the clutches of a tackler and falling when all of a sudden he stuck out his left arm, pushed himself off the turf, regained his balance, cut back and raced away in the opposite direction.

Or the one where he froze that Minnesota Vikings defensive back with an outside-inside juke en route to a long gain.

Or the one where he had the New England Patriots defender turning in circles trying to locate his man, let alone tackle him.

Or the one where he exploded through the right side of the Indianapolis Colts' defense as if it were nothing but party streamers.

Or the one ...

There were so many "ones."

But while Sanders reveled in personal triumphs, the Detroit Lions were hard-pressed to be average. During the Sanders years, the Lions were 78-82 and made the postseason five times. Only once did they win a playoff game. In that contest, a 38–6 trouncing of the Dallas Cowboys in the 1991 season, Sanders scored on a 47-yard run in the final minutes. The following week,

Barry Sanders rushes for yards at Lambeau Field on November 21, 1993.

Detroit was crushed 41–10 by the Washington Redskins, with Sanders kept to 44 yards on 11 carries.

The Lions' shoddy postseason record, combined with Sanders's drop in yardage, opened the doors for critics to claim the Hall of Fame running back was largely over-rated. Their argument was based on Sanders playing the bulk of his career inside a domed stadium and that once outdoors, in the playoffs, he was far less effective. (Sanders scored a touchdown for every 35 touches in his 153 career regular-season games, while aver-aging a touchdown for every 112 touches in his six career playoff games.)

Sanders left himself wide open to detractors when he retired late in July 1999. It happened in the most unanticipated fashion, with Sanders faxing a letter to his hometown newspaper, the *Wichita Eagle*. In his statement, he said, "The reason I am retiring is very simple. My

desire to exit the game is greater than my desire to remain in it."

Sanders declined to elabo-rate, which prompted a run of conspiracy theories. He wanted more money, wanted to be traded, disliked his coach Bobby Ross, hated the Lions for releasing his friend Kevin Glover two years earlier and for not doing enough to field a winning team.

Sanders said little even when the media argued he owed his teammates a definitive explanation, especially with him only 1,457 yards shy of breaking Walter Payton's then-record for most career rushing yards.

It took Sanders time to articu-late his reasons for quitting: "I'm very competitive when it comes to winning and losing and playing well," he said. "And I did put up big numbers. There were some times in 1997 when I could have gone back in to pad my numbers, but I wasn't as competitive with the numbers as

I was about winning and losing."

There was always talk that Sanders would return to the NFL, but he never did. Like Jim Brown, Sanders stepped away from the field, ensuring a lifelong debate that he could have played longer and done more amazing things had he chosen to stick around.

"Ten years is a lot of football," he said.

It was enough for him — and much too little for his fans. ■

College: Oklahoma State University
Drafted: 1989, Detroit Lions, 3rd overall
Years active: 1989–1998
Top honors: NFL All-Rookie Team (1989), NFL AP Offensive Rookie of the Year (1989), First Team All-Pro (1989–91, 1994, 1995, 1997), NFL AP Offensive Player of the Year (1994), NFL AP MVP (1997)
Hall of Fame induction: 2004

GALE
SAYERS RB

G	Att	Yds	Avg	TD
68	991	4,956	5.0	39

GALE SAYERS DIDN'T MERELY RUN WITH THE football, he slalomed. He was a restless wave of a running back, shifting to and fro, weaving in and out, until at last he found an open portal in the defensive line — and then he was gone.

"He's the only guy I think could be running, stop on a dime, tell you whether it was heads or tails and not even break stride," said Green Bay Packers defensive back Herb Adderley.

Apparently hemmed in and then changing direction, slithering out of the desperate grasp of tacklers and making his cut at precisely the right instant, Sayers left bamboozled defenders clawing at air. Pro football had not seen his like before. Watching old film of Sayers today, he gives you, more than anything, this exhilarating sense of freedom.

To defenders he must have seemed an almost ghostly presence, an apparition clad in white or black and wearing No. 40. As difficult to contain as a drop of mercury, Sayers could run with power and purpose, certainly, but what we remember most is his speed and elusiveness.

It sounds absurdly simple and clichéd, but it was nonetheless true: he just made people miss. Sayers once said he could instinctively "feel" defenders getting close to him. Certainly there seemed to be some form of special intuitive power at work.

"Magic," as they came to call him in Chicago. The legendary Papa Bear, coach George Halas, dubbed him the greatest back since Red Grange. Although their styles were different, Sayers became heir apparent to the great Jim Brown in a heartbeat.

Nicknamed the Kansas Comet, he had come out of the University of Kansas as the fourth overall pick in the 1965 NFL Draft, snubbing a more lucrative offer from the Kansas City Chiefs of the upstart AFL to join the Chicago Bears.

In his second regular-season game, Sayers touched the ball once — and scored a touchdown. By Game 4, he couldn't be kept out of the starting lineup. That day, one screen pass in particular trumpeted the arrival of a new star in the pro football firmament: an 80-yard touchdown ramble after latching onto the ball, shedding Los Angeles Rams along the way.

"I hit him so hard that I thought my shoulder must have busted him in two," said L.A.'s All-Pro defensive lineman Rosey Grier. "I heard a roar from the crowd and figured he'd fumbled, so I started scrambling around looking for the loose ball. But there was no ball and Sayers was gone."

The rookie also threw a touchdown pass that day from an option play. The Bears won 31–6. Gale Sayers had arrived. And there was more to come.

The afternoon of December 12, 1965, was a cold, wet day at Wrigley Field. Some people have labeled the game that day as "the greatest individual game ever played." In the bog of Wrigley, Sayers piled up 336 all-purpose yards and scored a phenomenal, record-tying six touchdowns — despite being pulled by Halas for most of the fourth quarter, with the Bears well on their way to a comfortable 61–20 over the San Francisco 49ers.

"I think in the mud I ran more flatfooted, made my cuts not on my toes but on the balls of my feet and my heels," recalled Sayers. "That kept me on balance."

Sayers captured Rookie of the Year honors in 1965 for his 867 yards rushing, 507 yards receiving and an NFL-record 22 touchdowns. His second season was no less spectacular. Sayers rushed for 1,231 yards, caught passes for 447 more and scored 12 touchdowns — eight via the run, two through the air and two more on kickoff returns.

His stats dipped in 1967, mostly because the Bears were a team in decline. Then, the next season, the unthinkable happened. After nine games, Sayers had amassed 856 yards rushing and was averaging 6.2 yards a carry. But on November 10, 1967, in mid-cut, he was tackled by the 49ers' Kermit Alexander. Sayers crumpled to the field in pain. He'd torn multiple ligaments in his right knee.

Surgery ended Sayers' season and, at that time, cast doubt on his career. But if he was a man of few words,

he was also nothing if not incredibly courageous and single-minded. A punishing rehabilitation followed. Looking back on that time, he said, "I learned if you want to make it bad enough, no matter how bad it is, you can make it."

When Sayers returned to the Bears the next season, he wasn't the same player. He could still "feel" the defenders, yes. But avoiding them proved a far greater challenge. That electric speed, the impossible-to-explain elusiveness, had been compromised. More and more yards had to be won down in the trenches, between the tackles, in the tough areas.

Sayers still led the league in rushing. It was arguably his greatest accomplishment in the game. A second knee operation, in 1970, did what few defenders had been able to do in four and a half unforgettable seasons: cut down Gale Sayers in his tracks.

"The Comet," they had christened him in his prime, and a comet he proved to be — flashing across the sky, burning oh-so-brightly and taking our breath away, only to fade from view too soon, leaving us awed and unfulfilled at the same time.

Only 34 when enshrined, Sayers remains the youngest man ever voted into the Pro Football Hall of Fame. ■

College: University of Kansas
Drafted: 1965, Chicago Bears, 4th overall
Years active: 1965–1971
Top honors: NFL AP Rookie of the Year (1965), First Team All-Pro (1965–69)
Hall of Fame induction: 1977

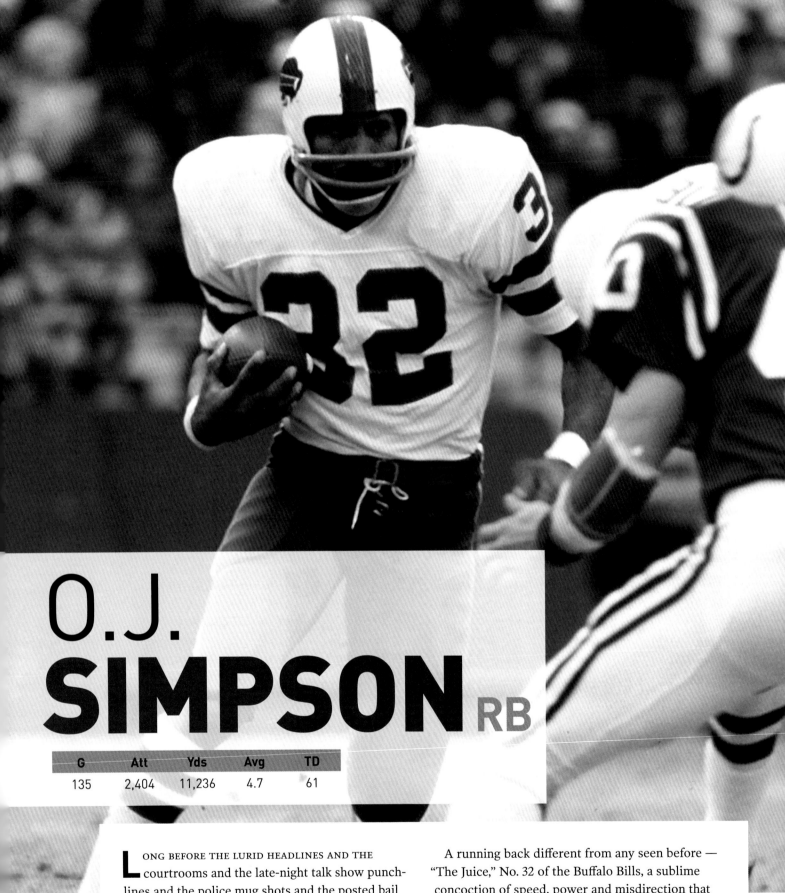

O.J. SIMPSON RB

G	Att	Yds	Avg	TD
135	2,404	11,236	4.7	61

Long before the lurid headlines and the courtrooms and the late-night talk show punchlines and the police mug shots and the posted bail and the almost cartoonish-buffoonish persona, Orenthal James Simpson was known far and wide as a running back.

A running back different from any seen before — "The Juice," No. 32 of the Buffalo Bills, a sublime concoction of speed, power and misdirection that ran through NFL defenses as easily as he dashed through airports in Hertz Rent-a-Car commercials. Simpson was the first rusher ever to top 2,000 yards in a season — and in only 14 games, at that. He was a man who established records for yards along the ground in a game (273) and touchdowns during a season (23); a three-time UPI Player of the Year, four-time leading rusher, All-AFC and All-Pro for five consecutive years, he participated in six Pro Bowls and was the NFL's MVP in 1973.

Here was an athlete so extraordinary, so unique, that legendary University of Southern California coach John McKay declared, "Simpson was not only the greatest player I ever had — he was the greatest player *anyone* ever had."

Watching videos of Simpson now still has the power to amaze and delight. He provides viewers with the same sort of goosebumps that Gale Sayers did before him: the dramatic, seemingly impossible changes in direction, that rare inexplicable ability to make opponents miss, as if he alone were enacting a dance of joy.

"The fear of losing is what makes competitors so great," he said of the game he came to dominate. "Show me a gracious loser, and I'll show you a permanent loser."

For the length of his stay there, O.J. Simpson turned frigid Buffalo into Broadway on Sunday afternoons or Monday nights, providing the greatest theater in the state outside of the Great White Way.

Because of the benevolent, charming façade Simpson studiously built during his decade as a superstar with the Bills, people forgot, or never knew, that he grew up in the rough Potrero Hill section of San Francisco and was raised by his mother, Eunice, after his dad walked out on the family.

Early on, Simpson hardly seemed a candidate for football immortality. He developed rickets at just two years old, leaving his legs skinny and bowed. He joined his first gang at 13, and at 15 Simpson landed in a Youth Guidance Center for a week after one of many fights. There had always been a dark side to O.J. Simpson the kid-from-the-shabby-side-of-the-tracks side.

But football ability, the great equalizer, was his ticket out of the squalor and into the limelight of mainstream American culture. He only ever wanted to play collegiately, for the Trojans at USC. And it was there his legend began to take shape. During his phenomenal Heisman Trophy–winning senior season, Simpson set NCAA records for most rushing yards in a season (1,709) and most carries (355). USC won the Rose Bowl that year. In 17 of his 21 career games for the Trojans, he ran for over 100 yards; in five of them, for over 200.

Chosen first in the 1969 college draft, Simpson languished for three seasons in Buffalo, unhappy with how he was being used. When Lou Saban took over as head coach in 1972, though, he built his offense around the workhorse back and was rewarded with 1,251 yards — the NFL high that year.

Simpson exploded into the national consciousness in 1973. He had 1,000 yards by the midway point of the season, and people began to speak openly about his chances of hitting 2,000. In Buffalo's next-to-last start, he rambled for 219 yards, leaving him 197 short of the mythical mark. On a bitter, snowy, windswept New York day at Shea Stadium, "The Juice" bulled and finessed for 200, giving him

2,003 on the season. He was carried off the field on the shoulders of his teammates.

During his 11 NFL seasons, Simpson ran for over 11,000 yards and, while he never brought the Super Bowl title to Buffalo, his accomplishments were many and lauded. He was inducted into the Pro Football Hall of Fame in 1985, and he remained an amiable and familiar presence on TV and in film. That is, until June 12, 1994, when his wife Nicole Brown Simpson and her friend Ron Goldman were found dead outside her condominium.

O.J. Simpson, football icon, was charged with the double murder. Following a year-long trial that gripped a nation and divided public opinion, he was acquitted. Later, Simpson was found financially liable in a civil trial for damages to the grieving parties, and in 2008 he was sentenced to 33 years in prison for kidnapping and armed robbery in Las Vegas. For that conviction, he served nine years in prison before his release on October 1, 2017.

His legacy as one of the game's great running backs, however, remains wistfully uncompromised. ∎

College: University of Southern California
Drafted: 1969, Buffalo Bills, 1st overall
Years active: 1969–1979
Top honors: First Team All-Pro (1972–76), NFL AP MVP (1973), NFL AP Offensive Player of the Year (1973)
Hall of Fame induction: 1985

EMMITT
SMITH RB

G	Att	Yds	Avg	TD
226	4,409	18,355	4.2	164

PLAY-BY-PLAY MAN BRAD SCHAM'S CALL OF THE MOMENT on October 27, 2002, is as instantly familiar to Texans as Al Michaels's call of the Miracle on Ice is to the nation: "I-formation, two receivers right. Second and seven from the Dallas 30. [Chad] Hutchinson hand-off. Smith at left guard — 35, 40-yard-line! [pause] Right on the mark! That should do it! Move over, Sweetness! Make a place for Emmitt!"

Nobody had to make a place for Emmitt Smith. He made his own.

"Thirteen years ago a rookie walked into my room. He was my roommate. We talked about the things we wanted to accomplish on the field," recalled wideout Michael Irvin during an emotional postgame celebration after Smith passed Walter Payton atop the NFL's all-time rushing list. "The first thing he said to me — and we were not a good team at the time — was that he wanted to win Super Bowls for you guys, and he did that. He said he wanted to win rushing titles, and he did that. He said he wanted to win MVPs, and he did that. His last goal, which I thought was fantasy, was to become the all-time leading rusher in the NFL.

"And today he did that."

On that October afternoon against the Seattle Seahawks, in front of the home fans at Texas Stadium, Smith ran into the record books.

"He personifies everything that's good about football," said Seahawks coach Mike Holmgren. "He's a gentleman, a good guy and a great player."

What people conveniently forget now, in the soft glow of hindsight, is by that point in his career Smith was generally thought to be a spent force. Observers had

begun wondering aloud if he hadn't stayed too long at the fair.

As he reached out to history, Smith was en route to his lowest rushing total since his rookie season, a count below the Herculean standards he'd set with 11 consecutive years of at least 1,000 yards. There were opinions voiced that maybe he should've had the good sense to retire. Luckily, Smith didn't have the sense to listen to others.

If he had, he might've also believed the scouts who had written him off as too small and too slow when he came out of the University of Florida. He might've agreed with all those teams that so cavalierly bypassed him in the 1990 NFL Draft. If he had had that kind of sense, Smith might never have passed Payton or left an indelible mark on pro football.

What Smith had, in abundance, was more powerful than sense. It was self-belief — an inner faith that if a person wants something badly enough, they can get it.

"For me, winning isn't something that happens suddenly on the field when the whistle blows and the crowds roar," said Smith. "Winning is something that builds physically and mentally every day that you train and every night that you dream."

As philosophies go, that carries a powerful motivational punch.

When Smith arrived in Big D in 1990, the Cowboys were hardly America's Team. They weren't, in fact, much of a team at all. Coach Jimmy Johnson had the gargantuan task of trying to rebuild a 1-15 loser.

With Smith running and Troy Aikman playing catch with Irvin, the Cowboys would go on to glory.

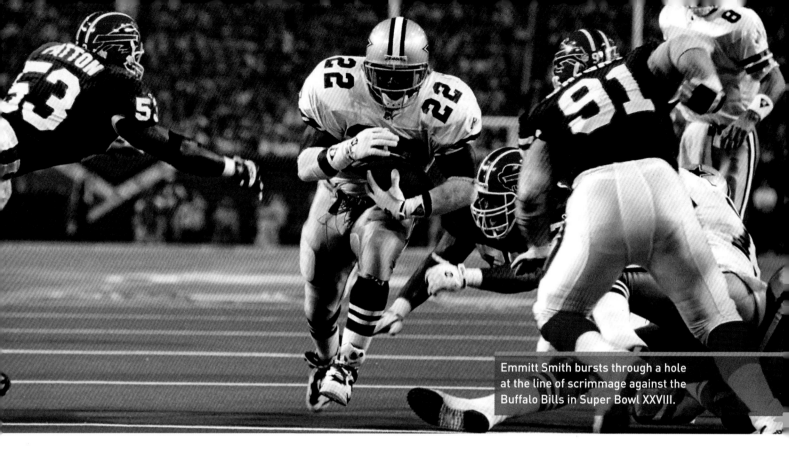

Emmitt Smith bursts through a hole at the line of scrimmage against the Buffalo Bills in Super Bowl XXVIII.

Smith thrived in a decade that also included the phenomenal Barry Sanders. Just as Ali had Frazier, Wilt had Russell and Nicklaus had Watson, Emmitt had Barry. The two men differed stylistically, and arguments raged throughout the 1990s about who was the better back. But there's little doubt that the greatness of one drove the greatness of the other.

In the final analysis, though, Smith was the one to persevere, the one to pass Walter Payton.

"You can just look at my age and say, 'Yeah, he's 33, he should go,'" said Smith as he approached Payton's all-time mark (16,726 yards). "Yeah, I'm 33. But have I lost my step? Have I lost my vision? Have I lost my power? Have I lost my ability to make a person miss? If I answer yes to all those questions, you might be right, but don't tell me I should quit just because of my age. That's what makes this frustrating. You have to know who you are. I know who I am."

In his career, Smith would win three Super Bowls and play in eight Pro Bowls. Like his hero, the man he supplanted at the summit of football's Olympus, Smith did it all with class and distinction. Here was someone who had his head screwed on right, someone who was a man of his word. When Smith came out of Florida early for the NFL Draft, he told his mother he'd get an education. He kept that promise, returning to school during the off-seasons in Dallas and earning his bachelor's degree in public recreation.

Appropriately, after spending 2003 and 2004 with Arizona to close out his career, the Cardinals released Smith and he signed a one-day contract with Dallas to retire as a Cowboy.

Deep inside, Smith — the guy many believed was too slow and too small — never wavered in his conviction that he had a date with destiny.

"I think about it all the time," said Smith as he closed in on the man they called Sweetness. "I'm chasing after legends, after Walter Payton and Tony Dorsett and Jim Brown and Eric Dickerson. After guys who made history. When my career's over, I want to have the new kids, the new backs, say, 'Boy, we have to chase a legend to be the best.' And they'll mean Emmitt Smith."

The 18,355 yards Smith amassed in 15 seasons remains the touchstone figure that all backs are still trying to catch. ◼

College: University of Florida
Drafted: 1990, Dallas Cowboys, 17th overall
Years active: 1990–2004
Top honors: NFL AP Offensive Rookie of the Year (1990), NFL All-Rookie Team (1990), First Team All-Pro (1992–95), Super Bowl Champion (1992, 1993, 1995), Super Bowl MVP (1993), NFL AP MVP (1993)
Hall of Fame induction: 2010

BART
STARR QB

G	Att	Comp	Yds	TD	Int
196	3,149	1,808	24,718	152	138

T HE MOMENT REMAINS AS FROZEN IN TIME AS THE minus-13-degree, minus-36-with-the-windchill conditions on the final day of December 1967 at Lambeau Field — a day so frigid, it prompted Dallas Cowboys owner Clint Murchison Jr. to quip, "If I owned Green Bay, I'd dome the whole town."

As the Packers' offense trotted onto the field, trailing 17–14 with five minutes and no timeouts

remaining in that NFL Championship Game, Green Bay's carnivorous linebacker Ray Nitschke fixed his gaze on his quarterback and hollered: "Don't let me down!"

No need to fret.

The drive, of course, ended with 13 seconds remaining on the clock and two feet from the end zone, on the now legendary third-down quarterback sneak that killed off the Cowboys. That day, Bart Starr dove into history.

Controlled. Precise. Economical. Humble. Cerebral. Efficient. Bryan Bartlett Starr came to embody the perfect Vince Lombardi quarterback. He was the ultimate game manager — the brain center of those legendary Packers teams of the 1960s that had folks in tiny Green Bay answering their telephones with "Hello, Titletown USA!"

Starr arrived in Green Bay as a 17th-round draft choice in 1956. He signed for $6,500 and languished on the bench in his first season. In 1957 he finally started and the Packers went 3-9-0. The next year they were 1-10-1. Then Lombardi came over from the New York Giants.

In the beginning, Lombardi was far from convinced that Starr was his guy. Largely lost in the mists of the time — and the almost mythic reverence in which that Packers era is held — is a moment from the 1960 title game. The emerging Pack lost 17–13 to the Philadelphia Eagles, thanks to Starr failing to spot a wide-open Max McGee at a critical point in the game. The missed opportunity gnawed away at Lombardi long after Eagles linebacker Chuck Bednarik stuffed running back Jim Taylor at the Philadelphia 9-yard line to end Green Bay's bid.

"Yeah, some guys see them and some guys don't," groused Lombardi to NFL executive director Jim Kensil during dinner early in 1961. "Then," recalled Kensil, "he told me, 'I'd really like to get that guy [Don] Meredith.' He told me he'd offered the Cowboys, who had just played their first season, any

two players on the Packers roster. I said, 'Any two?' He said, 'Any two.' He really didn't think that Bart Starr was what he wanted in a quarterback. I thought that was very interesting when Starr started seeing *every* receiver. I always meant to ask Vinnie what happened to that two-for-one deal."

Over the course of his 16-year career, Starr threw for more than 24,000 yards, won the 1966 NFL MVP and played in four Pro Bowls — most of which came during Lombardi's nine seasons in Green Bay. But the most telling testament to the man and his capabilities were the five championships he captured, including the first two Super Bowls.

In retirement, however, the success Starr enjoyed as a player proved elusive. His own nine years as head coach in Green Bay were a struggle, and he was fired in 1983. Away from the field, he suffered physical challenges, including an ischemic stroke, a hemorrhagic stroke, a mild heart attack, seizures and a broken hip. In 1988 his oldest son, Bret, battling a cocaine addiction, died of a heart attack that doctors believed was brought on by drug use.

Often, life leaves us no control. On the field, though, with those other men who also became legends of a truly dynastic era in Green Bay, Starr — who passed away in May 2019 — was in complete control. There he truly remains frozen in time.

"Earlier in my career," wrote Starr in his autobiography, "many fans misinterpreted my calm demeanor for lack of imagination."

Lack of imagination?

Late in that memorable game against the Cowboys, it was Starr

Starr came to embody the perfect Vince Lombardi quarterback.

who came up with the idea of the sneak option — the first run by the Pack all year. He pitched the idea to Lombardi on the sidelines late in the game (now known as the Ice Bowl), even though halfback Donny Anderson had slipped on the two previous plays and an incomplete pass would at least give Starr time to run a final play.

Instead Starr suggested a simple dive right over offensive guard Jerry Kramer.

"I told Coach Lombardi there was nothing wrong with the plays we had run," said Starr. "It's just that the backs couldn't keep their footing. I said, 'Why don't I just keep it?' All he said was, 'Let's run it and get the hell out of here.' That's all he said."

They ran it and got the hell out of there. All the way to Miami, where two weeks later the Packers paddled the Oakland Raiders to claim their second straight Super Bowl. ■

College: University of Alabama
Drafted: 1956, Green Bay Packers, 200th overall
Years active: 1956–1971
Top honors: NFL AP MVP (1966), First Team All-Pro (1966), Super Bowl Champion (1966, 1967), Super Bowl MVP (1966, 1967)
Hall of Fame induction: 1977

ROGER STAUBACH QB

G	Att	Comp	Yds	TD	Int
131	2,958	1,685	22,700	153	109

I N AN ERA OF CHANGE AND REBELLION, ROGER STAUBACH was a welcome, old-fashioned superhero, representing less turbulent times. Genial. Straitlaced. Rigidly conservative. Devoutly Catholic. To push the theme, you might almost say "prim." He came to symbolize those great Cowboy teams that went to four Super Bowls in an eight-year span.

Somehow, Roger Staubach seemed above it all.

In an interview aired on CBS in 1975, though, he showed he wouldn't let the image compromise his sense of humor.

"Everyone in the world compares me to Joe Namath, you know," he told interviewer Phyllis George. "As far as off the field, he's single, a bachelor, a swinger; I'm married with a family, and he's having all the fun. I enjoy sex as much as Joe Namath, you know, only with one girl. It's still fun."

The remark, coming from Staubach the Square, had all of America talking. Just as the man's quarterbacking had all of the NFL talking through 11 seasons of excellence.

As conventional as he was outside the white lines in his personal life, Roger Staubach could be considered a bit of a hell-raiser on the football field. He wasn't christened "Roger the Dodger" for nothing. His ability to avoid trouble netted him 2,264 rushing yards and 20 touchdowns during his seasons in Texas.

Armed with a dizzying array of offensive weapons — former Olympic gold medal sprinter Bob Hayes and Drew Pearson on the outside; pocket-sized dynamo Robert Newhouse, Calvin Hill and the sublime Tony Dorsett charging out of the backfield — Staubach was the choreographer of a brilliant ensemble.

His uncanny knack for bringing the Cowboys back from the abyss transformed the son of a Cincinnati salesman into NFL royalty. He directed 23 come-from-behind victories in the fourth quarter during his career, 14 of those in the final two minutes or overtime.

"Roger," said former Dallas tight end Billy Jo DuPree, "never knew when the game was over."

Staubach's Hail Mary pass to Drew Pearson, with the Cowboys trailing the favored Minnesota Vikings in the 1975 NFC divisional tilt with virtually no time left on the score clock, has gone into the realm of legend.

But as Staubach knew, the last-minute theatrics were born not so much out of inexplicable inspiration as through preparation, repetition and the readiness to hold his nerve in any situation. As a field general, he was tough, single-minded, commanding and innovative. Tom Landry, the taciturn coach of the Cowboys, called Staubach the greatest leader he had ever had the good fortune to come across.

"Confidence," Staubach once said, "doesn't come out of nowhere. It's a result of something ... hours and days and weeks and years of constant work and dedication. Spectacular results come from unspectacular preparation."

Roger Staubach certainly arrived to the NFL prepared. His path to football immortality was hardly a conventional one, but that makes the story all the more compelling. Originally selected by the 'Boys in the 10th round of the 1964 draft as the reigning Heisman Trophy recipient, he was unable to play pro football until his naval commitment, including a voluntary one-year tour of duty in Vietnam, had ended.

Roger Staubach runs with the ball during a November 1977 game against the Washington Redskins.

In his junior year, he led the Naval Academy's Midshipmen to a 9-1 record and the No. 2 ranking in the nation. Coach Wayne Hardin called him the finest quarterback the Navy had ever seen.

So the talent was obvious, but the timing was troublesome.

Undoubtedly that's why he went so late in the draft. The wait, however, was ultimately worth it for the Cowboys.

When Staubach left the Navy in 1969, he was a 27-year-old rookie. By 1971 he was the starter in Big D, taking control from incumbent Craig Morton after Dallas sputtered out of the gate 4-3.

Staubach guided the Cowboys to 10 consecutive regular-season victories and finished an astounding NFL debut season as a starter by beating the Miami Dolphins 24–3 in Super Bowl VI. His 119 yards passing and two TDs at the New Orleans Superdome that afternoon earned Roger Staubach MVP laurels. He'd taken his sweet time getting there, but he arrived in style.

The next decade would see Staubach and the Cowboys set standards for other quarterbacks, other franchises, to emulate.

Staubach would engineer Dallas's marches to three more Super Bowl appearances, beating Denver 27–10 in 1978 back in New Orleans, while losing a pair of title clashes to the Terry Bradshaw-led Pittsburgh Steelers, both times at Miami's Orange Bowl, in 1976 and 1979.

Upon retiring at the close of the 1979 season, in part over concerns of possible lingering aftereffects from a series of concussions, Staubach became more engrossed in a business he'd begun while still playing: real estate. In that, like anything else he has ever thrown his energies into, Staubach made a rousing success.

During his years at the helm of "America's Team," Captain America threw for 22,700 yards and 153 touchdowns. His career passer rating of 83.4 was, at the time, the highest career mark ever. He played in six Pro Bowls (although,

ironically, was never chosen All-Pro), led the league in passing four times and took home the NFL Players Association MVP Award in 1971.

He'd proven his versatility a hundred times over, winning games and championships with his arm and his feet and his head. In his first year of eligibility, 1985 — to no one's surprise — Roger the Dodger took his place in Canton, Ohio, alongside the greatest in the game.

Roger Staubach may have gotten a late start, but it'd be difficult to argue that he hadn't made up for lost time. ∎

College: New Mexico Military Institute
Drafted: 1964, Dallas Cowboys, 129th overall
Years active: 1969–1979
Top honors: Super Bowl Champion (1971, 1977), Super Bowl MVP (1971), NFL Walter Payton Man of the Year (1978)
Hall of Fame induction: 1985

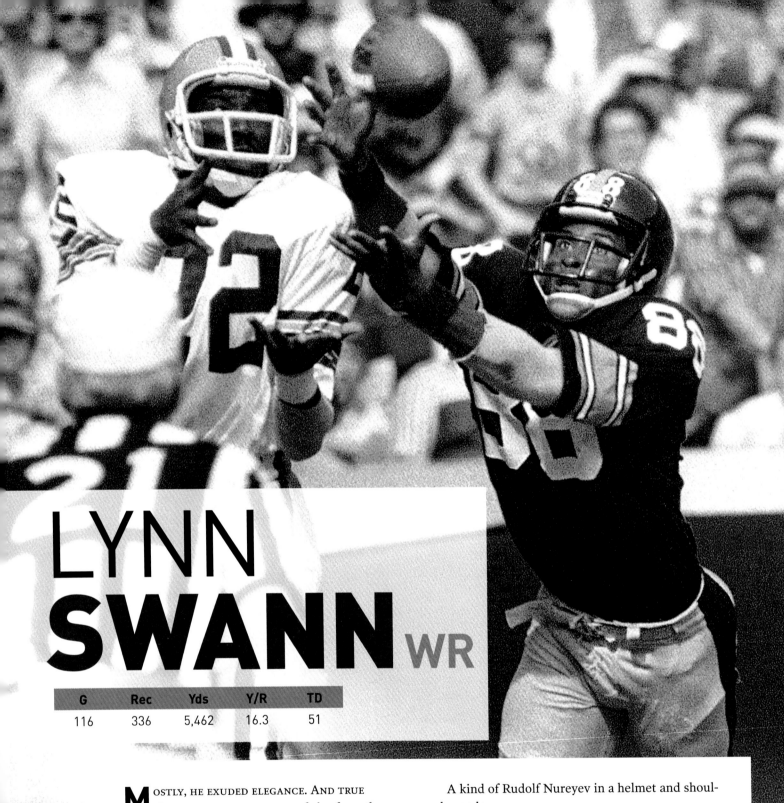

LYNN
SWANN WR

G	Rec	Yds	Y/R	TD
116	336	5,462	16.3	51

MOSTLY, HE EXUDED ELEGANCE. AND TRUE elegance, once seen, never fades from the imagination.

Up he'd go — up, up, up — No. 88 in the Pittsburgh Steelers' signature black, as if held aloft by invisible wires, body twisting, hands extending and ... *snap!* Body control and hang time reminiscent of M.J. attacking the hoop.

Ball as secure as a baby in a mother's arms at church.

A kind of Rudolf Nureyev in a helmet and shoulder pads.

"I took several years of dance lessons that included ballet, tap and jazz," Lynn Swann once recalled. "They helped a great deal with body control, balance, a sense of rhythm and timing."

Makes perfect sense. He was, after all — in each leap, every cut — a ballet unto himself for nine seasons and four Super Bowl celebrations.

Swann Lake.

A kind of Rudolf Nureyev in a helmet and shoulder pads.

Among the receivers generally included in the pantheon of all-time greats, Swann perhaps personifies the quality-over-quantity theory. Those accumulated 336 catches for 5,462 yards and 51 touchdowns don't rank him anywhere near the top in any receiving category.

Yet his continuing impact remains indisputable.

Swann arrived in Steeltown as the 21st pick of the 1974 draft, following an All-America college career at the University of Southern California, coached by the legendary John McKay. After being a part of the undefeated national championship Trojans team of 1972, Swann joined a Steelers team on the brink of a dynasty.

During his stay at Three Rivers Stadium, Swann didn't put up eye-popping regular-season numbers; he had to share the pass-catching wealth with another standout receiver, John Stallworth, and watch as the ball kept being handed off to Franco Harris.

Yet ask anyone who ever watched Lynn Swann rise for a pass or to a challenge, and they'll tell you what he meant.

When it mattered most, the man delivered. Over his four Super Bowl appearances, he amassed 364 receiving yards and 398 all-purpose yards — both records at the time of his retirement.

"People say I perform well in the 'big' games," Swann once said. "Maybe that's because I have more fun in those games … when there is no next week, when six months of work is riding on every play and

you come through, that's the ultimate.

"That's the rush we're all in this for."

Since quitting nearly four decades ago, Swann has, among other ventures, worked as a pundit for ABC Sports, ran as a Republican candidate for governor in Pennsylvania, been appointed athletic director at USC, and even had a guest spot on *Mister Rogers' Neighborhood*.

What he'll be forever remembered for, though, is that image of elegance caught and held forever in the mind's eye: the burnished grace that set him apart from anyone of his era. Of any era, really.

"Without Lynn Swann," said Pittsburgh's Hall of Fame defensive back Mel Blount, with flat certainly, "the Steelers don't win four Super Bowls."

Astoundingly, it took an eternity — 14 years — after his calling it quits for Swann to be enshrined in Canton. That relatively short career span and those rather modest regular-season numbers were an ongoing problem for many voters.

"The mark of a good player is being able to play in big games, and nobody played better in big games than Lynn Swann," parried former Steelers coach Chuck Noll. "If we had thrown the ball more (during regular seasons), he would have been in the Hall of Fame a long time ago."

Indeed, Swann was one of the rare few whose impact, whose legacy, goes far beyond numbers and into the realm of artistic achievement.

His near-poetic diving snare of a ball deflected upward by Dallas DB Mark Washington in Super Bowl

X remains one of the most iconic moments ever. With 2:53 left in the second quarter and the 'Boys from Texas ahead 10–7, Swann produced his stunner, reaching out to juggle and then latching onto a Terry Bradshaw heave of 53 yards down to the Dallas 37-yard line.

To this day, many fans and analysts refer to it as the greatest catch in Super Bowl history.

He made four catches for 161 yards and a touchdown that afternoon at Miami's Orange Bowl, paving the way for a 21–17 Pittsburgh victory and his selection as game MVP — the first receiver ever to be so honored.

"Whatever shortcomings people think my career has had or whatever their reasons why they could justify me not being in the Hall of Fame the past 14 years," Swann told the *Pittsburgh Post-Gazette* on the cusp of his induction in 2001, "it's withstood all of that, and I'm in the Hall of Fame.

"There's a sense of completion. It's done." ∎

College: University of Southern California
Drafted: 1974, Pittsburgh Steelers, 21st overall
Years active: 1974–1982
Top honors: NFL All-Rookie Team (1974), Super Bowl Champion (1974, 1975, 1978, 1979), Super Bowl MVP (1975), First Team All-Pro (1978), NFL Walter Payton Man of the Year (1981)
Hall of Fame induction: 2001

FRAN
TARKENTON QB

G	Att	Comp	Yds	TD	Int
246	6,467	3,686	47,003	342	266

IT WOULD BE TOO CONVENIENT TO MAKE THE CLAIM THAT Fran Tarkenton reinvented the quarterbacking position. But it would by no means be out of line to say he stretched its limits, in much the same way he stretched the defenses of his day.

Back then, in the 1960s and '70s, quarterbacks dropped back in the pocket to throw the football and stayed there, come hell or high water. That was the accepted way to play. Inside the pocket they felt safe and protected.

Tarkenton changed all that. He broke containment. He created chaos. He gave defensive coaches new dangers to consider.

"People looked down on scrambling quarterbacks when I broke in," said Tarkenton. "Now those who can't scramble are at a disadvantage."

Born the son of a preacher in Richmond, Virginia, Tarkenton was coming off a fine college career at Georgia, mentored by the legendary coach Wally Butts, when the Minnesota Vikings took him in the third round of the 1961 NFL Draft.

Right from the get-go, Tarkenton showed immense potential. His first pro start resulted in a 250-yard passing day and a 37–13 upset of the Chicago Bears.

He'd spend six seasons with the Vikings at old Metropolitan Stadium in Bloomington, bickering with head coach Norm Van Brocklin about the effectiveness of his scrambling style, before requesting — and receiving — a trade to the New York Giants in time for the 1967 campaign.

In the Big Apple he provided an interesting contrast to the brash, outspoken quarterback of the other team in town, Joe Namath. The Giants were no powerhouse, but by 1970 Tarkenton had them at least fighting, if unsuccessfully, for a playoff spot. They wound up 9-5. It would be a career highlight for his time in New York.

By 1972 Tarkenton was back in the Twin Cities, but these weren't the same sad-sack Vikings he'd left in '67. Bud Grant, a steely-eyed coaching recruit from the Winnipeg Blue Bombers of the Canadian Football League, had been installed on the sidelines, and Minnesota was putting the pieces in place for a concerted championship push.

These were to be Tarkenton's years of greatest glory and most profound disappointment. Always a bridesmaid, never a bride, the Vikings were among the regular-season elite over the next few seasons, but they could somehow never hit pay dirt come Super Bowl time.

In one stretch of inexplicable agony, Minnesota lost three Super Bowls in a four-year span. In January 1974 the Vikes were paddled 24–7 by the Miami Dolphins. Then the next year, in Super Bowl IX, the Pittsburgh Steelers beat them 16–6. Two years after that, it was the Oakland Raiders, 32–14.

In three trips to the Big Dance, Tarkenton's offenses had delivered a paltry 27 points.

The most punishing non-Super Bowl disappointment of Tarkenton's career came squished in among those title challenges. In the 1975 season, the Vikings finished with a chart-topping 12–2 record. The Purple People Eater defense, headed by Carl Eller, Alan Page and Jim Marshall, was at its ravenous best, and the elusive Tarkenton had never been more effective, winning the MVP award for his brilliance.

Fran Tarkenton passes in a December 1978 game against the Philadelphia Eagles.

But the Minnesota dream, riding hot on the heels of a stellar regular season, came cruelly undone during the NFC divisional playoff, when a controversial Roger Staubach-to-Drew Pearson Hail Mary touchdown pass helped Dallas slip past Minnesota 17–14. (To this day, Vikings partisans claim Pearson interfered with defensive back Nate Wright while running his pattern.) The play would only add to the image of Tarkenton as quarterback of the damned and the unluckiest man in pro football.

After his third shot at a Super Bowl, Tarkenton played two more seasons before walking away from the game at the close of the 1978 campaign, after prepping his successor, Tommy Kramer.

"If it's not fun," said Tarkenton, "you are not doing it right."

And football was simply not as much fun anymore. At 39, he knew instinctively that the time had finally arrived.

Even outside the game, Tarkenton continued to keep his feet moving.

In retirement, Scramblin' Fran did a stint on ABC's *Monday Night Football* and hosted the cultish *That's Incredible!* TV show alongside John Davidson and Cathy Lee Crosby. He was also shrewd enough to get into the computer software business on the ground floor.

In the opinion of some analysts, Tarkenton's three Super Bowl defeats in four years — the perceived inability to win that magical "big one" — automatically prevents him from joining the ranks of the elite all-time NFL quarterbacks. Yet at the time of his retirement, Tarkenton owned every major passing record of worth: yards passing (47,003), completions (3,686) and touchdowns (342). Add to that his 3,674 yards rushing, 125 regular-season victories and nine Pro Bowl appearances, and the stats make a mighty persuasive counter-argument in his favor.

This is a Hall of Famer, never forget, someone whose jersey — that famous No. 10 — has been retired by the Vikings. For his part, Tarkenton refused to let the one blemish on his résumé color his career.

"Success, in my view, is the willingness to strive for something you really want," said Tarkenton. "The person not reaching the top is no less a success than the one who achieved it, if they both sweated blood, sweat and tears and overcame obstacles and fears. The failure to be perfect does not mean you're not a success."

Tarkenton may have never won a Super Bowl, but neither did Dan Marino. If success were to be solely measured in blood, sweat and tears, Tarkenton would be as successful as they come. ■

College: University of Georgia
Drafted: 1961, Minnesota Vikings, 29th overall
Years active: 1961–1978
Top honors: NFL Offensive Player of the Year (1975), NFL AP MVP (1975), First Team All-Pro (1975)
Hall of Fame induction: 1986

THURMAN
THOMAS RB

G	Att	Yds	Avg	TD
182	2,877	12,074	4.2	65

FEW PLAYERS HAVE SMOLDERED THE WAY THURMAN Thomas did. He could bristle during practices. He glowed red-hot during games. His intensity was a three-alarm blaze waiting for a strong wind to make it uncontrollable.

It didn't matter if you were friend or foe — if you got near Thomas's blast furnace, you got scorched. Even Jim Kelly, the Buffalo Bills star quarterback, felt the sting of Thomas's ire if he didn't play up to his potential.

"He brings an edge to the team because he's not afraid to get in anybody's face," Buffalo linebacker Darryl Talley once said of Thomas. "In my opinion, he was the best back I've ever seen at being able to catch the ball out of the backfield and being able to run the ball at the same time."

He could run, he could catch and he bubbled with a desire that matched his versatility. Thomas is one of only six running backs to have over 400 receptions and 10,000 yards rushing and one of just six to run for over 1,000 yards in eight consecutive seasons, along with holding the record for most consecutive playoff games with a touchdown: nine.

A central cog in Buffalo's famed "no-huddle offense," Thomas led the league in total yards from scrimmage for four consecutive seasons and scored a touchdown in four consecutive Super Bowls.

And he was one of a rare breed of backs known for their hands as well as their feet; by the close of his career, Thomas had rushed for 12,074 yards and 65 touchdowns while catching 472 passes, 23 of those for a major.

"I don't believe there has ever been a more complete player at his position than Thurman," Bills coach Marv Levy said when he delivered Thomas's induction speech at the Pro Football Hall of Fame in 2007.

Branded the "Thurminator," teammates marveled at his varied skill set, including the way he blocked.

"I swear to God, I watched film of it at times to remind myself of the proper way to do things," said Buffalo center Kent Hull. "If Thurman had been bigger, he would have made a heck of an offensive lineman."

Thomas was such an outstanding running back at Oklahoma State University he kept Barry Sanders glued to the bench — a pretty neat trick considering how good Sanders was.

In four seasons at OSU, Thomas ran for 4,595 yards and 43 touchdowns. He had 21 100-yard games. By the time he left for the NFL, Thomas was his school's all-time leading rusher and a likely first-round draft pick in 1988. But a knee injury sent Thomas's stock plummeting. He was taken in the second round, 40th overall, by the Bills.

Sensing what they had drafted, the Bills revamped their attack to maximize his skills. They became the masters of the hurry-up offense and used it, not just as time was winding down late in the second and fourth quarters, but as a change-of-pace tactic.

"One [game] that really started the no-huddle was when he caught a playoff record against the Cleveland Browns, like 13 catches or something," recalled Kelly. "Defensive coordinators really didn't know how to guard against what we had."

Propelled by their multifaceted offense, the Bills won four conference titles in a row to earn four consecutive Super Bowl trips.

Unfortunately, their first Super Bowl appearance in 1991 was their best, and it was still a loss. Thomas totaled 190 yards rushing and receiving and scored a touchdown, but the Bills were left heartbroken when kicker Scott Norwood's 47-yard field goal sailed wide right, sealing their 20–19 loss to the New York Giants.

A year later in Super Bowl XXVI, everything went wrong for the Bills. At the start of the game, Thomas couldn't find his helmet and had to miss two plays. He didn't touch the ball until 12 minutes had been played. That set the tone, as the Bills lost to the Washington Redskins 37–24. In their next two Super Bowl appearances in 1993 and 1994, the Bills would be drubbed by the Dallas Cowboys by a combined score of 82–30. It was a bitter experience for Thomas, who would, years later, joke about the case of the missing helmet:

"You always sent me out well-equipped," Thomas told Levy at the Hall of Fame ceremony, "except for that one time when you played tricks on me with my helmet."

When it came to giving his best in a number of ways, from performing to keeping his teammates honest, few players in history were better equipped than Thomas.

On October 29, 2018, his signature number, 34, was retired by the Bills on national TV. ■

He could run, he could catch, and he bubbled with a desire that matched his versatility.

College: Oklahoma State University
Drafted: 1988, Buffalo Bills, 40th overall
Years active: 1988–2000
Top honors: First Team All-Pro (1990, 1991), NFL AP MVP (1991), NFL AP Offensive Player of the Year (1991)
Hall of Fame induction: 2007

LaDAINIAN
TOMLINSON RB

G	Att	Yds	Avg	TD
170	3,174	13,684	4.3	145

SCANNING THE APPOINTED SECTION IN THE STANDS at Cleveland Browns Stadium (now FirstEnergy Stadium), LaDainian Tomlinson's gaze at last picked out the 73-year-old, still ferocious-looking man among a sea of 73,000 faces. Tomlinson pointed up in acknowledgment, tapped his chest in reverence and saluted in tribute.

An 11-yard tote had just pushed the San Diego Chargers tailback past an authentic living legend, the peerless Jim Brown, and into eighth place on the NFL's all-time rushing list. Right in Cleveland, where for nine incredible seasons Brown had set the standard for all those at the position to follow.

"As a kid playing football in the yard, I looked up

> *For every Chargers fan of the generation and beyond, Tomlinson was their own No. 21 ... The ultimate lightning bolt.*

to all the great running backs, but there were a lot of days I was Jim Brown out on the football field," said Tomlinson. "To do it here in Cleveland is extra-special. I can't even tell you what it means because it seemed like it was supposed to happen being here in Cleveland. I'm just excited we were able to get it done. He transcended generations.

"Everyone loved Jim Brown and rightfully so. Even today when you talk about great running backs, the majority of the people say Jim Brown is the best ever."

By the time L.T. retired, on June 18, 2012, he had thrust himself into that conversation: fifth all-time with a career aggregate of 13,684 rushing yards, third in total touchdowns with 162 and second in rushing TDs with 145.

The kid born in Rosebud, Texas, who only got into football after joining a Pop Warner Little Scholars program at age 9, scored a touchdown the first time he laid hands on a football.

An omen if ever there was one.

Over his final two seasons of college ball, after enrolling at nearby Texas Christian University as the starting tailback, Tomlinson led the NCAA in rushing with 1,850 and 2,158 yards, respectively, and a cumulative 42 touchdowns.

The San Diego Chargers selected Tomlinson fifth in the 2001 NFL Draft after acquiring that pick from Atlanta in exchange for No. 1 overall, which the Falcons used to land quarterback Michael Vick.

The effect at Qualcomm Stadium was immediate and electric. In his rookie season, Tomlinson rushed for 1,236 yards on a lousy 5-11 Chargers team. Two years later he became the first player in history to run for 1,000 yards and catch 100 passes, while piling up a league-record five games of more than 200 yards from scrimmage. In 2005, against the Oakland Raiders, he became the seventh player to run, catch and throw for a touchdown in the same game.

But all of that was nothing more than foreplay for 2006, a season for the ages.

"I guess the way I describe it is when basketball players talk about being in the zone and they feel like they can't miss," said Tomlinson. "That's the way a running back feels when the game is in slow-motion. It feels like every cut is right, every run is going to be at least 10 yards. You see what the defense is doing. You know what they're trying to do to you.

"It's *awesome.*"

So, indisputably, was Tomlinson.

That season he struck for an NFL-record 31 touchdowns, a record 28 along the ground, and piled up the most points ever scored in a single season with 186.

After Tomlinson broke the touchdown record in a game against Denver, the Chargers' offensive linemen lifted him up on their massive shoulders and the home crowd chanted "L.T.! L.T.! MVP! MVP!"

Turns out they were onto something there.

Unsurprisingly, Tomlinson was later named the runaway winner of that NFL MVP award, collecting an astonishing 44 of 50 ballots.

Tomlinson had long spoken of his wish to retire as a Charger. But, unhappy due to an increasingly prickly relationship with general manager A.J. Smith, he made an uneasy decision to test free agency in 2010.

His final two seasons in New York, decked out in Jets green-and-white, were worthy but seemed odd. For every Chargers fan of the generation and beyond, Tomlinson was their own No. 21, biding his time, slowing the game down before sliding through the just-opened hole. The ultimate lightning bolt.

So it was only fitting, then, that in June 2012, Tomlinson returned to San Diego to sign a one-day contract and retire a Charger.

"I was a part of greatness," said offensive lineman Kris Dielman. "And it was awesome to be a part of it. It was awesome to watch.

"It was a fun time. I mean, I had the best seat in the house."

In truth, when L.T. was in the game, there was no such thing as a bad one. ∎

College: Texas Christian University
Drafted: 2001, San Diego Chargers, 5th overall
Years active: 2001–2011
Top honors: NFL All-Rookie Team (2001), First Team All-Pro (2004, 2006, 2007), NFL AP Offensive Player of the Year (2006), NFL AP MVP (2006), NFL Walter Payton Man of the Year (2006)
Hall of Fame induction: 2017

KURT
WARNER QB

G	Att	Comp	Yds	TD	INT
124	4,070	2,666	32,344	208	128

THEY MADE A MOVIE ABOUT KURT WARNER'S RISE FROM obscurity and called it *American Underdog*. It was a long time coming for a story that could have only been made in Hollywood.

How else would you explain Warner's tale — from the college backup who rode the bench for three years to the relentless dreamer who had a football epiphany in aisle 7 of a HyVee supermarket in Cedar Rapids, Iowa? It was there that Warner was inspired by a box of cereal with Miami Dolphins great Dan Marino on it.

More on that later.

His improbable stardom made Warner the NFL's feel-good quarterback. Even rival fans cheered for him, when he wasn't playing their team, of course. He represented everyone who wanted to be a pro quarterback, who wanted to lead a team to the Super Bowl and win it. As the game's MVP. As the league's MVP. Like it was meant to be when so many times it seemed a fool's pursuit.

Until the fool got a break. Actually, Warner got a couple of breaks. He found an NFL head coach who believed there was something special about this slow-footed 28-year-old with a live-wire arm. Plus, there was an injury to St. Louis Rams quarterback Trent Green, which opened the starter's role to Warner.

By then, Warner was an indomitable spirit ready to explode. He assumed control of the Rams' offense in 1999 and made it the Greatest Show on Turf. With receivers Isaac Bruce and Torry Holt and running back Marshall Faulk, Warner went right to work. He won his first six games, including a 42–20 drubbing of the San Francisco 49ers that saw him throw four touchdown passes in the first half. He finished the regular season with 4,353 passing yards and 41 touchdowns as the Rams went 13-3 to score their first playoff berth in 10 years.

That earned Warner his NFL MVP honors.

In Super Bowl XXXIV, he passed for 414 yards and two touchdowns in a tense 23–16 victory over the Tennessee Titans. That earned Warner his Super Bowl MVP honors. At that point, he became only the sixth player to win the NFL and Super Bowl MVP awards in the same season.

All of that was born from the telltale moment at the Cedar Rapids HyVee, where Warner was captivated by the Dan Marino cereal box. Warner wasn't shopping that night; he was working, earning $5.50 an hour stocking shelves and bagging groceries. At his Pro Football Hall of Fame induction speech, Warner said it was as if "Dan the Man's eyes followed me, like one of those creepy paintings in a horror movie ... Dan seemed to be asking me, 'Are you going to spend your life stocking someone else's cereal boxes? Or are you going to step out and make sure someone else is stocking yours?'"

Warner had been signed and then released by the Green Bay Packers before joining the Iowa Barnstormers of the Arena Football League. After his first season in the AFL, he was granted a tryout with the Chicago Bears but had to cancel it after being bitten by a spider and suffering an allergic reaction. The Rams signed Warner and then shipped him off to the Amsterdam Admirals of NFL Europe, where he topped the league in passing yards and touchdowns. Brought back by the Rams, he was named the starting quarterback when Green suffered a knee injury in the 1999 preseason. Head coach Dick Vermeil took a chance on

Warner and was rewarded beyond his expectations.

"I had a hunch he'd be a good player," said Vermeil, "but my hunch didn't take me to the category of [him being] a Hall of Famer, believe me."

The year after the Super Bowl win, Warner started hot but cooled off after suffering a broken hand. In 2001, he totaled 4,380 yards and 36 touchdowns to be named league MVP a second time. He also guided the Rams to Super Bowl XXXVI, where he scored a fourth-quarter touchdown and threw for another to tie the game at 17–17. As time ran out, New England Patriots kicker Adam Vinatieri booted a 48-yard field goal for the win.

Within three years, Warner lost his touch, lost his starting position and was released by the Rams. He ultimately ended up with the Arizona Cardinals, and in 2008 he accumulated 4,583 yards passing and 30 touchdowns. That resulted in the Cardinals' first playoff appearance in 10 years, then a spot in Super Bowl XLIII against the Pittsburgh Steelers. Warner completed 72 percent of his passes for 377 yards but it wasn't enough to defeat the Steelers. In January 2010, he retired and became an analyst for the NFL Network.

When reflecting on his playing career, Warner has always been adamant in crediting his wife for her unwavering support. Brenda Warner had been a corporal in the U.S. Marine Corps during her first marriage. She was given a hardship discharge to care for her infant son, Zack, who had suffered brain damage after being accidentally dropped by his father. Six years later, Brenda's parents were killed when a tornado destroyed their home in Mountain View, Arkansas.

Through it all, Warner and Brenda have relied on their faith in God and in each other. It was strong enough to make good on Warner's commitment to have someone else stocking cereal boxes with his face on them. The brand name? Warner's Crunch Time.

Kurt Warner throws a pass during a game against the Tennessee Titans on October 31, 1999.

College: University of Northern Iowa
Drafted: Undrafted
Years active: 1998–2009
Top honors: Super Bowl Champion, Super Bowl MVP (2000), NFL MVP (1999, 2001), First Team All-Pro (1999, 2001), Walter Payton NFL Man of the Year (2008)
Hall of Fame induction: 2017

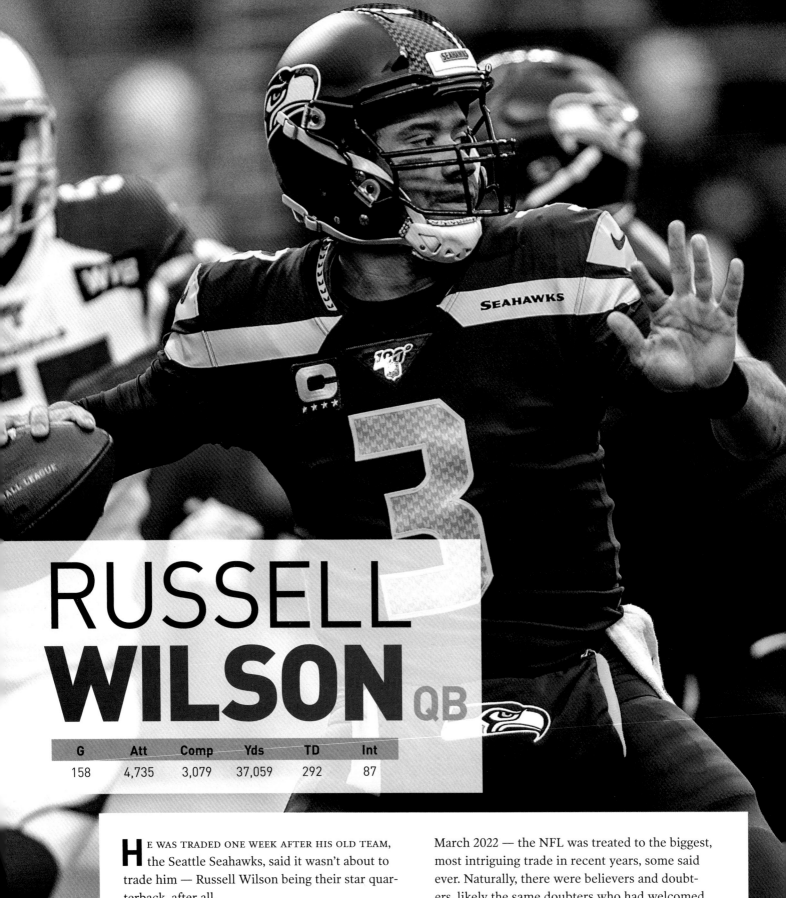

RUSSELL
WILSON QB

G	Att	Comp	Yds	TD	Int
158	4,735	3,079	37,059	292	87

HE WAS TRADED ONE WEEK AFTER HIS OLD TEAM, the Seattle Seahawks, said it wasn't about to trade him — Russell Wilson being their star quarterback, after all.

And yet, when the Denver Broncos offered three players along with five draft picks — and Wilson agreed to waive his no-trade clause in March 2022 — the NFL was treated to the biggest, most intriguing trade in recent years, some said ever. Naturally, there were believers and doubters, likely the same doubters who had welcomed Wilson to the NFL by saying the measure of an outstanding quarterback had to do with how tall he was, and Wilson was supposedly 5-foot-11. Too short compared with the majority of his peers.

Wilson paid no heed to the pessimists and went to work proving his worth. In 2012, he set a record for most wins at home by a rookie pivot, going 8-0 on the season. He also threw for 26 touchdowns to tie Peyton Manning's mark for most passing TDs by a rookie quarterback. Through his first seven seasons, Wilson never missed a start for Seattle. (That streak ended in 2021 when he underwent surgery for a torn tendon in the middle finger of his throwing hand. He missed five games.)

When it came to postseason accountability, Wilson took his team to back-to-back Super Bowl appearances, winning the Vince Lombardi Trophy in 2014 and then losing it in 2015 on a last-second pass play that never should have been called. That flub came in Super Bowl XLIX against the New England Patriots. With Seattle at the Patriots' 1-yard line, and the clock counting down the final moments of the fourth quarter, the Seahawks were poised to score the winning touchdown. The obvious decision was to hand the ball to running back Marshawn Lynch and then step back to watch the victory celebrations. Instead, Wilson threw a pass that was intercepted by New England's Malcolm Butler — and that was it. Championship lost.

In his postgame address, Seattle coach Pete Carroll said the play-calling was his fault. Not about to let his coach or anyone else accept the blame, Wilson did what he felt was right, saying he was responsible for what had happened.

"I'm the one that threw the pass, but I know I'll throw another one," he said. "And hopefully I'll be remembered for something different."

NFL scouts had a hard time remembering Wilson's glowing performances at the University of Wisconsin, how he led the Badgers to a Big Ten championship and an appearance in the 2012 Rose Bowl. The scouts couldn't get past Wilson's height. In a *Seattle Times* story, Daniel Jeremiah, a scout for the Philadelphia Eagles, recalled how Wilson asked for his phone number, then sent a text saying, "I know I can help the Eagles win."

Jeremiah admitted, "I hate the fact that because he came in under 5-foot-11, I dropped my personal grade [of Wilson] to the third round."

The third round of the 2012 NFL Draft was precisely where Wilson was claimed by Seattle, well back of the first two picks overall, quarterbacks Andrew Luck and Robert Griffin III. After a strong showing in training camp led to some promising efforts in the preseason, Wilson started his first NFL game and lost 20–16 to the Arizona Cardinals. Yet in December he led the Seahawks to a 5-0 record, which put them in the NFC playoffs. There, Wilson engineered a comeback win over the Washington Redskins before losing 30–28 to the Atlanta Falcons.

Those experiences would work to the Seahawks' advantage in 2013.

With a 13-3 regular-season record, Seattle defeated the San Francisco 49ers to secure a Super Bowl showdown against Peyton Manning and the Denver Broncos. By halftime, Seattle had a 22–0 lead. At game's end, the score was 43–8 for the Seahawks. It was quickly noted that Wilson was the shortest quarterback in NFL history to have won a Super Bowl.

Some of Wilson's most ardent supporters are his opponents, the very people who study his game looking for faults to exploit. Before facing him in Super Bowl XLIX, New England coach Bill Belichick spoke highly of Wilson and compared him to Dallas Cowboys Hall of Famer Roger Staubach.

"I remember a lot of Staubach's spectacular running plays where it looked like he was about to get tackled by three or four guys, and he would Houdini it out of there somehow," said Belichick. "You see Wilson doing some of the same things." That's part of the reason why Wilson has done some of the same things Tom Brady has done, such as share the record for most wins (86) by a quarterback in their first eight seasons, and why Wilson is one of only two men to hold a career passer rating of over 100.

Prior to his finger injury, Wilson had spoken confidently of what he planned to accomplish in the balance of his career. "No matter what the circumstances are," he said, "I believe my mindset is gonna take me further than anybody else has ever gone."

Now that's how you measure an outstanding quarterback. ▪

College: University of Wisconsin–Madison
Drafted: 2012, Seattle Seahawks, 75th overall
Years active: 2012–present
Top honors: Super Bowl Champion (2013), Walter Payton Man of the Year (2020)
Hall of Fame induction: N/A

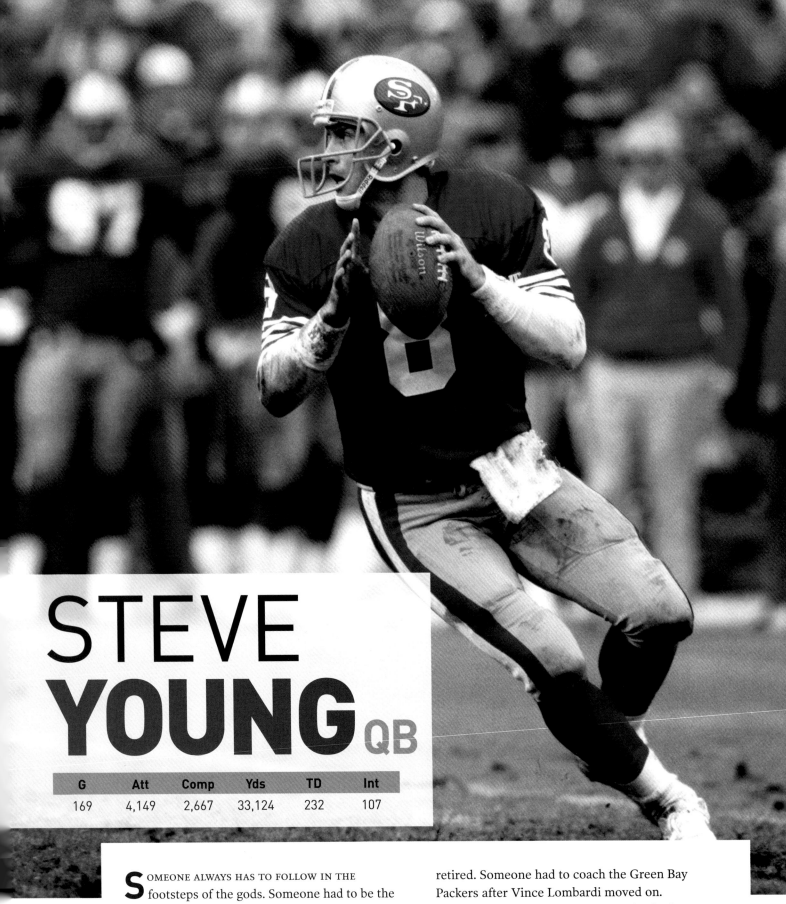

STEVE YOUNG QB

G	Att	Comp	Yds	TD	Int
169	4,149	2,667	33,124	232	107

S OMEONE ALWAYS HAS TO FOLLOW IN THE footsteps of the gods. Someone had to be the heavyweight boxing champ after Muhammad Ali was stripped of the title. Someone had to be the Chicago Bulls shooting guard after Michael Jordan retired. Someone had to coach the Green Bay Packers after Vince Lombardi moved on.

And someone had to play quarterback after Joe Montana was traded away by the San Francisco 49ers. Steve Young was that someone.

He was the follower who bore the brunt of comparative greatness. Montana was king — a four-time Super Bowl champion of mythical proportions. Young came after: someone who never seemed to measure up when it counted.

It stayed that way until 1995, when Young finally won a Super Bowl, won Super Bowl MVP honors and set a Super Bowl record by throwing six touchdowns (nosing out the previous record holder, the unparalleled Montana, who had once tossed five). In that glorious moment the comparisons ended, and the true appreciation commenced. Theoretically, it should have started sooner.

Young was jaw-droppingly good with the 49ers before his win in Super Bowl XXIX. He could run like a fullback and deke like a halfback. He could throw off the run or from deep in the pocket. Either way, he was utterly proficient, always completing a high percentage of his passes.

"Steve is doing things no other quarterback has ever done," 49ers tight end Brent Jones said. "But there are still people who think they can only like Joe. Steve can't please all the people in the world. There's never going to be another Joe, and Steve knows that. What more can he do?"

Young certainly waited for his chance to succeed Montana. After spending two seasons in the USFL, then another two with the Tampa Bay Buccaneers, Young was traded to the 49ers where he waited another four years before becoming a starter. He got his chance when Montana was sidelined with an elbow injury. Unfortunately, Young suffered a knee injury that limited his playing time.

Still, there were signs that Young was the one to eventually replace Montana. In 1992, despite a serious concussion, Young passed for 3,456 yards and 25 touchdowns and won the NFL's MVP award.

Montana was traded to the Kansas City Chiefs in 1993, clearing the way for Young, who overcame a sluggish start to finish the year with 4,023 passing yards and 29 touchdowns. Losing to the Dallas Cowboys in the playoffs for the second year in a row revved up the critics who thought of Young as a flawed substitute to you-know-who. It didn't help that when Montana's Chiefs played Young's 49ers in September 1994, the Chiefs won 24–17.

"I really feel like, in being after Joe, I've learned how to be a great quarterback and now I have a chance to go prove it," Young said of his situation. "I think a lot of people feel they have untapped potential in their bodies and don't get a chance to bring it out. In San Francisco, with the pressure, I have a chance to see how good I really can get."

The Chiefs game was the last tough loss San Francisco endured that season. Young threw for 35 touchdowns, led his team past Dallas in the playoffs and would need just one minute and 24 seconds to begin his Super Bowl rout of the San Diego Chargers. He hit receiver Jerry Rice for a 44-yard touchdown, and then found running back Ricky Watters for a 51-yard touchdown on the 49ers' second possession.

"All along, I felt I was playing against the past," Young said afterward. "Honestly, I have distanced myself from all [the Montana comparisons]. I did so a couple of years ago. I want my performance to stand for myself and my teammates."

That it did. Although several more concussions forced an early retirement, his numbers stood tall, throwing for more than 3,000 yards in a season six times and for 20 or more touchdowns five times. He held the NFL record among retired quarterbacks for the highest career passer rating (96.8), and he held the record for most rushing touchdowns by a quarterback (43) until it was broken by Cam Newton.

In 2005 Young was inducted into the Pro Football Hall of Fame — the first left-hander to be so honored. Arguably, the 49ers' decision to retire his No. 8 jersey meant just as much.

The day Young retired, five years earlier, his old pitch-and-catch partner Jones labelled him one of the five greatest NFL quarterbacks ever.

"And none of those other four, whoever they may be, followed a Hall of Famer," Jones reminded everyone. "That, to me, is the single greatest accomplishment in sports."

Like the man before him, Young left behind some mighty fine footsteps for the next guy to follow. ■

College: Brigham Young University
Drafted: 1984 (NFL Supplemental Draft), Tampa Bay Buccaneers, 1st overall
Years active: 1985–1999
Top honors: NFL AP MVP (1992, 1994), NFL AP Offensive Player of the Year (1992), First Team All-Pro (1992–94), Super Bowl Champion (1994), Super Bowl MVP (1994)
Hall of Fame induction: 2005

Defensive Greats

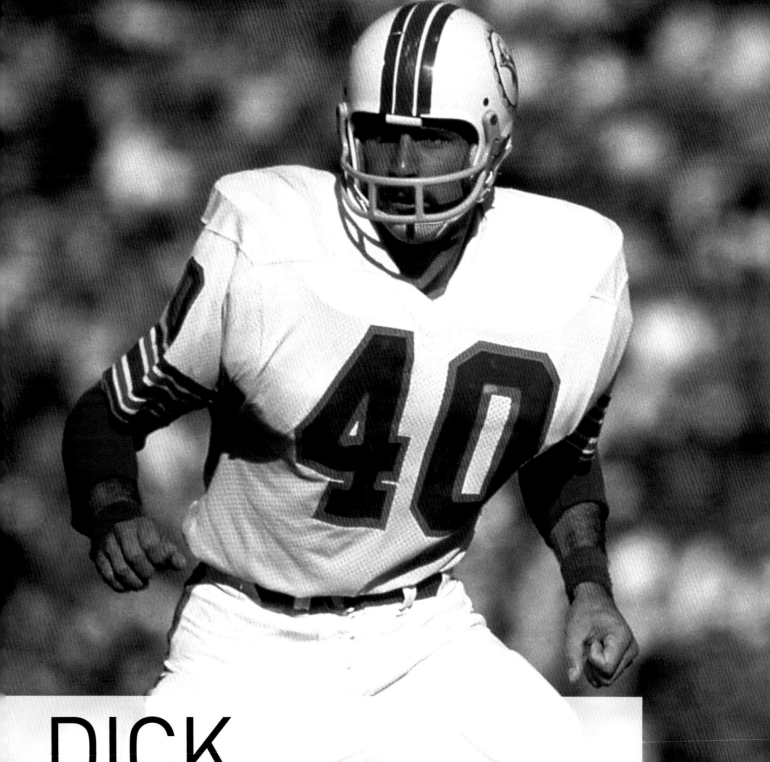

DICK
ANDERSON DB

G	Int/Yds	FR	TD
121	34/792	16	3

MAYBE YOU REMEMBER HIS NAME, or even one of his 30-plus interceptions. If you spend enough time online, you'll find the archived tales of safety Dick Anderson. He was a celebrated member of the Miami Dolphins' No-Name Defense, as were Jake Scott, Nick Buoniconti and Manny Fernandez.

Their job was to frustrate and annihilate the opposition's offense. The Dolphins did that so well, it carried them through an undefeated year that encompassed 14 regular-season games and three playoff games, including Super Bowl VII.

The New England Patriots gave such excellence a close shave, losing Super Bowl XLII off the miraculous helmet catch by New York Giants receiver David Tyree. Anderson congratulated the Patriots for going 18-1 overall. That left the Dolphins' undefeated mark intact, and that suited Anderson just fine.

"It's nice to have a record," said Anderson. "You always want to see it stand for as long as it can. It's what you work so hard to achieve."

Anderson's work was especially key to the Dolphins' pass coverage. During his nine seasons in Miami (missing 1975 because of a knee injury), Anderson studied his rivals around the league and got to know their tendencies. He crafted his style of play as an opportunist who could run with and take out the best receivers. His list of accomplishments includes multiple Pro Bowl and First Team All-Pro selections and being selected Defensive Player of the Year in 1973 after tying for the league lead with eight interceptions.

Anderson was a one-man Swiss Army knife. For his career, he had 34 interceptions (with three going for touchdowns) for 792 yards. He recovered 16 fumbles, gained 100 yards on them and added another touchdown. On kickoffs and punt returns, he ran for 438 yards. He even punted nine times when called to duty.

Anderson's most memorable game occurred on December 3, 1973. The Pittsburgh Steelers tried to set the tone early, only to play into Anderson's hands. By halftime Miami had four interceptions — three by Anderson, who returned two of them for touchdowns. He added another pick in the second half.

It was a stunning display, but hardly unexpected given the defensive game plans thought up by assistant head coach/defensive coordinator Bill Arnsparger. Although Arnsparger asked for player input before making his game calls, the players had full faith in his ability to sniff out the other side's weaknesses and how best to attack them.

"We knew it would be the right defense ... We understood that his system was designed to get help and give help," said Anderson. "Teamwork was the key to having a defense be exceptional."

For Anderson, there could be no better teammate than fellow safety Jake Scott. Together they were double migraines for quarterbacks and receivers. They'd fake one defense, then rush with another. They loved to blitz with unusual twists, like having defensive lineman Fernandez drop back into pass coverage. It's been written that New York Jets quarterback Joe Namath was so exasperated by the Dolphins duo that he would come to the line of scrimmage and curse them.

Don Shula could get angry at Scott, too. The Dolphins head coach didn't appreciate much of what Scott had to say, some of which could've sent him to the showers, the practice roster or on a flight headed to his home state of Colorado. But Shula decided it was best to have Scott and Anderson doing their best for Miami rather than trading one of the two, most likely Scott, and creating a hole in the Dolphins' defensive backfield.

"I loved Jake on that [1972] team, and I know the kind of player he was," said Shula. "I don't think there has been a better safety combination than him and Anderson."

During their time together with the Dolphins, Anderson and Scott proved their worth time and time again. They were the last line of defense, and they took their jobs seriously.

After football, Anderson continued to make a name for himself in golf. He has competed in the American Century Championship, an annual event that pits sports and entertainment celebrities against one another on the links. Anderson won it in 1994 and has had 11 finishes in the top 10.

He's not yet been hailed as the No-Name golfer. ▪

College: University of Colorado
Drafted: 1968, Miami Dolphins, 73rd overall
Years active: 1968–1977
Top honors: Super Bowl Champion (1972, 1973), First Team All-Pro (1972, 1973), NFL AP Defensive Player of the Year (1973)
Hall of Fame induction: N/A

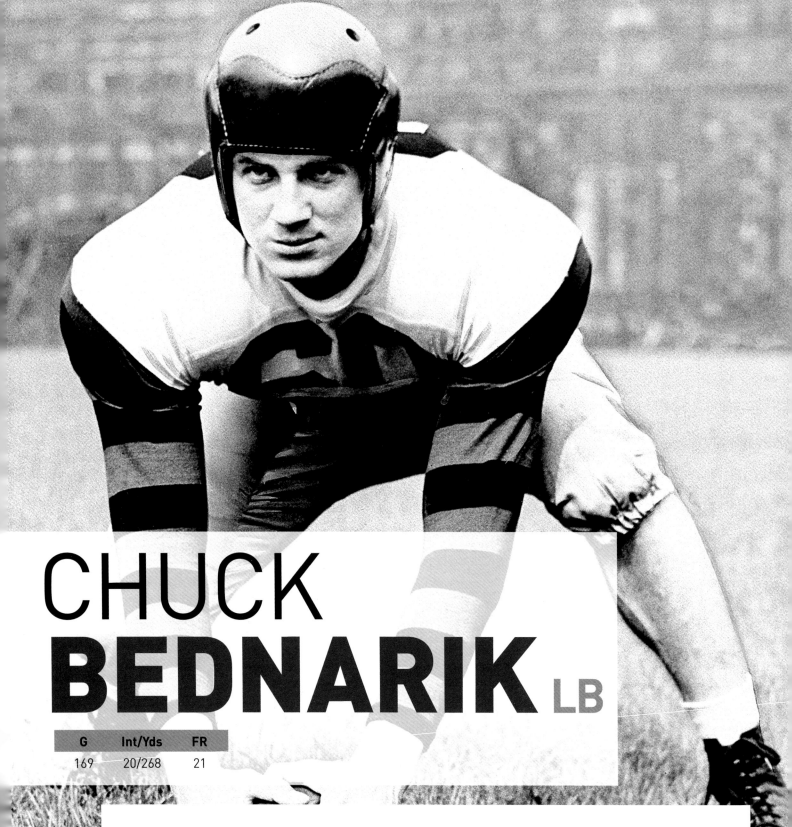

CHUCK
BEDNARIK LB

G	Int/Yds	FR
169	20/268	21

THIS ONE NIGHT, CHUCK BEDNARIK WAS THE featured speaker at a roast of former New York Giant Frank Gifford. Just before he was to deliver his speech, Bednarik instructed the manager to turn off the lights for five or six seconds. Then he told the audience, "Now you know what Frank Gifford felt like when I hit him."

They called him Concrete Charlie, not just because he hit the other team's players like a sack of cement, but because his part-time job was selling concrete. It was the perfect occupation for the last of the NFL's full-time, 60-minute players, the Philadelphia Eagles centre, linebacker and hellion whose surname suited his nature and his era.

His on-field exploits became instant classics. In the 1960 NFL Championship Game, at the age of 35, he played on offense and defense and made the clinching tackle on Green Bay Packers running back Jim Taylor, holding him down at the Philadelphia 10-yard line until the clock ran out. A photographer captured a grinning Bednarik coming off the field with his arm draped over Taylor's shoulders, as if they were the best of buds.

But it was the November 20, 1960, hit that nearly ended Gifford's career (and some say his life) that earned Concrete Charlie his enduring notoriety. Gifford lay motionless on the field and was still unconscious when he was carried to the dressing room on a stretcher. In his brilliant Bednarik bio piece in *Sports Illustrated*, John Schulian recounts how that hit played out then and in the decades that followed. Gifford's wife was standing outside the New York dressing room when the team physician opened the door and announced, "I'm afraid he's dead."

The doctor was talking about the security guard who had been rushed to the same room, having suffered a heart attack. Many wouldn't have been surprised had Gifford drawn the same pronouncement. Giants linebacker Sam Huff called it "the greatest tackle I ever saw." Eagles defensive back Tom Brookshier said the impact "sounded like an axe splitting a piece of wood."

The hit was a combination of calamities: the ball was thrown behind Gifford, who turned his head to reach back and make the catch and was completely blindsided; the 6-foot-3, 233-pound Bednarik unloaded a high hit that dropped Gifford on the spot. As if to make matters worse, a photographer captured Bednarik standing over a prone Gifford, shouting at that very moment, "This game is over."

Bednarik proved prophetic as the Eagles defeated New York en route to their league championship. The hit reverberated throughout the NFL. New York fans hated Bednarik, calling him barbaric and classless. Bednarik said it was all done in the heat of the moment and that he had no idea where Gifford was sprawled on the field. Although the hit was considered legal, the passage of time made it clear to many that Bednarik's ruthlessness was deserving of a penalty and a suspension. One of those who spoke up in support of Bednarik was the man he ran over.

"He didn't hurt me," said Gifford. "When he hit me, I landed on my ass and my head snapped back. That was what put me out — the whiplash, not Bednarik." Either way, Gifford missed the balance of the 1960 season and all of 1961, having suffered a concussion.

Bednarik was born in 1925 to a working-class family from Siroke, Slovakia, that had immigrated five years earlier to Bethlehem, Pennsylvania, where his father worked for Bethlehem Steel.

After a sterling high school football career, the 18-year-old Bednarik enlisted in the U.S. military, settling in with the Eighth Air Force, where he was a waist gunner on a B-24 bomber. Bednarik flew in 30 bombing runs over Germany in World War II and received the Air Medal with four oak leaf clusters, four battle stars and the European–African–Middle Eastern Campaign Medal.

Bednarik insisted his war experiences gave him an appreciation for life that carried over to his football career.

"You go through combat, you develop a killer instinct," said Bednarik. "You become — what's the term? — hard core. Did I take that on the field? Yes, to be honest, [I] did."

After the war ended, Bednarik returned home and enrolled at the University of Pennsylvania. The Eagles made him the first pick in the 1949 NFL Draft. He was chosen ahead of such future luminaries as Doak Walker, Norm Van Brocklin and George Blanda. When his 14 years in the NFL ended, Bednarik had left a lasting impression. Ten times he was named a First Team All-Pro. He was inducted into the Pro Football Hall of Fame in 1967 and voted a member of the NFL 50th Anniversary All-Time Team, the 75th Anniversary Team and the 100th Anniversary Team.

Bednarik retired after the 1960 season; Gifford played three more seasons before hanging up his cleats. The two ex-rivals became friends, with Gifford never once accusing Bednarik of a dirty hit. "If I'd had the chance I would have done the same thing to Chuck," said Gifford many times. He never got that chance. Maybe saying what he felt was enough for Gifford to move on and return to the game he loved. ■

College: University of Pennsylvania
Drafted: 1949, Philadelphia Eagles, 1st overall
Years active: 1949–1962
Top honors: NFL Champion (1949, 1960), First Team All-Pro (1950–1957, 1960, 1961)
Hall of Fame Induction: 1967

MEL
BLOUNT CB

G	Int/Yds	FR	TD
200	57/736	13	2

The story never grows old — not in Pittsburgh, anyway.

It happened in 1982, when a collection of NFL scouts stopped by the city's Three Rivers Stadium to chart the progress of Renaldo Nehemiah, then the world record holder in the 110-meter hurdles. The possibility of a proven sprinter pulling away from his tacklers was simply too good to ignore, even if Nehemiah didn't play a down of college football.

Pittsburgh Steelers veteran cornerback Mel Blount happened to walk by and asked what that mark made high on a wall represented. He was told it had measured Nehemiah's vertical leap. At the age of 31, dressed in street clothes, Blount jumped higher and said, "That's the Steelers' mark."

That was Blount — a 6-foot-3, 205-pound athletic marvel who always left a mark on his rivals if they so much as passed through his corner of the Steelers' defense. To protect that air space, Blount liked to "bump" receivers. Of course, his bumps had a habit of separating an opposing player from the football, if not his head from consciousness.

It was all part of the Blount credo that no receiver that lined up across from him got a free pass. Everything had to be earned. Naturally receivers complained, and the NFL responded in 1978 by putting in the bump-and-run rule, which restricted how far downfield a cornerback could molest a receiver. Offenses were delighted. The Mel Blount rule had saved them from the man who was single-handedly (sometimes two-handedly) rerouting their passing game.

That's how domineering Blount was. In 1972, his third season in black and gold, Blount worked his position to near-perfection. He intercepted three passes, recovered two fumbles, returned one for a touchdown and did not give up a single touchdown pass in 14 games. In 1975 Blount intercepted a league-leading 11 passes and was named the NFL's Defensive Player of the Year. It was proof positive that Blount's role in the fabled Steel Curtain defense couldn't be overstated. If a ball carrier could slip past Mean Joe Greene in the Pittsburgh defensive front and then avoid linebacker Jack Lambert, he was bound to run into Blount, who played the running game the same way he covered receivers — with an edge.

Hundreds of NFL players, if not thousands, have come from humble beginnings. Blount came from a place that made humble beginnings look like the Hamptons. He grew up on a farm in Georgia, the youngest of 11 children. The house had no plumbing or electricity. His first job was stacking tobacco on a wagon in the early morning hours before going to school.

Blount learned to take pride in the hard work and his father's praise. On Sundays the Blount boys and their friends went to church and then played football. In high school Blount starred in basketball, baseball and track, and earned a football scholarship at Southern University in Baton Rouge, Louisiana.

Earning Southwestern Athletic Conference All-Star status, Blount was chosen by the Steelers in the third round of the 1970 draft (quarterback Terry Bradshaw was taken in the first). Soon after he arrived in Pittsburgh, Blount settled in at right corner and stayed there for 14 seasons, helping the Steelers win four Super Bowls.

His biggest championship moment came in Super Bowl XIII, when his interception of a Roger Staubach pass led to a key Pittsburgh touchdown in its 35–31 win over the Dallas Cowboys.

When Blount wasn't making things difficult for opposing teams, he was taking on the Steelers organization.

Pittsburgh head coach Chuck Noll had accused Oakland Raiders defensive back George Atkinson of being part of the NFL's "criminal element" for using a forearm hit to knock out Steelers receiver Lynn Swann. Atkinson sued, and Noll testified that the criminal element included Blount.

Blount's response was to file a $5 million defamation suit against his own coach. It was dropped when Blount ended a 56-day contract holdout (the Atkinson suit was dismissed). The coach and his cornerback patched up their differences.

"It was never anything personal," Blount told the *Pittsburgh Post-Gazette*. "I showed my character by being the type of player I was after I came back. Chuck showed his character by never holding it against me."

Blount's football accolades included such niceties as being named to the NFL's 1980s All-Decade Team, the league's 75th- and 100th-anniversary All-Time Team rosters and, of course, his inclusion in the Pro Football Hall of Fame in 1989.

His retirement in 1983 was celebrated by receivers everywhere. ◾

College: Southern University
Drafted: 1970, Pittsburgh Steelers, 53rd overall
Years active: 1970–1983
Top honors: Super Bowl Champion (1974, 1975, 1978, 1979), NFL AP Defensive Player of the Year (1975), First Team All-Pro (1975, 1981)
Hall of Fame induction: 1989

> *It was all part of the Blount credo that no receiver that lined up across from him got a free pass. Everything had to be earned.*

NICK
BUONICONTI LB

G	Int/Yds	FR
183	32/312	6

THERE WAS ALWAYS A CAUSE THAT CALLED FOR A FIGHT. A fight that must be won. A win for those who needed something to believe in.

That was Nick Buoniconti's approach to football. His career and all its wins were meaningful, even spectacular. And the undefeated season of 1972? It has been challenged over the decades, yet still stands strong as a monument to teamwork. Certainly it helped guide Buoniconti, from his time as co-captain of the Miami Dolphins to his work as a registered player agent, to his role as a father whose son was carried off the field with a damaged spinal cord, never to play football again.

Marc Buoniconti was 19 years old when he was playing his dad's position, middle linebacker, for The Citadel, a military college in South Carolina. On the afternoon of October 26, 1985, the opposing team from East Tennessee State University had the ball on a third-and-one situation. Marc threw himself at the ball carrier.

"I've made that tackle 1,000 times in my life," he recalled. "There was nothing dangerous about it ... [But] I knew I was paralyzed before my body hit the ground."

Marc was rushed to the nearest hospital, where doctors found two bones had been dislocated at the top of his spine. There was no feeling in his body below his shoulders. He was a paraplegic.

There were tears and fears in the early going as father and son tried to adjust to a new reality. Together, they motivated one another to keep going.

During their time at the hospital, Marc and his dad heard about the Miami Project to Cure Paralysis, an ambitious plan to create a renowned spinal cord injury (SCI) research center by gathering the best medical minds in one place. Funding the project became the elder Buoniconti's next pursuit. He teamed with co-founder Dr. Barth Green, and while Buoniconti handled the fundraising aspects by working the boardrooms, Dr. Green took care of the operating room.

It was a formidable partnership, but people expected nothing less from an All-Pro player who co-helmed the only undefeated championship team in the post–World War II era.

Nicholas Anthony Buoniconti was born in Springfield, Massachusetts. His parents operated a bakery, and he grew up loving football. He played at Cathedral High School and was good enough at a number of positions to be recruited by Notre Dame. As a senior in 1961, he was co-captain of the Fighting Irish and the only member of the team to receive All-American status.

The vast majority of Dolphins fans can tell you what came after that: Buoniconti was drafted by the American Football League's Boston Patriots in 1962. He became a fixture at the AFL All-Star Game and, as a Patriot, was selected to the AFL All-Time First Team. In 1969 Buoniconti was traded to the Dolphins, where success kept following him.

He was an integral part of Miami's No-Name Defense, which also included Manny Fernandez, Dick Anderson and Jake Scott. They were a collection of team players, not "me" guys, who played for the stats and what that would mean at contract negotiation time.

With a reliable defense, the Dolphins had more than enough offense to take a run at the Super Bowl. They ended up playing in three consecutive Super Bowls and winning two of them, with 1972 as the

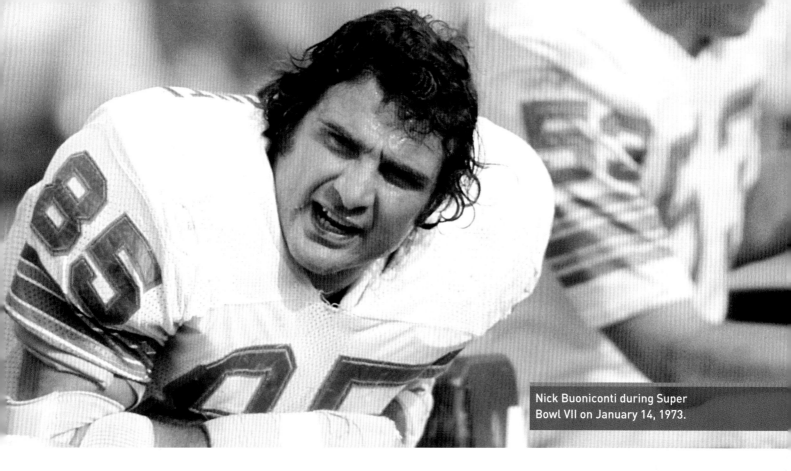

Nick Buoniconti during Super Bowl VII on January 14, 1973.

topper. The Dolphins beat the Washington Redskins 14–7, with Miami gift-wrapping the Redskins' lone touchdown. It came off a horrible-looking pass attempt by Dolphins kicker Garo Yepremian.

During his tenure in Miami, Buoniconti was voted the Dolphins' MVP three times and once held the franchise record for most tackles in a season (162). All totaled, he played 14 seasons of pro football, played in six AFL All-Star Games and two Pro Bowls and was a five-time First Team All-Pro selection.

There were other jobs for Buoniconti. He finished the law degree he had been working on during his time in Boston. He became a sports agent and represented 30 professional athletes, such as baseball players Bucky Dent and Andre Dawson. He became the president of the United States Tobacco Company. He even co-hosted the HBO series *Inside*

the NFL for 23 years until 2001, the year he was inducted into the Pro Football Hall of Fame.

Marc delivered the introductory speech for his father in Canton, Ohio. Eighteen years down the road, there would be another emotional piece Marc would need to write about his father.

Nick Buoniconti died on July 30, 2019, at the age of 78, after a slow battle with dementia. Buoniconti didn't cower from his diagnosis. In 2017 his family released a short video showing him struggling to put on a T-shirt. In November of that same year he announced he was donating his brain to Boston University's Chronic Traumatic Encephalopathy (CTE) center.

After his father's death, Marc Buoniconti once again gave a stirring account of his father's accomplishments.

"Today, with a heavy heart and profound sorrow, my family and the entire Miami Project to Cure

Paralysis and Buoniconti Fund community mourn the loss of a man who was truly larger than life: my father, NFL Hall of Famer Nick Buoniconti," Marc wrote on the Miami Project website.

"My dad has been my hero and represents what I have always aspired to be: a leader, a mentor and a champion. He selflessly gave all to football, to his family and to those who are less fortunate. We can best honor his dedication and endless commitment by continuing with our work until ... a cure is found." ■

College: University of Notre Dame
Drafted: 1962 (AFL Draft), Boston Patriots, 102nd overall
Years active: 1962–1976
Top honors: First Team All-Pro (1964–67, 1969), Super Bowl Champion (1972, 1973)
Hall of Fame induction: 2001

KEVIN
BYARD s

G	Int/Yds	Tkl	Sk	FR
97	23/279	519	4.0	3

K EVIN BYARD CAN DO ALMOST ANYTHING HE PUTS his mind to, so he figured he should exercise his brain. To stay ahead of the competition.

Along with lifting weights and working on his physical dexterity, Byard figured the intellectual aspect of his game could stand some improvement. That put him in touch with a California company and its virtual reality technology designed to improve an athlete's peripheral vision, decision making and mental clarity. It seemed to work for

Byard, who led the Tennessee Titans' defense in 2020 with a career-best 111 tackles.

He followed that with a sparkling start to the 2021 NFL season. In a nine-game span, he recorded five interceptions and a touchdown, helping him regain the form that made him the highest-paid safety in NFL history ($70.5 million over five years). It was another chapter in the story of a player who has taken matters into his hands and worked his way to the top. Just like he did at Middle Tennessee State

University, where he set school records for interceptions.

It was there, at the school's Pro Day, that he caught the eye of the NFL scouts who had bothered to check him out. Byard didn't have a big reputation at that time. He was selected to play in the 2016 Senior Bowl but wasn't one of the 60 defensive backs invited to the NFL Combine. What convinced the Titans to draft him in the third round was the 40-yard dash he ran at Tennessee State's Pro Day. His clocking? A sizzling 4.46 seconds.

That got scouts and personnel directors digging into his background story. This was once a young teen who helped raise his five younger siblings while his single mom worked 13 hours a day as a waitress. When his parents divorced, Byard took care of his two brothers and three sisters and helped make lunches while his older brother would take the youngest to daycare.

As a child, Byard and his family lived in eight different locations, even staying in the basement of a friend's home on one occasion. Byard would come home after school to clean the place they were living in and then return to school for football practice. He was just 14 years old. It was a lot to ask of a kid his age.

Byard went to university on a football scholarship and produced as both an athlete and a student. He signed with the Titans and used his $900,000 signing bonus to buy his mother a home, one that could fit the entire family.

"She has always been my biggest supporter," said Byard. "I had her back."

By his second season in the NFL, Byard had earned his salary and then some. He totaled 87 tackles and 16 pass deflections and tied Darius Slay of the Detroit Lions for the league lead in interceptions with eight — five of which came in a two-game tour de force. For his work, Byard was chosen to the Pro Bowl and named a First Team All-Pro.

In the 2017 playoffs, Byard and the Titans gathered some valuable postseason experience. The Kansas City Chiefs offered serious opposition but fell to the Titans by one point, 21–20.

Tennessee's second playoff game was against the New England Patriots and quarterback extraordinaire Tom Brady. Prior to the game, Byard was asked for his thoughts on Brady and was surprisingly candid. He said Brady didn't have the arm strength he once did when he was going long to receiver Randy Moss.

"His deep ball across the middle is not getting there," said Byard. "I hope he would [try to make that pass against the Titans' defense]."

Some in the media took Byard's comments as poor gamesmanship; others liked seeing him step into the spotlight to take some of the pressure off his teammates. Brady replied the best way he knew how: with 35 completions in 53 attempts for 337 yards, three touchdowns and no interceptions in a 35–14 win for the Patriots.

Byard took his lumps and was gracious in defeat.

"He played a better game than we did," said Byard. "He's a great quarterback, and we didn't give our offense a chance to get going."

The gains kept coming in 2018 when Byard threw a touchdown pass off a fake punt against the Houston Texans. He raised eyebrows in Dallas

This was once a young teen who helped raise his five younger siblings while his single mom worked 13 hours a day as a waitress.

when he celebrated a win over the Cowboys by dancing on their star logo after his game-ending interception. Years before, San Francisco 49er Terrell Owens was the first to mock the Cowboys by posing on their star. It started a full-on battle royal.

In July 2019, Byard signed his mega-million-dollar contract extension and once again faced Brady and the Patriots in the playoffs. This time Byard and his defensive teammates said little, played loud and scored the clinching touchdown off a Brady interception. In the next two rounds, the Titans pounded out a 28–12 decision over the Baltimore Ravens before losing to the eventual Super Bowl champion Chiefs.

In the hopes of winning a Super Bowl for Tennessee, Byard continues to train his brain with this overriding thought: "At this point in my career, it is more about sharpening the mental part of your game ... I think anything you can do to help you improve and sharpen your mind, it's a good thing." ∎

College: Middle Tennessee State University
Drafted: 2016, Tennessee Titans, 64th overall
Years active: 2016–present
Top honors: First Team All-Pro (2017, 2021)
Hall of Fame induction: N/A

FLETCHER
COX DT

G	Sk	Tkl	FF	FR
156	58.0	443	14	12

THERE IS NO BETTER WAY TO EXPLAIN WHAT FLETCHER Cox does than this description from Chicago Bears defensive lineman Akiem Hicks: "He terrorizes offensive strategies."

That means Cox, the Philadelphia Eagles' defensive stalwart, does more than bash blockers, crash quarterbacks and smash running backs; he takes all their careful week-long game planning and feeds it to a paper shredder. As Hicks elaborated: "[Cox] has a knack for being a disruptor."

At 6-foot-4, 310 pounds, Cox has a knack like few others in the NFL. From the defensive tackle position, where the majority of his peers are asked to clog the middle of the field and open lanes for pass-rushing defensive ends, the man known as Fletch is not content with being a plug-the-gap player. He wants to be a difference maker. A guy who turns offensive coordinators into walking ulcers.

He does it exceedingly well. A six-time Pro Bowl honoree, he was named to the NFL 2010s All-Decade Team. In 2020, he maintained his disruptive ways with 6.5 sacks, 28 tackles and a forced fumble. And while hobbled with a groin injury late in Philadelphia's 2021 preseason, he was in his familiar spot creating havoc when the Eagles faced the Atlanta Falcons in their season opener.

"When he wants to be Fletch," said defensive teammate Brandon Graham, "that boy is a monster."

Eagles fans have loved Cox's game from the moment they saw him deconstructing offenses. A three-sport star at Yazoo City High School in Mississippi, Cox arrived in Philadelphia via Mississippi State University,

"I can see the fear in the faces of the offensive linemen going against him all the time."
— Former Eagles safety Malcolm Jenkins

where he earned All-American status in his junior year after turning in 103 total tackles, 11 quarterback sacks and two interceptions. His senior year numbers were almost identical: 104 tackles, 10 quarterback sacks and one interception.

That hooked Philadelphia's interest to the point where the Eagles traded up in the 2012 NFL Draft to take Cox with the 12th selection overall. In his first season in the NFL, he played defensive tackle. In his second, the Eagles went with a 3-4 defense, which shifted Cox to defensive end. It was a move designed to give Cox more room to maneuver, and he used it to make 61 tackles and four sacks while recovering three fumbles. In 2015, he returned to his tackle position and made 71 tackles and 9.5 sacks and forced three fumbles.

The high point in Cox's career came in the 2017 season. His play earned him a ticket to his third straight Pro Bowl, but he had to turn it down because the Eagles had a date with destiny.

At Super Bowl LII, Philadelphia faced the New England Patriots in a rematch of Super Bowl XXXIX, when the Pats trimmed the Eagles by a field goal, 24–21.

This time, however, the Eagles would come out on top,

Fletcher Cox pressures San Francisco 49ers quarterback C.J. Beathard during an October 2017 game.

41–33, to give Philadelphia its first Super Bowl victory in franchise history. Comedian Kevin Hart, a Philly native, was so giddy — also inebriated — he crashed Cox's postgame interview with the NFL Network. Cox was more than happy to let the little man speak for the big man, and Hart summed up the sentiment for Eagles fans.

"We're lucky to have this guy a part of this team," said Hart. "I've been drinking. I'm on cloud nine. I started the celebration early ... This was supposed to happen. We've got a great unit, we've got a great team, we've got a great defensive line."

Hopes were high for a repeat in 2018, but a sluggish start did a lot of damage. The Eagles lost six of their first 10 games, including a 48–7 thrashing by the New Orleans Saints. It was the worst loss by a defending Super Bowl champion in NFL history.

Cox got his game going in time to help the Eagles pull together a 9-7 record and beat the Chicago Bears by a single point in a 2018 NFC wild-card matchup. The Saints took the Eagles out of the playoffs the following weekend.

By the start of the 2019 season, Cox had established himself among the elite defensive linemen in the game, and his peers had taken notice. Los Angeles Rams defensive tackle Aaron Donald said of Cox, "For him to be as big as he is, he's explosive, he's quick, he's got some technique with him too, but the power he got is ridiculous."

Cox had his share of difficulties in 2021. He sat out the regular-season finale due to COVID-19, and he was dogged by trade rumors for months on end. That aside, there were still times when he was the difference maker eager to trash the opposing team's game plan.

"It's crazy because I can see the fear in the faces of the offensive linemen going against him all the time," said former Eagles safety Malcolm Jenkins.

They know the bashing is about to begin. ■

College: Mississippi State University
Drafted: 2012, Philadelphia Eagles, 12th overall
Years active: 2012–present
Top honors: NFL All-Rookie Team (2012), Super Bowl Champion (2017), First Team All-Pro (2018)
Hall of Fame induction: N/A

AARON
DONALD DT

G	Sk	Tkl	FF	FR
127	98.0	441	23	6

THEY COULD HAVE DEDICATED THEIR CHAMPIONSHIP pursuit to the quarterback who had spent more than a decade in Detroit without winning a single playoff game. They could have rallied around their head coach, Sean McVay, or the two prime additions — one on defense, the other on offense — whose presence was a clarion call that the Los Angeles Rams meant business. Super Bowl business.

But it was the veteran defensive tackle who became the Rams' touchstone, the man they turned to for inspiration. It worked for them against the Tampa Bay Buccaneers and quarterback supreme Tom Brady. It worked against the San Francisco 49ers and quarterback Jimmy Garoppolo in the NFC Final. And in Super Bowl LVI it worked against passer Joe Burrow and the Cincinnati Bengals.

In each of those encounters, Aaron Donald unleashed his dominance; in two of them he produced the game-clinching turnover to fulfill the vow the Rams organization had made. "We want to win it for Aaron," said L.A. defensive coordinator Raheem Morris before the 23–20 Super Bowl triumph. "Everyone in this building wants to create more for his legacy."

Winning an NFL championship had been the missing gem for one of football's greatest defensive players. His list of accomplishments includes multiple All-Pro selections, a spot on the 2010s All-Decade Team and three Defensive Player of the Year Awards. Yet, Donald's only previous Super Bowl experience had been a 13–3 loss to Brady and the New England Patriots in 2018. That disappointment, countered by the 2021 acquisition of Detroit Lions quarterback Matthew Stafford, Denver Broncos linebacker Von Miller and free-agent receiver Odell Beckham Jr., helped harden Donald's resolve.

It wasn't the first time the Pennsylvania native pushed himself to a higher level. His father, Archie, was responsible for getting things started years ago. Archie Donald played college football and was said to attack with such ferocity that his hits occasionally broke opponents' helmets. In his freshman year at Norfolk State, Archie fell victim to a serious knee injury. He worked out every day, morning, noon and evening, hoping he could return to play the game he loved. It never happened.

Despite the setback, he never surrendered the discipline and determination he'd forged at the gym. Years later, as a father, he would watch his youngest son, Aaron, take after him and succeed as a fullback and defensive lineman.

The gym, however, was a different story. As much as he resembled his dad on the field, the son was unlike the father when it came to working out. Aaron was chubby and uninterested in getting into shape. Archie knew that had to change.

After transforming the basement of their modest Pittsburgh home into a downstairs gym, Archie coaxed Aaron into improving his health and overall fitness. It didn't take long for his son to see the results. Aaron was soon strong enough to tangle with anyone who thought he was just a big throw pillow. In one memorable showing with the University of Pittsburgh, Donald did what many defensive linemen have dreamed of doing but could never pull off. He wasn't sure which Duke Blue Devil had the ball — the quarterback or the running back — so he dropped both of them at the same time.

That two-for-one tackle had NFL scouts wondering, "Was that a sign of future greatness? Could anyone else have been so athletic and strong?" The St. Louis Rams didn't wait long to affirm their belief in Donald, selecting him 13th overall in the 2014 NFL Draft. He went on to win Defensive Rookie of the Year.

Four years later he was remaking the position. While it's difficult for any defensive tackle to break free from the constant double-team blocking they face, Donald was able to record a mind-blowing 20.5 sacks from his interior position. It was the confirmation of his greatness and the culmination of what his father had initiated. Little wonder Donald's peers throughout the NFL have stood in line to express their awe.

"He's been a beast as soon as he stepped into the NFL," said Miller, a friend before they became teammates. "If you look at his game, it's not only his pass rush; he's a beast on the run game. He chases the ball down. He gets tackles for a loss."

He demonstrated that in Super Bowl LVI. His final stats read two quarterback sacks, three QB hurries and a crucial tackle late in the fourth quarter that prevented a Cincinnati first down. He also snuffed the Bengals' last offensive play when he chased Burrow and forced him into throwing an incomplete pass. Within minutes of that, Donald was doing interviews on the field, answering what it was like to be a Super Bowl champion and whether this was his last game in the NFL at age 30.

"I promised my daughter when she was five years old [she'd get] to play in the [postgame celebration] confetti," he said. "I'm just in the moment right now."

It was Miller, who also won a Super Bowl with Denver, who gave the most insightful commentary on Donald and his future, saying, "He's done so much, but I tell you, this feeling is great. It just makes you want it more and more and more ... I just can't see him walking away from this."

Three days after that, Donald said of another Super Bowl quest, "Why not run it back?" ▪

College: University of Pittsburgh
Drafted: 2014, St. Louis Rams, 13th overall
Years active: 2014–present
Top honors: NFL All-Rookie Team (2014), NFL AP Defensive Rookie of the Year (2014), First Team All-Pro (2015–19), NFL AP Defensive Player of the Year (2017, 2018, 2020), Super Bowl champion (2022)
Hall of Fame induction: N/A

STEPHON GILMORE CB

G	Int/Yds	Tkl	Ast	Sk	FR	TD
132	27/465	427	53	1.0	3	2

PARTING IS NOT ALWAYS, DESPITE THE OLD SAYING, such sweet sorrow.

Sometimes anger lingers, too.

"I learned a lot there," star cornerback Stephon Gilmore told sportswriters of his contentious exit from New England, in early November 2021, while settling in to life as a Carolina Panther.

"There are a lot of friends there, a lot of great coaches. I wasn't ready at the beginning of training camp, I'll be completely honest with you, but the only thing I just didn't like [was] how they handled my situation with my injury. You know, a lot went on with that, that I didn't agree with."

Despite two seasons of turmoil and injury, even at 31, there can be no doubting the man's game-changing abilities.

Gilmore wasn't just idly boasting when, during his Patriot days, he explained his dare-you mentality to the NFL Network, saying:

"I'm in a rhythm and I'm just daring the quarterback to throw at me and I'm just trying to make them pay ... Playing against the best guy, you have to really focus, every play is important — if you don't play well on one play, it can cost your team.

"I try to focus each and every play, be in tight-coverage, try to be in great shape."

Great shape has been an elusive target for the Rock Hill, South Carolina, product for the past couple of seasons.

The injury issues began in December of 2020, Gilmore suffering a partially torn quadriceps muscle in Week 15 of the Patriots' season, requiring surgery. Placed on the NFL's physically unable to perform (PUP) list ahead of the next campaign, he missed training camp in order to continue his recovery.

With the final year of a five-season, $64 million mega-contract looming, the Patriots — unable to persuade Gilmore to restructure his deal — released their foundational corner and then before he could actually hit the waiver wire dealt him on November 6, 2021, to Carolina in exchange for a sixth-round draft pick.

Excitement at the news around the Carolinas was palpable.

"Everyone in this building," proclaimed Panthers defensive tackle DaQuan Jones that day, "believes we can win now."

Intelligence. Athleticism. Quiet attitude. An insatiable appetite for success.

Those characteristics are why the Pats had splashed the cash — including $31 million up front and a signing bonus of $18 million — to lure Gilmore away from the Buffalo Bills in March of 2017.

To remember his dynamism, New Englanders need only flash back to Super Bowl LIII in Atlanta's Mercedes-Benz Stadium and the Pats' 13–3 defense-dominated victory over the Rams.

L.A. is trailing only 10–3, second and 10 from New England's 27-yard-line — just the second time in the second half that they've managed to infiltrate New England's side of the field — and time is winding relentlessly down. With visions of a game-tying TD drive dancing in the Californians' imaginations, Gilmore delivers what turns out to be the coup de grâce by intercepting Rams quarterback Jared Goff at the 3-yard line with 4:17 remaining.

Or the spectacular fourth-down, climb-the-ladder, one-handed, win-securing knockdown of a Blake Bortles pass intended for Dede Westbrook in the dying embers of the 2017 AFC Championship Game versus Jacksonville.

Or flash forward to the entirety of the 2019 season, one that saw Gilmore deliver 53 tackles and a league-topping six INT, two of which were turned for touchdowns. For such excellence, he was named AP's NFL Defensive Player of the Year.

"I mean, my play speaks for itself," Gilmore told the *Boston Globe* of the honor. "If you really watch the tape each and every game, it's no question."

Gilmore starred for South Pointe High School as a three-sport athlete, playing quarterback as well as defensive back and winning Mr. Football for the state of South Carolina along the way. Sticking close to home, he was wooed and won over by the University of South Carolina, and he started all four seasons on the corner for the Gamecocks.

The retooling Bills then chose Gilmore 10th overall in the 2012 draft, planning to build their secondary around him. An

immediate starter, he spent five seasons at Orchard Park, establishing himself as one of the rising cornerbacks in the league and snaring 14 interceptions.

The Bills never reached the postseason during his stay, though, and Gilmore went in search of greater opportunities, more ambitious challenges

After free-agent negotiations with the Chicago Bears broke down early in 2018, New England stepped in.

Gilmore's first season at Bank of America Stadium in Charlotte, North Carolina wasn't what anyone expected, individually or collectively. Things had begun well enough: Gilmore's Carolina debut after being taken off PUP was highlighted by a late pick of a Matt Ryan pass that helped the Panthers lay claim to a 19–13 win at Atlanta to end a four-game losing streak.

A groin injury and COVID-19 protocol issues arose, compromising Gilmore's impact. The Panthers wound up 5-12.

And with his contract up at season's end, another chapter of uncertainty began in the Stephon Gilmore saga. ▪

College: University of South Carolina
Drafted: 2012, Buffalo Bills, 10th overall
Years active: 2012–present
Top honors: NFL AP Defensive Player of the Year [2019], First Team All-Pro [2018, 2019], Super Bowl Champion [2018]
Hall of Fame induction: N/A

JACK HAM LB

G	Int/Yds	TD	FR
162	32/218	1	21

ARGUABLY THE BEST JACK HAM STORY COMES COURTESY of teammate Andy Russell.

Remembering the burnished excellence of his six-season linebacking cohort, Russell recalled with relish the Steelers' season opener versus the Chargers in 1975. Late in the game, with Pittsburgh handily pitching a shutout at San Diego Stadium, both men had been substituted. As they stood on the sidelines, talking about Ham's involvement in the coal business, the Chargers intercepted a pass and lugged the ball to the Pittsburgh 3-yard line. Steelers coach Chuck Noll promptly broke up the conversation and fired Ham back onto the field to try and hold onto the whitewash.

"The first play the Chargers ran was a sweep to the right," wrote Russell in his book *Andy Russell: A Steeler Odyssey.* "Bad idea. Ham took their giant tight end, threw him aside, speared the runner behind the line of scrimmage causing him to fumble, which of course Jack recovered. As he slowly walked off the field, he casually flipped the ball to the ref.

"Returning to our position on the sideline, Jack turned to me smiling and said, 'Where was I?'"

A legendary lot, the Steel Curtain defense defined a generation of excellence in the Steel City: the menacing Front Four of "Mean" Joe Greene, L.C. Greenwood, Dwight White and Ernie Holmes. On the back end, halfback Donnie Shell and all-world corner Mel Blount. And in between, the tungsten-tough Jack Lambert anchoring the second level with Russell and, with his quiet yet devastating style, Ham.

"I prefer to play consistent, error-free football," said Ham. "If you're doing your job well and defending your

"I have never seen anyone play the outside linebacker position better than Jack Ham."
— Super Bowl–winning coach Tony Dungy

area, you might not get tested that often or get a chance to make big plays."

Destined to be a Steeler, Jack Raphael Ham Jr. was born two days shy of Christmas, 1948, in the hardscrabble city of Johnston, Pennsylvania, 67 miles east of Pittsburgh. He would go on to play college ball at Penn State, starring for the Nittany Lions for three seasons. It's no coincidence they went 29-3 during that span.

Selected in the second round in the 1971 NFL Draft, Ham earned a starting job on the outside as rookie. There he helped propel the Steelers to four Super Bowl victories over a dynastic six-season span in Pittsburgh.

He was renowned for being a fearsome tackler with great track-down speed. Noll called him "the fastest Steeler for the first 10 yards — including wide receivers and running backs." Many peers singled out Ham's ability to read the game, sniff out opposition plays and make the right split-second decision as his most decisive attributes.

In 1976 the now-fabled Steel Curtain reached its zenith. The team struggled 1-4 to open the season. By the finish, however, that Steelers defense had surrendered a miserly 9.86 points per game and only 3.22 yards

Jack Ham in action during a 1978 game against the New Orleans Saints.

per rush attempt. During a remarkable nine-game regular-season stretch, they allowed only two touchdowns and 28 points *total*. Eight of their 11 starters, including Ham, were Pro Bowlers that season, and Lambert won Defensive Player of the Year — the third year in a row that a Steeler took home the award.

Still, they were upset 24–7 by the Oakland Raiders in the AFC Championship and denied the chance at a Super Bowl three-peat.

As the years rolled on, Ham continued to excel. A man who played briefly alongside him on that ferocious Steelers D, Super Bowl–winning coach Tony Dungy, put Ham in a class all of his own.

"I have never seen anyone play the outside linebacker position better than Jack Ham," said Dungy. "Fundamentals, technique, awareness and athleticism were all exceptional. He was the total package."

Ham retired following the 1982 season and was inducted into Canton in his first year of eligibility.

"It's a great feeling to be selected into the Hall of Fame with players who are the all-time greats," said Ham on the big day.

Two years later he was enshrined in the College Football Hall of Fame.

Today, nearly four decades after stepping away from a dynasty he helped form and an era he had a hand in defining, Ham's 53 career takeaways still stand as the most in league history by a non-defensive back. ▪

College: Penn State University
Drafted: 1971, Pittsburgh Steelers, 34th overall
Years active: 1971–1982
Top honors: Super Bowl Champion (1974, 1975, 1978, 1979), First Team All-Pro (1974–79)
Hall of Fame induction: 1988

JUSTIN
HOUSTON LB/DE

G	Int/Yds	Sk	TD	FR
149	4/52	102.0	1	14

THE BALTIMORE RAVENS DIDN'T have a lot to celebrate on October 18, 2021, when they dropped a 22–10 decision to the Miami Dolphins. But there was one special moment, and it came from their 32-year-old pass rusher making a beeline for Miami quarterback Jacoby Brissett.

On the Dolphins' opening drive of the second half, Brissett went to deliver a third-down pass only to be bowled over by the Baltimore defense. It was Justin Houston who got there first before another Raven charged into Brissett, forcing him to leave the game with a knee injury.

Not wanting to make it look as if he was applauding another player being hurt, Houston thrust his arms in the air and then went right back to work. At game's end, he sought out Brissett and the two men exchanged jerseys. For Houston, the aqua, white and orange jersey with the No. 14 on it will always commemorate a triumphant occasion — the 100th sack of his NFL career.

"I'll frame it and give it to my son," said Houston. "He says I can't retire until I get 130 [sacks]."

For eight seasons, every NFL quarterback who played against the Kansas City Chiefs' defense knew the deal: that guy over there wearing No. 50, expertly anticipating the snap count so he could explode off the line, he was shrewd and dangerous and he was coming for them.

Houston had earned his rivals' respect by totaling 78.5 sacks during his time in Kansas City. His game was straightforward. He overpowered blockers and punished quarterbacks. As former Oakland Raiders running back Darren McFadden said of Houston, "He [came] off the edge with a bad attitude on every play."

Houston was a beast as far back as his high school days in Statesboro, Georgia. He helped his teammates advance to three consecutive state championship games, winning one in 2005. That said, he showed his true strength away from the football field in 9th grade when he ran back into his burning home to rescue two of his brothers too scared to leave their bedroom. It was a harrowing experience that left Houston's mom and six of her other nine children without their belongings or a place to live. Friends, neighbors and local churches offered their support. So did Statesboro High, the school Houston took to three state title games.

From there, he enrolled at the University of Georgia and proved to be a quick study. He had seven sacks his sophomore year and 10 as a junior. He was later voted All-South Eastern Conference and a first team All-American.

In the 2011 NFL Draft, Kansas City took Houston in the third round. He responded by recording 5.5 sacks and 56 tackles in his rookie season. By 2013 he was listed as one of the NFL's top 100 players, and by 2014 he was a First Team All-Pro.

"He's not just a pass-rusher," said Bob Sutton, then the Chiefs' defensive coordinator. "He's involved in multiple roles in [pass] coverage. We move him around to both cover and to pressure ... The nature of the beast would say sack, sack, sack, but this guy played really good football in a lot of areas for us."

One of those areas is the strip sack. That was when Houston not only wrapped up the quarterback but also stripped the football away on a forced fumble. Houston had four of those in 2014 to rekindle the memories of the late Derrick Thomas, a superb pass rusher and arguably the franchise's greatest player.

Houston finished that season with 22 sacks, good enough to break the previous franchise record of 20 set by the legendary Thomas and just a whisker away from equaling Michael Strahan's NFL single-season record of 22.5 sacks. It elevated Houston to a higher status.

Houston was so dominant in 2014 that at season's end the Chiefs signed him to a six-year contract worth $101 million, making him the highest-paid defensive player in NFL history at the time. Unfortunately, the ink was barely dry on the deal when injury woes began to curtail Houston's effectiveness. A knee injury partway through 2015 shut him down for the rest of the season, requiring ACL surgery. The following season, he made only five appearances.

When Houston turned 30, Kansas City tried to trade him but was unable. The Chiefs released him, allowing Houston to sign a two-year, $24 million deal to play for the sack-deprived Indianapolis Colts. His 11 sacks with his new team were his highest total since that glorious 2014 season. For 2021, he jumped to Baltimore and kept chasing quarterbacks until he reached the 100-sack plateau. That made him one of four active players to achieve such a lofty goal.

Houston's son thinks his dad is good for another 30. ■

College: University of Georgia
Drafted: 2011, Kansas City Chiefs, 70th overall
Years active: 2011–present
Top honors: First Team All-Pro (2014)
Hall of Fame induction: N/A

LUKE
KUECHLY LB

G	Int/Yds	Sk	TD	FR
118	18/168	12.5	1	9

LUKE KUECHLY WAS DESCRIBED IN MANY WAYS DURING his playing time with the Carolina Panthers. Some were understated ("he's a tackling machine"), some were overstated ("he turns into Superman on Sundays") and some were decidedly funny.

"It's just like that fly," said former NFL tight end Martellus Bennett. "When you're in the restaurant there's just one fly in the restaurant, but it's only flying in your food."

That was Kuechly, the 6-foot-3, 238-pound middle linebacker who was the fly in most every team's lasagna. That was because he studied the videos of his opponents' games until he didn't just guess what they were going to do offensively, he knew. He prepared himself so completely he would recognize formations and tendencies and shout out what the quarterback was going to do before the snap of the ball.

It produced another Kuechly label — the smartest linebacker in the game.

With his physical abilities and his mental acuity, he recorded his 1,000th career tackle on October 6, 2019, needing just 107 games to do so, an NFL record. When he retired months later, he was smart enough to acknowledge how critical his teammates were to his success.

"You try to do everything you can to put yourself in position to be successful," said Kuechly. "And a lot of that goes to the coaches and especially the big guys in front of me. Ever since I've been here, we've had fantastic guys inside. And if you ask any inside linebacker what makes our job easier, it's those guys."

The traits that became so familiar to Panthers fans first drew national attention when Kuechly took to the field for the Boston College Eagles. There was little doubt he was going to be a football star. As a freshman, Kuechly started for the Eagles and led the NCAA in tackles. By the end of his junior year, he had taken home just about every award a college linebacker could win: the Vince Lombardi Award as the best lineman/linebacker in U.S. college football, the Lott IMPACT Trophy as defensive player of the year, the Bronko Nagurski Trophy as the best defensive player in the NCAA and the Dick Butkus Award as the top linebacker at the collegiate level. He was also a two-time consensus first-team All-American.

Destined for stardom, Kuechly made good on all those awards and honors after Carolina selected him with the ninth pick overall in the 2012 NFL Draft.

"I call him Clark Kent, and he can turn into Superman on Saturdays and Sundays," said Mike Mayock, who worked as an analyst for the NFL Network ahead of that draft and was until recently the general manager of the Las Vegas Raiders. "His instincts and his pass-coverage ability might be the best of any linebacker I've seen come out of the draft."

By the 2012 season opener, Kuechly was a starting outside linebacker. But when Jon Beason tore an Achilles tendon, Kuechly was moved into the middle spot, where he finished his rookie season atop the NFL with 164 tackles.

In a 2013 game against the New Orleans Saints, Kuechly was credited with 24 tackles, which tied the NFL record for most tackles in a single game. The Panthers reviewed the video of that game and found two more tackles by Kuechly, giving him the solo record with 26.

Luke Kuechly in action in a September 2018 game against the Dallas Cowboys.

The following season Kuechly led the league again in tackles with 153 and added 11 pass deflections, three sacks, a forced fumble and an interception.

"If I had to do a quarter of what he does, I'd need an oxygen tank," said former Carolina center Ryan Kalil. "You'd have to bring me out in a golf cart."

For both Kuechly and Carolina, 2015 almost touched the heavens. Following a 15-1 regular-season record, in the divisional round of the playoffs versus Seattle, Kuechly had a pick 6 against Seahawks quarterback Russell Wilson that established a 14-0 lead. He added another interception major late in the Panthers' 49–15 NFC Championship win over Arizona.

Carolina may have ultimately fallen 24–10 to the Denver Broncos in Super Bowl 50, but Kuechly did his part, homing in on 10 tackles and adding a sack.

In the four years that followed, Kuechly continued to anchor the Panthers' defense. By the end of the 2019 season he had been named a Pro Bowler seven times, a First Team All-Pro five times and Defensive Player of the Year.

After eight NFL seasons, however, the ferocity of the game and the nature of his playing style had exacted its toll on Kuechly. There had been off-season shoulder surgery in 2018 and, more tellingly, concussion issues to deal with from 2015 through 2017.

In a stunning announcement,

Kuechly called it quits in January 2020 at the age of 28. He accepted a pro scouting job with the Panthers but walked away from that in May 2021. He said he wanted to hunt and fish and spend time with friends and family. ■

College: Boston College
Drafted: 2012, Carolina Panthers, 9th overall
Years active: 2012–2019
Top honors: NFL All-Rookie Team (2012), NFL AP Defensive Rookie of the Year (2012), NFL AP Defensive Player of the Year (2013), First Team All-Pro (2013–15, 2017, 2018)
Hall of Fame induction: N/A

JACK
LAMBERT LB

G	Int/Yds	Sk	FR
146	28/243	23.5	17

JOHN ELWAY WAS A ROOKIE QUARTERBACK FOR THE Denver Broncos when he looked across the line of scrimmage and almost wet his football pants. There, in the cold heart of the Pittsburgh Steelers' defense, was the scariest man he had ever seen. Count Dracula from Pittsburgh, Transylvania: Jack Lambert.

With his pronounced bicuspids and snarling mood, Lambert played middle linebacker like a lion tearing into a fallen gazelle. Just the look of him was enough to send a trickle of fear through the young quarterback.

"He had no [front] teeth, and he was slobbering all over himself," recalled Elway. "I'm thinking, 'You can have your money back, just get me out of here. Let me go be an accountant.' I can't tell you how badly I wanted out of there."

> **"We've got a rookie who's so mean he doesn't even like himself."**
> **— Steelers defensive line coach George Perles**

Elway wasn't alone in his fear of Lambert, who would sometimes play up his evil image, saying, "I am very aggressive and very physical. On the field I guess I am just plain mean."

Lambert was a brutal hitter. He'd drive himself into the ball carrier, then sort through the pieces to find the ball. In his second season in Pittsburgh — in the Super Bowl, no less — Lambert went after Dallas Cowboys defensive back Cliff Harris, who had tapped Steelers kicker Roy Gerela on the helmet after a missed 33-yard field goal and said, "Way to go." Lambert took offense, tossed Harris to the ground, and then had to talk his way out of being ejected by the officials.

Lambert also had a trio of run-ins with the Cleveland Browns after flattening their quarterback, Brian Sipe. He was penalized three times for a late hit on Sipe, ejected twice and fined by the league. All three times, Lambert was mobbed by Cleveland players who took exception to his actions. A week later Lambert told Howard Cosell on *Monday Night Football*, "Quarterbacks should wear dresses."

The Steelers drafted Lambert from Kent State, where he had played a rambunctious game at linebacker despite weighing only 204 pounds. It was assumed that Lambert lost his teeth playing football, but he actually had them knocked loose by a teammate during a high school basketball practice. (Was he a good basketball player? He averaged 17.9 points and 13 rebounds per game.)

By then, Lambert's image as a menacing predator was already well established. On the eve of training camp in 1974, Steelers defensive line coach George Perles told one of his players, "We've got a rookie who's so mean he doesn't even like himself."

Being drafted by the Steelers afforded Lambert two early opportunities. Pittsburgh is only a 90-minute drive from where he was born in Mantua, Ohio, so he was able to drive to the team's office every weekend to watch game film before his first training camp in 1974. When starting middle linebacker Henry Davis got hurt in the preseason, Lambert moved into the position and never stepped out.

By 1976 Lambert already had a pair of Super Bowl rings, and the Steelers' defense had become one of the best in league history. Led by Lambert, Pittsburgh allowed just two touchdowns in a nine-game span that season, recorded five shutouts and finished first in almost every defensive statistic kept by the NFL. Overall, the Steelers gave up just 9.9 points per game over a 14-game schedule, and eight of their 11 defensive starters were selected to the Pro Bowl. Lambert was named Defensive Player of the Year.

"Jack had the image of a wild man, but he killed opponents with his perfection," said linebacking partner Andy Russell. "His greatness has nothing to do with his popular image."

The bloodsucking, wild-man persona was awfully tough to get past, though. Lambert was as fiercely private away from the game as he was punishing during it, which simply added to his myth. He didn't like to talk much, either. His teammates recalled how Lambert would cringe when he was recognized in public. Once, when spotted by some young fans, he was asked, "What's your sign, Jack? You know, astrology."

"Feces," he said.

Lambert once joked that he was from Buzzard's Breath, Wyoming. Some people took him seriously.

In the end, the man who almost turned Elway into an accountant finished with more than 1,400 tackles, 23.5 sacks, 28 interceptions and four Super Bowl rings, and played in nine consecutive Pro Bowls.

In 1990 Lambert achieved the ultimate recognition when he was inducted into the Hall of Fame. His acceptance speech was delivered with the passion and purpose that punctuated the way he played his position.

"If I could start my life all over again, I'd be a professional football player," he said. "And you damn well better believe I would be a Pittsburgh Steeler." ◼

College: Kent State University
Drafted: 1974, Pittsburgh Steelers, 46th overall
Years active: 1974–1984
Top honors: NFL AP Defensive Rookie of the Year (1974), NFL All-Rookie Team (1974), Super Bowl Champion (1974, 1975, 1978, 1979), NFL AP Defensive Player of the Year (1976), First Team All-Pro (1976, 1979–83)
Hall of Fame induction: 1990

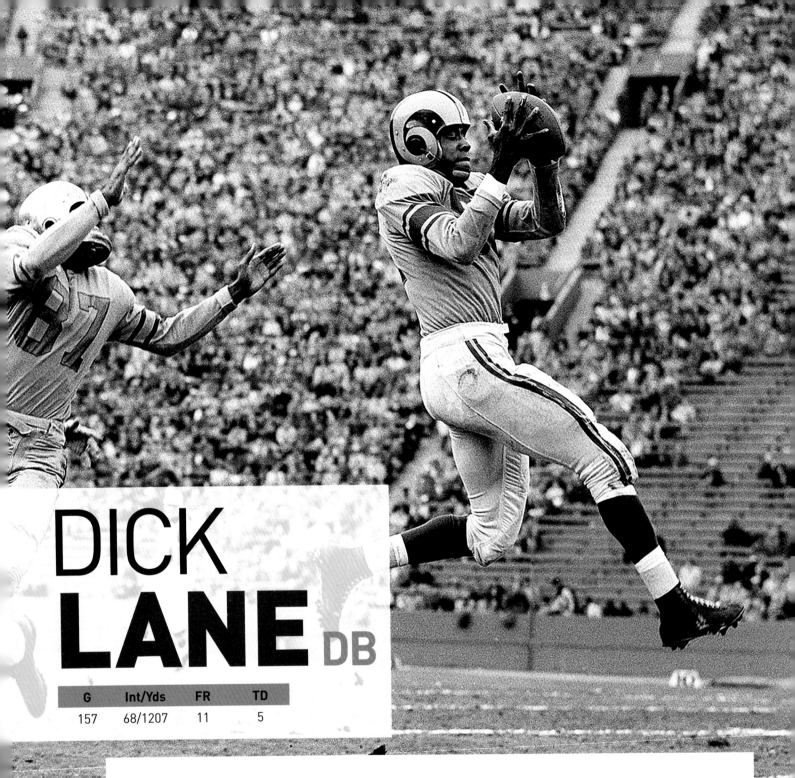

DICK
LANE DB

G	Int/Yds	FR	TD
157	68/1207	11	5

Y OU HAD TO ACKNOWLEDGE THE MAN'S INGENUITY, if not his taste for carnage. Dick (Night Train) Lane used to corkscrew ball carriers into the ground by grabbing their facemask as they tried to run past him. Complaints reached the NFL office, and in quick order facemasking was banned.

Lane responded by grabbing ball carriers by the back of their shoulder pads and jerking them to the ground. It became known as the horse-collar tackle, and the NFL banned that, too.

Unable to facemask or horse collar, the inventive Lane developed a forearm maneuver nicknamed the Night Train Necktie. It was a clothesline hit that hung so many players out to dry the league banned its practice hoping it would make Lane a little more gentle. It worked to a degree but not nearly enough to soften his reputation as the most fearsome defender of the early 1950s to the mid-1960s.

With his size [6-foot-1, 194 pounds) and speed, Lane played cornerback the way it had never been played before. He could cover receivers as easily as he knocked down oncoming running backs. "I've never seen a defensive back like him," said Green Bay Packers' Hall of Fame cornerback Herb Adderley. "I mean, take them down — whether it be Jim Brown or Jim Taylor."

That he could mug opponents and separate them from their senses was only half of his destructive power. His ability to read situations and disrupt passes was unparalleled, especially for a player who was signed by the Los Angeles Rams having never before lined up at cornerback.

Lane was four years removed from serving in the US Army and working at a dead-end factory job when he decided to ask the Rams for a tryout armed only with a scrapbook full of his high school and college football heroics. Lane was interested in being a receiver, but head coach Joe Stydahar had two future Hall of Fame pass catchers in Tom Fears and Elroy (Crazy Legs) Hirsch. Still, Stydahar was so impressed by Lane's athleticism he put him on defense. Little did anyone suspect Lane was about to set the standard that exists to this day.

"Train will always be the Godfather of cornerbacks," said former Detroit Lions defensive back Lem Barney. "He was as large as some linemen of his era. He was also agile and very fast. His tackling was awesome. He did the clothesline and other tackles that just devastated the ball carrier."

In 1952, as a 24-year-old rookie, Lane did the ridiculous and intercepted 14 passes in a 12-game regular season, an NFL record that still stands. During his 14-year career,

he also played for the Chicago Cardinals and with Detroit. He was selected to multiple Pro Bowls and was a seven-time First Team All-Pro.

His final statistics included 68 interceptions for 1,207 yards, five touchdowns, 11 fumble recoveries for another touchdown, and he added eight catches for 253 yards and a touchdown as a receiver.

"I was a small, very wiry kid, so therefore nobody gave me a ghost of a chance of making it," said Lane. "But I had a big heart."

Lane wasn't given much of a chance of making it beyond the first three months of his life after being abandoned in a trash can in Austin, Texas. His birth mother had been a prostitute; his father, a pimp. The people who heard baby cries coming from the trash can thought a cat had been trapped inside. The woman who found the infant Lane wrapped in newspaper was Ella Lane, a widow who took the baby home and mothered him along with her two other children.

Lane starred in high school football and at Scottsbluff Junior College in Nebraska, where he spent one season before joining the Army. It didn't take long for Lane to settle in with the Rams and prove his worth. His teammates started calling him Night Train, which was the name of a popular R&B song by Jimmy Forrest. At first, Lane wasn't enamored with the moniker. He finally warmed up to it when he saw it used in a newspaper headline that included Washington Redskins' star Charlie 'Choo Choo,' Justice, "Night Train Derails Choo Choo."

Lane had another technique to instill fear in the receivers he covered — his execution of the

Cornerbacks aren't supposed to frighten their opponents, but Lane did.

bump and run. It has been said that Lane invented the practice of jamming the receiver as he comes off the line of scrimmage then running downfield with him. Today's defensive backs can do anything to a receiver, except hold him, within a 5-yard bump zone. Lane's bumps were powerful enough to knock some receivers flat, a result that always made him feel good.

"My object is to stop the guy with the ball before he gains another inch," said Lane, who figured it was far more effective if he flattened receivers before they got their hands on the ball. It was a strategy that saw him voted to the NFL's 50th, 75th and 100th Anniversary All-Time Team. He was inducted into the Pro Football Hall of Fame in 1974.

Lane worked in the Lions' front office and later at two universities when his playing career ended. He left Central State University in Ohio to be a bodyguard and personal assistant to comedian Redd Foxx. Being Foxx's guardian angel meant Lane could facemask, horse collar, Night Train Necktie and bump whenever the situation called for it.

It was safe to say he enjoyed the job. ■

College: Scottsbluff Junior College
Drafted: undrafted
Years active: 1952-1965
Top Honors: First Team All-Pro (1956-1957, 1959-1963)
Hall of Fame induction: 1974

WILLIE LANIER LB

G	Int/Yds	TD	FR
149	27/440	2	18

THE NICKNAME — CONTACT — PRETTY MUCH illustrates the spirit of the man.

"Those who evaluated me never thought I was as good as I thought I was," confessed Willie Lanier while in retirement.

"You see, I came into pro football with a heckuva purpose. I looked at it as a helluva challenge to prove something.

"Being the first black middle linebacker placed me in an unusual position."

The Kansas City Chiefs, smarting from a 35–10 clubbing courtesy of the Green Bay Packers in the very first Super Bowl, were in search of defensive reinforcements when they used their second-round pick in the 1967 NFL Draft to select Lanier.

Little could anyone in Clover, Virginia, (where Lanier was born) or Richmond (where he grew up) imagine what kind of a career he was embarking on. At the end of it all, Lanier would be a three-time First Team All-Pro selection, a six-time Pro Bowler, a selection on both the league's 75th and 100th anniversary teams and a member of the Pro Football Hall of Fame's class of 1986.

That first camp, Lanier had been tagged to compete with the team's top pick in the draft, Jim Lynch, for the starting middle-linebacking spot. Lynch, off playing the College All-Star Game, arrived late, only to find Lanier had already nailed down the job.

Besides being renowned for his hitting ability, as his second nickname — the Honey Bear — indicates, Lanier was noted for being a clean and fierce tackler, wrapping opponents up tightly with his arms rather than dangerously attacking with his helmet. And his tackles always came with purpose.

"My reality was that if there was a defenseless player, if that player didn't touch the ball, I would not hit them," Lanier said.

"I was not going to strike if you if you didn't have the opportunity to get the ball."

Of all the Willie Lanier moments that continue to linger in memory for lifelong Chiefs fans, one perhaps rises above them all: the 1969 AFL divisional playoff game versus the Broadway Joe Namath–propelled New York Jets. Trailing 6–3 late in the third quarter in front of a sellout throng at Shea Stadium, the Jets, who were the reigning Super Bowl champs, found themselves first and goal from the 1-yard line following a pass interference call against the Chiefs.

A seismic swing in momentum seemed in the offing. Over the growing din, though, one man's voice could be heard clearly on the defensive side of the line of scrimmage.

"They're not going to score!" bellowed Lanier at his teammates, as much a command as a plea. "They're *not* going to score!"

And, on three cracks, the Jets failed to score, settling for a field goal to tie matters. Buoyed by the stalwart defensive stand, quarterback Len Dawson and the Chiefs marched down the field on the ensuing, and the K.C. quarterback found wideout Gloster Richardson on a 19-yard TD pass to regain the upper hand.

Final score: Kansas City 13, New York 6.

The Chiefs would then go on to trim the Raiders 17–7 in Oakland and then down the favored Minnesota

Willie Lanier tackles Pittsburgh Steelers running back John Fuqua.

Vikings 23–7 in Super Bowl IV at Tulanc Stadium in New Orleans.

"We had the kind of team that didn't back down from anybody," reflected Lanier years later. "If they wanted to intimidate us, we could intimidate as well as they could. Our team was too big and too good to intimidate."

The Chiefs' defensive setup of that era represented a veritable who's who of ball-tracking talent — Aaron Brown, Curley Culp, Jerry Mays and Buck Buchanan up front; Lanier, Bobby Bell and Lynch prowling the second level; and Jonny Robinson, Jim Marshall, Emmitt Thomas and Jim Kearny on the back end.

Six of them — including the iconic No. 63 at the hub of the resistance — are now enshrined in the hallowed Pro Football Hall of Fame in Canton, Ohio.

Gradually, as the Chiefs continually failed to follow up the glory of '69 with another World Championship or two, the inevitable changes began to occur.

Following a disastrous season in 1974, head coach Hank Stram, the architect of the great teams, was fired. Bell retired; Buchanan followed him the next year; Dawson announced his retirement in May 1976.

Then, in the wake of a miserable 2-12 debacle that was the 1978 season, Lanier announced his decision to

walk away from the game after 11 years. His rights were subsequently dealt to the Baltimore Colts, but try as they might, they couldn't coax him to wear another team's colors.

A Chief, one of the greatest, to the end. ∎

College: Morgan State University
Drafted: 1967, Kansas City Chiefs, 50th overall
Years active: 1967–1977
Top honors: First Team All-Pro (1968, 1972, 1973), Super Bowl Champion (1969), NFL Walter Payton Man of the Year (1972)
Hall of Fame induction: 1986

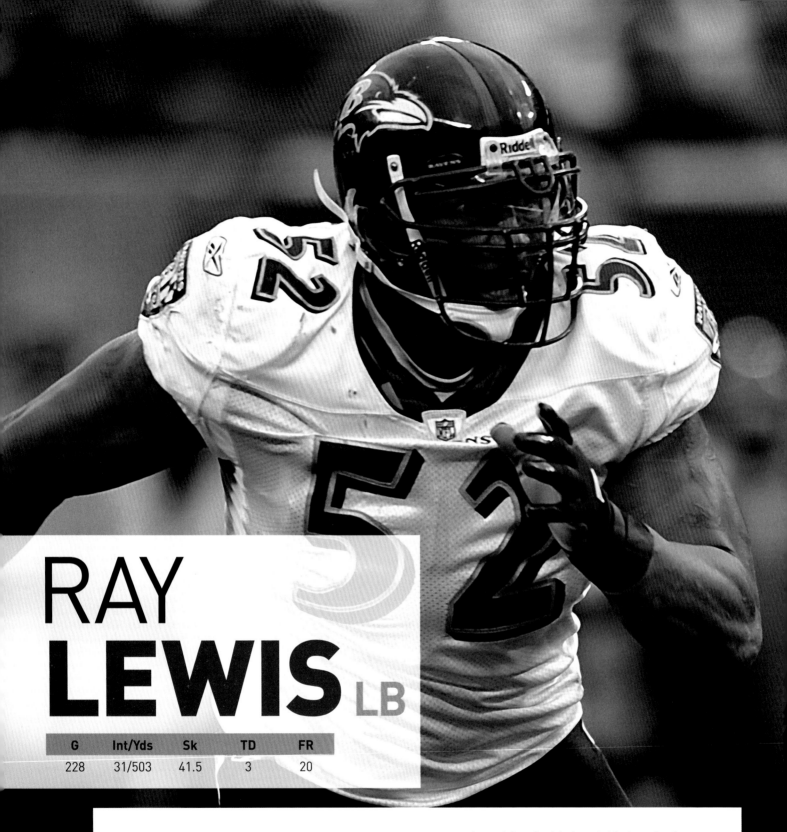

RAY
LEWIS LB

G	Int/Yds	Sk	TD	FR
228	31/503	41.5	3	20

IN 2006 SPORTS ILLUSTRATED GAVE RAY LEWIS A front cover pulpit, proclaiming him to be "God's linebacker." It was a calculated decision by the magazine. Anyone who has followed Lewis's life knows he is a polarizing individual.

There are those who are convinced he was wronged when he was arrested and charged in connection with a double homicide in suburban Atlanta in 2000. Then there are those who believe the spiritual Baltimore Ravens linebacker got away with his part in the killing of Jacinth Baker and Richard Lollar, who were stabbed to death outside a nightclub. The murder charges were dropped as part of Lewis's plea bargain, which meant he had to sing like a free bird about what had happened that night and how two of his friends were involved. His friends were eventually acquitted of the murder charges and Lewis reached a financial settlement with the murder victims' families, the terms of which were undisclosed.

Lewis's antics made for rousing disagreements. Depicted on the front of *SI*, the sporting world's bible, God's linebacker had his hands clasped together and his eyes looking up in heaven's direction as the protector of the Baltimore franchise. On the field, there was never any doubt what guided Lewis: he wanted to win all of the time, not just some of the time. That was why he played with a fervor that inspired as much as it made some people cower. Enough, for Lewis, was never enough.

Born in Bartow, Florida, he became the star of his high school football team and a state champion in wrestling for his weight class. He went to the University of Miami and starred at middle linebacker from his freshman year right up until he left after his junior year to play in the NFL. He was drafted by the Baltimore Ravens in 1996, 26th overall.

Between 1996 and 2000, Lewis won dozens of awards while the Baltimore defense set a league record for fewest points allowed. What proved even more amazing was how, within one year, Lewis went from murder suspect to conquering hero when his Baltimore Ravens won Super Bowl XXXV. That season he was named Defensive Player of the Year and Super Bowl MVP after the Ravens defeated the New York Giants 34–7.

After the murder allegations, many of his fans rushed to his defense as he pledged his innocence, as he had from the very start. They reminded everyone of the many acts of kindness Lewis had done for the less fortunate. There were celebrity auctions, bowling tournaments, food drives and youth camps in Baltimore and also in Angola and Ethiopia, where he helped war victims and championed their need for help all the way to U.S. Congress.

Much of that will be part of Lewis's legacy. So will his competitive nature.

Say what you will about Lewis's ways, from his religious ramblings to how he manhandled ball carriers like a Central Park mugger — he was the NFL's most daunting interior linebacker, as tough as he was relentless. From his 1996 rookie season right up until his Super Bowl swan song in New Orleans in 2013, Lewis was renowned for pillaging offenses and convincing people he was one scary dude. Boastful, too.

"I already believe I am the best linebacker in the game," he has said. "Now I have to show one more thing: that I am the most dominating, influential person in the game and the best football player to ever put on a pair of cleats."

Even when it was suggested he was losing a step at the age of 32, Lewis managed 120 tackles, 10 pass deflections, two sacks, two interceptions and a touchdown to earn his ninth Pro Bowl selection. If that's what losing a step means, there are plenty of NFL linebackers longing for a decline in speed.

"It's amazing that as long as he's been playing in this league, the amount of explosion he has, the strength ... [it's with]

the physicality of a 25-year-old," Rashard Mendenhall, former Pittsburgh Steelers running back, said of Lewis before his retirement.

Even being injured was no excuse for not getting the job done. In Week 6 of the 2012 season, Lewis suffered a torn triceps muscle. He was 37. The doctors proclaimed he was done for the year, perhaps for good. Lewis didn't agree, and by December he was telling everyone he'd be back. And back he came to help his team win Super Bowl XLVII, a remarkable finale to a career spiked with platitudes and controversy.

He retired as the only defender in league history to record more than 40 career sacks and 30 interceptions. He was voted to the league's 2000s All-Decade team, was named to the NFL's All-Time Team roster, has been a multiple Pro Bowler and All-Pro selection, and was inducted into the Pro Football Hall of Fame in 2018. He did it all, and it defied conventional thought.

After winning the first of two Super Bowls and an MVP award, Lewis summed up what he'd learned from the past year by saying, "If the world wants to see me stumble now, I'll stumble with a [Super Bowl] ring on my finger." ∎

College: University of Miami
Drafted: 1996, Baltimore Ravens, 26th overall
Years active: 1996–2012
Top honors: First Team All-Pro (1999–2001, 2003, 2004, 2008, 2009), NFL AP Defensive Player of the Year (2000, 2003), Super Bowl Champion (2000, 2012), Super Bowl MVP (2000)
Hall of Fame induction: 2018

HOWIE
LONG DE

G	Sk	FR
179	84.0	10

For the longest time, Howie Long was a massive contradiction. He played a prickly game for the NFL's nastiest team, the Los Angeles Raiders. Yet he was funny and engaging out of uniform, a media darling who charmed his way into acting and broadcasting.

As a kid, Long didn't care for school. Yet his high school tutor was surprised to hear him speak with perfect grammar — a gift from his grandmother, who raised Long in one of Boston's working-class neighborhoods.

When younger, Long secretly wanted to play hockey like Bobby Orr, but he enjoyed football as well. The problem was that he hated playing it in front of big crowds with people watching and counting on him to produce. He loathed that kind of pressure.

"I had no confidence," said Long. "None."

Still, Long matured into a good high school player, a better college player and one of the NFL's most formidable defensive linemen, easily able to separate his football actions and transgressions from his desire to be just an everyday normal guy, with good grammar.

It was that fully developed, fully secure, 6-foot-5 and 268-pound defender who became a Raiders mainstay.

Long terrorized offenses to the point where he once walked into an opposing team's huddle during a time-out and yelled at their trainer, "Give me that water. They don't need it. They're not doing anything." Then there was the game against Chicago where Long screamed at a Bears offensive lineman, "I'm going to get you in the parking lot after the game and beat you up in front of your family!"

This guy could be prickly.

"I think the moment you're content is the moment you're heading backward," said Long. "It's the proverbial quest for perfection, which is unattainable, and therein lies the dilemma."

Long's childhood was rife with hardship. At 12 years old, he was turned over to his grandmother after his parents separated and later divorced. He had to overcome some early ailments.

"I was sick a lot, and doctors told my grandmother I'd never grow up to be big and strong," recalled Long. "Isn't that ironic?"

Long was shipped to an uncle who lived in the suburbs, and there he was fortunate to meet a high school football coach who not only believed in him but had his wife, a math and English teacher, tutor him. Long responded by becoming a Scholastic Coach All-America defensive player in 1977, his senior year.

Long was spotted by a coach from Villanova and offered a scholarship. In the 1980 Blue-Gray Football Classic, an annual college football all-star game, he was named Defensive MVP. A year later he was drafted by the Raiders in the second round.

Not having played at a major Division I school, Long's inexperience became obvious when he arrived at training camp. In no time he was taken to the woodshed by the Raiders' veteran offensive linemen and later by rival offensive linemen. Aware that he had much to learn, Long turned to meticulous preparation.

Long took a VCR with him on the road and watched game tape while staying in hotels. He started the last five games of the 1982 season and became a regular in 1983, when he went to the Pro Bowl for the first time

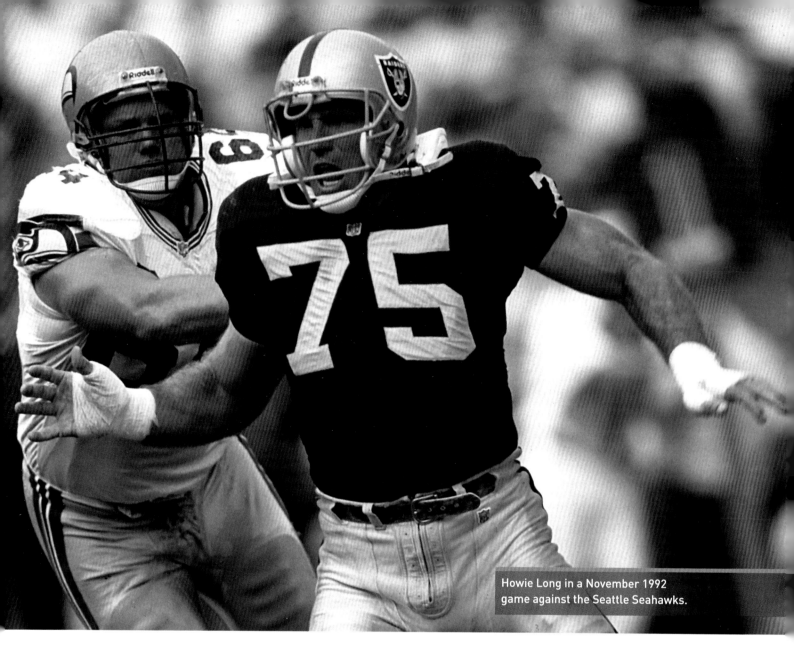

Howie Long in a November 1992 game against the Seattle Seahawks.

after recording what would be a career-high 13 quarterback sacks.

The Raiders made it to Super Bowl XVIII that season against the Washington Redskins and won handily, 38–9. Long recorded five tackles as the Raiders forced two interceptions and a fumble and allowed just 90 yards rushing.

By the time Long retired in 1993, he had made seven more visits to the Pro Bowl in a career that included 84 sacks, two interceptions, 10 fumble recoveries and a 1980s All-Decade Team nomination.

Long had earned the admiration of his NFL peers and coaches.

Raiders defensive line coach Earl Leggett spoke for many: "In those 13 years I thought that he became the most disruptive force in pro football."

Once finished as a player, Long jumped into acting. He became an action hero, starring in the movies *Firestorm*, *Broken Arrow* and *3000 Miles to Graceland*. He has become a mainstay as an analyst for the FOX Network and also authored the book *Football for Dummies*, teaching the basics to Joe Fan.

At his induction into the Hall of Fame in 2000, Long thanked his

family, friends, coaches and teammates, and then his grandmother, Ma Mullan, who "is up there somewhere saying, 'See, I told you you'd be somebody special.'"

Turned out she was right on the mark. ▪

College: Villanova University
Drafted: 1981, Oakland Raiders, 48th overall
Years active: 1981–1993
Top honors: Super Bowl Champion (1983), First Team All-Pro (1984, 1985)
Hall of Fame induction: 2000

RONNIE
LOTT s

G	Int/Yds	TD	Sk	FR
192	63/730	5	8.5	17

THE STORY OF RONNIE LOTT AND HIS LEFT PINKY finger has become as mangled as the defensive back's damaged digit.

Some say the finger was so badly fractured during a game that doctors cut it off at halftime and let Lott return to action. Others insist Lott hacked it off when doctors told him his finger was a goner.

"It's like Babe Ruth pointing to center field," Lott said of his legendary tale. "That's the kind of story it's turned out to be."

It's a telling saga, even if the facts have been mutilated over the years. What is without any doubt is Lott's deserved reputation as a fearless, ball-seeking missile who played it rough as a Pro Bowl cornerback and even rougher as a Pro Bowl safety. He was as vital to the San Francisco 49ers' four Super Bowl wins as Joe Montana and Jerry Rice. He would do anything — make any hit, intercept any pass, create fumbles and score touchdowns — to ensure the 49ers' success.

Even lop off a finger? The acknowledged version of events goes like this:

In San Francisco's last game of the 1985 regular season, the baby finger on Lott's left hand was crushed in a full-bore collision with Dallas Cowboys running back Tim Newsome. Lott's hand was caught between his chest and Newsome's helmet and "exploded," according to Lott. A piece of his finger was left on the field as Lott was taken to the dressing room, done for the day.

He refused to miss the following week's playoff game and played with his hand taped up. The 49ers lost to the New York Giants and, in the off-season, doctors gave Lott the choice of undergoing an intricate surgical procedure involving pins and skin grafts or having the tip of the finger removed.

"The doctors thought it would be better for me to [have part of the baby finger amputated] since I was continuing to play," said Lott, who was told the surgery would require months of recovery and rehabilitation. "It wasn't like I was going to have a good-looking finger, because it was pretty much destroyed."

By agreeing to have his finger pruned, Lott was ready for the start of the 1986 season — one that would see him snare a career-high 10 interceptions, make 77 tackles, force three fumbles and record two sacks, despite missing the final two games of the regular season with a leg injury.

"That shows [Lott's] dedication to the game," said Dennis Thurman, who played for the Cowboys and was Lott's teammate at the University of Southern California. "I think it's a tremendous story about courage, determination and grit, and how important football was to Ronnie, and still is."

Lott arrived at USC as a potential running back. He lost out to Marcus Allen and was asked to play safety, which turned out to be a good thing for the Trojans. Lott helped his school garner enough votes to win a share of the 1978 national championship alongside Alabama. He played in two Rose Bowls and was a team captain and a unanimous All-America selection.

Drafted in the first round by the 49ers, he stepped in as a rookie cornerback and made seven interceptions, returning three for touchdowns — tying an NFL record for a rookie defender. In 1985 he switched to safety, and was able to punish receivers and running backs from his new vantage point.

One of his best mood-altering hits took place on January 27, 1989, in Super Bowl XXIII. Cincinnati Bengals runner Ickey Woods was gaining significant yardage early in the game, when Lott promised his teammates that was about to stop. The tackle he put on Woods was so nasty it should have come with a warning: "Viewer discretion is advised."

"It just knocked Ickey's spark right out of him," said 49ers defensive coordinator Ray Rhodes. "The game turned right then because Ickey just didn't run with the same authority after that."

Lott did the same thing to a number of other players over the years, but he was also quick and heady enough to intercept 63 passes in his career. He was even better in big games, notching 89 tackles, nine interceptions, a fumble recovery and two touchdowns in 20 playoff games.

"He's like a middle linebacker playing safety," Dallas head coach Tom Landry once said. "He's devastating. He may dominate the secondary better than anyone I've seen."

Lott was showered with awards and honors, voted to the 1980s and 1990s All-Decade Teams and the NFL's All-Time Team and elected to the Pro Football Hall of Fame in 2000.

Asked if he had made the right decision about his left pinky being shortened, Lott replied, "All in all, yes. I don't have any regrets. You do that because you just love playing the game of football ... That's the ultimate compliment to pay to your teammates, to play hurt."

With nine-and-a-half fingers, no less. ■

College: University of Southern California
Drafted: 1981, San Francisco 49ers, 8th overall
Years active: 1981–1994
Top honors: First Team All-Pro (1981, 1986, 1987, 1989–91), Super Bowl Champion (1981, 1984, 1988, 1989)
Hall of Fame induction: 2000

He would do anything — make any hit, intercept any pass, create fumbles and score touchdowns — to ensure the 49ers' success.

KHALIL
MACK LB

G	Int/Yds	Sk	TD	FR
117	3/66	76.5	0	10

YOU'D ASSUME AN OTHERWORLDLY OUTSIDE LINEBACKER who's made a habit of picking the remains of quarterbacks out of his teeth would list one of the many incarnations of *Godzilla*, say, or *Alien* as his favorite movie.

In Khalil Mack's case, it's actually *Mary Poppins* — everyone's favorite practically perfect British nanny. It makes more sense when you think of the sack master/chaos causer of the Chicago Bears as not simply great, or even really great, but as supercalifragilisticexpialidociously great.

That's precisely why the Bears signed him in 2018 to a six-year contract worth $141 million, immediately after swinging a blockbuster trade. The megadeal made Mack the highest-paid defender in NFL history at that time — truly a worthy successor to Dick Butkus and Mike Singletary, Brian Urlacher and Wilber Marshall in the rich lineage of Chicago linebackers.

And why the Chargers flipped two draft picks to Chicago to acquire him four years later, despite Mack missing most of the 2021 season following foot surgery.

"You don't really ever anticipate it, even if you know it's coming, or think it's coming," said Mack about the trade.

"It was weird to hear. But understanding the team, the coach, having a relationship with coach Staley, and knowing his mindset, knowing his passion for the game, I kinda went from bittersweet to kinda excited."

Mack, of course, is all about the hunt.

He has been ever since joining the University of Buffalo Bulldogs on a scholarship. During his stay in Buffalo, Mack set the NCAA record for most tackles for loss (75) and tied the mark for forced fumbles (16). He also set the school record for most sacks (28.5).

Highly coveted heading into the 2014 NFL Draft, Mack was chosen fifth overall by the Oakland Raiders.

As encouraging as his first two years in California turned out to be, the 2016 season was a professional epiphany for Mack. His ferocious display was largely responsible for the Raiders' first playoff appearance in 14 years. Individually dominating, he racked up 11 sacks, five forced fumbles and three fumble recoveries.

In Week 12 against Carolina, Mack recorded a sack, a fumble and a recovery on the afternoon around an interception that he returned 6 yards for a touchdown.

Naturally the individual accolades were swift and plentiful: a second Pro Bowl and another First Team All-Pro selection, along with the Butkus Award and Defensive Player of the Year laurels.

Not that self-satisfaction is part of the man's makeup. "If you get caught up in people saying you're good, people saying you're this or that, good or bad, it can kind of wear on you," said Mack. "Or it'll make you feel like you're better than you are."

Not many are better than Mack. And he knows it.

Seriously, how can you not like a guy who quips: "I have a big head, so I can appreciate a good hat"?

He was named to the Pro Bowl again for the 2017 season. But when Mack's four-year rookie deal expired, contract trouble began brewing between the organization and its star. When the team convened for mini-camp in Alameda, California, Mack was nowhere in sight.

Less than three months later, having made no significant headway, Mack was dealt to the Bears.

"He makes this defense just a little bit more ferocious,"

Khalil Mack battles with New Orleans Saints offensive tackle Ryan Ramczyk in an October 2019 game.

said Chicago defensive end Akiem Hicks. "Well, shoot, a lot more ferocious."

In Year 1 of the relationship, Mack's new employers received everything expected and more. Their new defensive linchpin generated 12.5 sacks, a career-high six forced fumbles and his second interception. For his exemplary work, Mack received the Butkus Award for a second time.

By only Year 2, such was his immediate impact that Mack was honored by inclusion, at No. 60, in a centenary list selected by Hall of Fame writers Don Pierson and Dan Pompei of the top 100 Chicago Bears in franchise history.

A give-back type of guy, he continued to pay back Bears fans both on and off the field. As Christmas 2019 approached, it came to light that he'd quietly paid off the remaining balances of every unpaid layaway account in a Walmart store in his hometown.

The 2020 season began brightly enough, Chicago flying 5-1 out of the gate, but ended poorly, the team finished 8-8 before being beaten 21–9 by New Orleans in the wild-card playoff round. Mack was named to his sixth straight Pro Bowl.

That loss was painful. Hinting at what would be a disappointing 2021 season for both player and team.

Hobbled by a foot injury suffered during a Week 3 loss to Cleveland in 2021, Mack played on through four more games before being shut down in Week 8.

Season-ending surgery followed.

The Bears missed the playoffs altogether. ∎

College: University at Buffalo
Drafted: 2014, Oakland Raiders, 5th overall
Years active: 2014–present
Top honors: NFL All-Rookie Team (2014), First Team All-Pro (2015, 2016, 2018), NFL AP Defensive Player of the Year (2016)
Hall of Fame induction: N/A

VON
MILLER LB

G	Int/Yds	Sk	TD	FR
150	2/68	115.5	1	9

THE GENERATOR WAS KEPT IN THE BACK OF THE family's Chevrolet Suburban, which was parked as close to the stadium as Gloria Miller could get. From there she would snake an orange extension cord through the stands, onto the sidelines and then over to the players' bench, where it powered a compressor for her son's nebulizer. That way, when Von Miller's asthma was getting the better of him,

he could come off the field, take his medication on the spot and not miss much of the action.

It was a great idea perfected over time, and it was his mother who put a lot of time into making sure her son was healthy enough to play football, from Pop Warner to his Dallas high school. He spent his university years at Texas A&M, starring in the classroom and on defense, all while receiving the best care available. The Denver Broncos had the second pick overall in the 2011 NFL Draft and showed their smarts by claiming Miller.

What happened over the next four seasons was testimony to Miller's determination. Not only did he keep rising through the ranks as one of the game's most dynamic defenders, he had to address two additional health concerns — failing eyesight and an allergy to natural grass. Miller's asthma and allergies were dealt with via the right medications and precautions. (He took to wearing long-sleeved T-shirts under his jersey to keep his arms from coming in contact with grass.) As for his vision, at one point he used prescription goggles to sharpen his eyesight and protect his eyes.

What others saw of Miller was clear cut and definitive.

"He's the best of the best [at taking down quarterbacks]," asserted Denver offensive tackle Garett Bolles, who practiced against Miller most every day. "He's a freak of nature."

At 6-foot-3 and 250 pounds, Miller has the bulk to beat down blockers all game long. His speed is second to few at his position. In his rookie debut on Denver's home field, Miller forced the Oakland Raiders into a fumble. A week later he registered his first sack. He would go on to post 11.5. The next season he set a Broncos best of 18.5 sacks. It earned him First Team All-Pro honors.

Everything seemed to be in place for a career breakthrough in 2013, but Miller was caught "violating league policy." ESPN reported that Miller used a urine collector to help him pass what was likely to be a failed drug test. The NFL initially

suspended Miller for four games because his urine sample came back positive for a banned substance but bumped it up to six games because Miller had used a facilitator to try to ensure his urine test would come back clean. Miller was back in the starting lineup on October 20, 2013.

Then, in Denver's second-last regular-season game against the Houston Texans, Miller's right knee buckled, ripping his ACL and sidelining him for the Broncos' appearance in Super Bowl XLVIII. That may have been a blessing since the Seattle Seahawks won by a colossal count of 43–8.

Denver returned to the Super Bowl to make up for its embarrassing 35-point loss to the Seahawks. The Carolina Panthers were the sacrificial offerings, and Miller's contribution was enormous. He had six tackles and 2.5 sacks, and he forced two fumbles that led to Broncos touchdowns. The first Carolina cough-up came when Miller ripped the ball out of the hands of quarterback Cam Newton and Denver recovered the ball in the Panthers' end zone. Miller also knocked the ball out of Newton's hand in midthrow later in the game, allowing Denver to add another touchdown and win comfortably, 24–10.

When the game ended with the Broncos celebrating their third Super Bowl title in franchise history, TV cameras zeroed in on Miller looking through the crowd, trying to spot his mom. There were big

hugs when he found her, and they shared a moment with the game MVP trophy.

It would take six years and a trade to the Los Angeles Rams for Miller to once again grace the Super Bowl stage, which he did in the game's 56th installment. He pressured Cincinnati Bengals quarterback Joe Burrow six times, putting him down twice to tie a Super Bowl record for most career sacks. Defensive end Charles Haley was the first to total 4.5 sacks in his illustrious days with the San Francisco 49ers. He reached his number in five Super Bowl appearances; Miller got his in two.

"I felt when I got here we had a special team," said Miller of the Rams. "We wanted to bring it to life, and it feels good to do it."

Little more than a month later, Miller scored a second monster win — he signed as a free agent with the Buffalo Bills for $120 million over six years. Big money for a big-time player. ■

College: Texas A&M University
Drafted: 2011, Denver Broncos, 2nd overall
Years active: 2011–present
Top honors: NFL AP Defensive Rookie of the Year (2011), NFL All-Rookie Team (2011), First Team All-Pro (2012, 2015, 2016), Super Bowl Champion (2015, 2022), Super Bowl MVP (2015)
Hall of Fame induction: N/A

RAY
NITSCHKE LB

G	Int/Yds	TD	FR
190	25/385	2	23

BORN IN ELMWOOD PARK, ILLINOIS, IN 1936, RAY Nitschke lost his father at age three, was orphaned at 13 when his mother died and was raised by an older brother.

Add to that growing up in a rough-and-tumble Chicago neighborhood, and it's a small wonder he turned out to be as tough as his last name. Nitschke. Just the sound of it, the hardness of the syllables, the spit-in-your-eye indomitable nationality of it, provided an understanding into the man. For the rest, you simply had to watch him at work. Balding, wild-eyed, missing his four front teeth and apparently some of his mind, Nitschke became the beating heart — and the obstinate backbone — of Green Bay's underappreciated defense during the glory decade of the '60s.

Legend has it that a metal tower on the Packers' practice field fell over on top of Ray Nitschke. Coach Vince Lombardi ran over to see what was going on. Informed that it was Nitschke underneath the structure, Lombardi barked, "He'll be fine. Get back to work." Nitschke's biography states that the tower actually drove a stake into his helmet, but he went unharmed. The helmet (complete with hole) is on display at the Packers Hall of Fame in Green Bay.

A caring man with a hard shell, Nitschke went from being a notorious hell-raiser to a happy family man, working in a bank during the off-season. His is one of the great success stories of football. Perhaps not as famous today as his linebacking contemporary Dick Butkus of the Chicago Bears, he was nonetheless every bit as visceral, as violent and as uncompromising between the lines on a football field.

Drafted by the Packers instead of his beloved hometown Bears, Nitschke took $300 of his $500 signing bonus, bought a used Pontiac and drove to Green Bay. He spent the next 15 seasons in Packers green-and-gold.

"Oh, that Nitschke was crazy as hell," said defensive back Emlen Tunnell of the early years. "He had the locker right next to mine. Tom Bettis was the middle linebacker then, so Nitschke didn't play much. And Ray used to get on Vinnie [Lombardi] about it. He'd say, real loud in the locker room, 'Just call me the judge. Just call me the judge. 'Cause I'm always on the bench.' Oooh, that would make Vinnie mad."

Under Lombardi's tough-love guidance, though, Nitschke channeled his rage and energy into football. The coach knew what he had in the raw, untamed beast prowling the middle of the field: one of the most competitive people ever to grace that highly competitive business.

Paul Hornung gleefully recounted a memorable nutcracker drill during practice one day. Future Hall of Fame fullback Jim Taylor was the ball carrier. "There was very little running room," said Hornung, "because the [blocking] dummies were up there tight and the blocker — some rookie — just screened Nitschke while Taylor slid by." Lombardi stopped the drill, walked over to Nitschke and said, "Mr. Nitschke, I have read that you are the best linebacker in the NFL, but after watching you just then I find it hard to believe. Now, do it again!" This time, continued Hornung, "Ray grabbed the rookie by the shoulder pads, literally lifted him up and threw him into Jimmy. All Vince said was, 'Next group.' It took them two minutes to get the rookie to come to."

The coach knew what he had in the raw, untamed beast prowling the middle of the field: one of the most competitive people ever to grace that highly competitive business.

Ray Nitschke beats a block against the St. Louis Cardinals in a December 1969 game.

Nitschke the indomitable met his match in his wife-to-be, Jackie. She provided balance and meaning to his life. "Getting married, settling down, getting responsibility for someone beside myself, having someone to love and later adopting the children — all those things were enough motivation for me to quit making a fool of myself," he wrote in his autobiography, *Mean on Sunday.*

Of all the great Packers players of that era, arguably the most loved in Green Bay was, and is, Nitschke. When he died unexpectedly at 61 in 1998 — his heart, of all things, giving out on him — the whole of Wisconsin mourned.

The brawler who used to pitch people through the windows of bars when the mood struck him would doubtless be astounded to learn that a six-inch NFL Legends action figure, No. 66, has been modeled in his image, and that both a bridge in Green Bay and the luncheon prior to induction at the Pro Football Hall of Fame are named in his honor. In 1999 *Sports Illustrated* named him the third greatest linebacker in history, behind only Dick Butkus and Lawrence Taylor. But people in Titletown, U.S.A., know better.

Ray Nitschke didn't just leave his imprint on anyone daft enough to dare to run between the tackles. He left it on the game. ■

College: University of Illinois
Drafted: 1958, Green Bay Packers, 36th overall
Years active: 1958–1972
Top honors: First Team All-Pro (1964, 1966), NFL Champion (1961, 1962, 1965, 1966, 1967), Super Bowl Champion (1966, 1967)
Hall of Fame induction: 1978

ALAN
PAGE DT

G	FR
218	23

How's this for splendid serendipity? Alan Page, the All-Pro defensive tackle who ruled his turf like a Supreme Court associate justice, became one after he retired from the NFL. He's also a Hall of Famer, which is only fitting considering he was born and raised in Canton, Ohio.

Better yet, when Page finished high school in 1963, he got a job working construction in his hometown — the project being the Pro Football Hall of Fame. The guy literally helped lay the groundwork and build the shrine that one day would honor him as a member.

By any measure, physical to statistical, Page ranked among the elite players of his time. For nine consecutive years he was named to the Pro Bowl. He made history in 1971 by being named Defensive Player of the Year and MVP — the first time a defensive player had ever won both awards in the same season. Only one other player has done so since: New York Giants linebacker Lawrence Taylor in 1986.

Page wasn't your standard-issue defensive tackle. He played for Notre Dame, where he helped the Fighting Irish win the 1966 national championship. He was a consensus All-American who, at 6-foot-4, had the height to deflect passes and block kicks.

Yet it was his weight that became a point of contention at the start of his pro career in 1967. The Vikings had drafted Page in the first round and wanted him to bulk up to more than his 240 pounds. Page, however, wanted to drop weight so that he could rely on speed more than size.

The quick attack was Page's specialty. He would often be in the other team's backfield as the running back was getting the handoff.

With great players alongside him, adding their talents to the mix, the Minnesota defensive front four was often the unit that took command and made opponents wish they were in a different division. Carl Eller and Jim Marshall lined up at end while Gary Larsen played tackle alongside Page. Together, they were dubbed the Purple People Eaters after a novelty song by Sheb Wooley that went to No. 1 on the pop charts in 1958. Marshall admitted he and his defensive linemates hated the moniker (and the song). They preferred the Purple Gang after the team's main color. Their motto was, "Meet you at the quarterback."

Whatever their nickname, the Minnesota four had an enjoyable time chasing down quarterbacks and building a reputation as one of the top defensive units in the NFL. Eller and Page were inducted into the Hall of Fame, and there has been a push to get Marshall in as well.

At their peak they were a grueling force to be reckoned with, especially Page. He finished his career with 23 fumble recoveries, 28 blocked kicks and a variance of quarterback sacks. Many of the NFL's older records weren't detailed enough, so the league doesn't have official tackle data prior to 2001. But several online football databases credit Page with 148.5 sacks, while the Hall of Fame has Page's sack count at 173.

However many he had, Page and his defensive linemates met in the backfield often. He was explosive coming off the line, and hit the quarterback every chance he got.

"My job is to go after [the opposition]," said Page. "A defensive player should think of himself as an aggressor, not as a defender."

Jerry Kramer, former division rival and now a fellow Hall of Famer, retired just two years after Page came into the league. In that short window, the veteran Green Bay Packers guard had seen enough of the Minnesota Vikings pass-rushing master to know he'd made the right decision.

"A lot of desire, a lot of heart, a lot of speed," Kramer said of Page. "Any time I think of coming out of retirement, I think of Alan Page."

With Page, the Vikings won four conference titles but lost every time in the Super Bowl. In a four-year stretch, they lost three times by a grand total of 45 points.

It was crushing for some players, but not for Page. He was taking classes at the University of Minnesota Law School while playing in the NFL. He graduated in 1978 and worked for a Minneapolis firm before being appointed special assistant attorney general and later an associate justice of the state Supreme Court.

Outsiders may have been surprised by Page's work in the field of law, but not his family, friends and teammates. This was Page as he dreamed and projected.

"He had instincts that were beyond the average football player," said former Vikings head coach Bud Grant. "Alan was a very bright guy, and he was always interested in why we did things. Not many football players would do that." ■

By any measure, physical to statistical, Page ranked among the elite players of his time.

College: University of Notre Dame
Drafted: 1967, Minnesota Vikings, 15th overall
Years active: 1967–1981
Top honors: First Team All-Pro (1969–71, 1973–75), NFL Championship (1969), NFL AP MVP (1971), NFL AP Defensive Player of the Year (1971)
Hall of Fame induction: 1988

PATRICK
PETERSON CB

G	Int/Yds	Tkl	Ast	Sk	FR	TD
167	29/317	544	63	4.0	12	4

I T HAS HAPPENED COUNTLESS TIMES BEFORE: A university football player, decorated with awards and bowl game victories, decides to forgo his senior year. He declares himself eligible for the NFL Draft. If he's as good as he believes he is, he'll be a first-round pick with a juicy contract.

All he has to do is crack the starting lineup and prove to his teammates and peers he can hold his own against some of the best athletes in the game. Sounds simple, right? It was for Patrick Peterson.

In one year, he went from being the best defensive player in U.S. college football to a first-round draft pick to a rookie defensive back who proved as unshakable as an auditor come tax time. That was Peterson, the former Louisiana State University star who lit it up in 2011 with a flair for the dramatic.

On his first play in his first preseason game, the Arizona Cardinals cornerback intercepted a pass against the San Diego Chargers and returned it 85 yards for a touchdown.

In one year, he went from being the best defensive player in U.S. college football to a first-round draft pick to a rookie defensive back who proved as unshakable as an auditor come tax time.

During the regular season, he became the first player in league history to return four punts for 80 yards or more in a single season. He scored four touchdowns on punt returns to tie a single-season record shared by three others (Devin Hester, Jack Christiansen and Rick Upchurch). One of those touchdowns covered 99 yards and sealed an overtime win for the Cardinals. That earned him a spot in the 2012 Pro Bowl as a return man.

But Peterson wasn't done there. When he wasn't returning punts to give the Arizona offense choice field position, he was defending his side of the field like a seasoned pro. He was credited with 59 solo tackles, 13 pass deflections, two interceptions, two fumble recoveries and a quarterback sack.

"He's a guy who makes an impact in every single game he's in," San Francisco 49ers tight end George Kittle told NFL.com. "It doesn't matter who he's playing. He's fired up and ready to roll."

"He baits you a lot; makes you think you're open, then closes quick," said Los Angeles Rams receiver Robert Woods. "You've got to be perfect [playing against Peterson]."

Things were going Peterson's way until 2014, a season that saw the Cardinals make the playoffs but lose to the Carolina Panthers. Peterson had an uncharacteristically poor season. He was criticized for appearing sluggish and out of step. Eventually, Peterson revealed he had been diagnosed with type 2 diabetes.

"It was very frustrating, very scary going through that situation and not knowing what the hell is going on," said Peterson, who put on what he called "massive weight" — 21 pounds, which increased his playing weight to 224.

"Not being able to move the way I was able to move in previous years. I believe that was definitely the cause of my struggle," he said. "As an athlete, we try to fight through those kinds of things. Obviously, I wasn't able to make it."

Peterson worked hard to return to his playing weight of 203 pounds. Once there, he was a force. In the 2015 playoffs, he picked off a pass from the Green Bay Packers' Aaron Rodgers and returned it 100 yards for a touchdown. A defensive holding call wiped out the play. Arizona still won and faced the Carolina Panthers in the NFC Championship Game. Peterson had another long interception return (70 yards), but the Cardinals made too many mistakes that day and lost 49–15.

For the next three seasons, he continued his Pro Bowl streak, topping out at eight consecutive selections.

On May 16, 2019, the NFL announced Peterson had violated the league's performance-enhancing drug restrictions. He was hit with a six-game suspension and forced to sit it out in full. Peterson was back in the lineup by mid-October.

Before his return, there were comments and social media outbursts indicating Peterson wanted out and was open to a trade. That went on until Cardinals GM Steve Keim told an Arizona radio station that he didn't understand why the Peterson trade speculation continued.

"I have addressed it multiple times — we are not trading Patrick Peterson," said Keim.

He didn't, but in 2021 Peterson chose to sign as a free agent with the Minnesota Vikings, where he brought a whole other level of expertise and leadership to his team's secondary. He proved that in the Vikings' last game of the season.

Having intercepted at least one pass in every season he had played, Peterson vowed to maintain that streak against the Chicago Bears. And sure enough he did, by stepping in front of an Andy Dalton pass and plucking it like low-hanging fruit. But the best part? Peterson ran the ball 65 yards, all the way to the Chicago end zone to clinch a Minnesota win. It wasn't enough to put the Vikings in the playoffs, but it was another superb addition to the Patrick Peterson highlight reel. ■

College: Louisiana State University
Drafted: 2011, Arizona Cardinals, 5th overall
Years active: 2011–present
Top honors: NFL All-Rookie Team (2011), First Team All-Pro (2011, 2013, 2015)
Hall of Fame induction: N/A

MEL
RENFRO CB

G	Int/Yds	FR	TD
174	52/626	13	3

THEY WERE A LEGENDARY LOT ON defense in Big D in those days.

Ed "Too Tall" Jones, Randy White, Bob Lilly and Harvey Martin along the line, causing havoc and inciting terror; Thomas "Hollywood" Henderson and Chuck Howley nestled right in behind them; and, dotting the secondary, names that would go on to lasting Dallas Cowboys fame — Charlie Waters, Cliff Harris, Benny Barnes and Everson Walls.

But none can forget Mel Renfro at both safety and corner — arguably the finest, purest athlete on a lavishly talented Cowboys team.

Doomsday, they dubbed 'em. And with ample reason.

"My whole game was beating the man in front of me," Renfro would recall. "It was a matter of studying the opponent as well as you can and knowing the tendencies.

"You had to have the speed, agility and quickness to get the job done."

A product of Houston, Texas, Renfro spent four seasons at the University of Oregon in Eugene, shredding defenses at tailback while branching out to run track. While at Oregon, he was also part of a world-record-setting relay team and found himself named to the All-America track and field team in both high hurdles and long jump.

On the gridiron, he led the Ducks in rushing for three consecutive seasons, finishing his collegiate career with 1,540 yards and 23 touchdowns. Clearly, this was a very special athlete.

An off-field injury in 1963 nearly ended Renfro's pro football career before it had even begun. President John F. Kennedy was assassinated on November 22 of that year, two weeks before the NFL Draft. Upon hearing the tragic news, Renfro impulsively slammed his fist into a mirror in anger and sorrow, severing a nerve in that hand and requiring surgery.

Renfro's injury made more than one potential team shy away from selecting him on draft day, and the Cowboys were able to wait until the second round to call his name with their 17th pick.

When Renfro arrived in Dallas in 1964, his expectation was to be used on the offensive side of the line of scrimmage as a running back or a receiver. Unfortunately, those positions were already filled.

"[Tom] Landry took me aside and explained that he had Frank Clarke as a receiver, and he had just made trades for Buddy Dial and Tommy McDonald," Renfro would explain later. "He didn't want me to sit on the bench, so he planned to use me as a safety until there was an opening on offense.

"I guess I made one fat mistake: I played defense too well."

True that.

In Renfro's rookie season, spent at safety, he led the 'Boys with seven interceptions and the entire NFL in punt/kickoff return yardage, including an eye-popping 273 in a game against Green Bay, which remains a franchise high.

He also had speed to burn — once clocking a 4.65-second 40-yard dash — and the intuition to shut down the most dangerous of receivers. Before too long, quarterbacks weren't throwing often in Renfro's direction. He still managed to top the INT charts in 1969, pilfering 10 passes.

Those attacking gifts that had entranced scouts during the lead-in precipitated a brief shift to running back in his rookie season.

But Renfro injured an ankle in his first game at the position, and by the time it had healed Landry had decided stopping big plays, not making them, was No. 20's forte.

The Cowboys, a bonafide title threat every year during Renfro's extraordinary stay, would go on to collect a pair of Super Bowl titles — one versus the Miami Dolphins in 1972 and another against the Denver Broncos a half-dozen seasons later. Over his 14-year career, he would pick off 52 opposition passes — a mark that remains the Dallas franchise career record. Renfro also made 10 trips to the Pro Bowl and was selected to the All-Pro team on seven occasions.

Aged 36, he retired following the Cowboys' 27–10 Super Bowl triumph over the Broncos at the Louisiana Superdome on January 15, 1978.

A fitting exit.

Eight years later, Renfro was honored with induction into the College Football Hall of Fame, and a decade after that, in 1996, the Pro Football Hall of Fame swung open its doors for one of the most accomplished secondary men of a generation.

"I'm just thrilled," he confessed in Canton. "I had to pinch myself to see if I were dreaming. This is monumental, fantastic."

In a defensive line littered with Hall of Famers, so was Mel Renfro. ■

College: University of Oregon
Drafted: 1964, Dallas Cowboys, 17th overall
Years active: 1964–1977
Top honors: First Team All-Pro (1969), Super Bowl Champion (1971, 1977)
Hall of Fame induction: 1996

DEION SANDERS CB-WR

G	Int/Yds	Tkl	Ast	Sk	FR	TD
188	53/1,331	512	20	1.0	13	9

G	Rec	Yds	Y/R	TD
188	60	784	13.1	3

URBAN MYTH HAD IT THAT THE DO-EVERYTHING DEION Sanders could cover 40 yards in 4.57 seconds — running backward.

Supposedly there were scouts and personnel directors at an NFL evaluation camp who got to clock Sanders for themselves. They also checked his 40-yard dash time running forward. Sanders turned in a 4.27. A younger Bill Belichick, then the defensive coordinator of the New York Giants, was quoted as saying Sanders ran "a sub-2."

That was how it started for Neon Deion, the left-handed, spray-hitting, base-stealing virtuoso, who hit a home run with the New York Yankees the same week he scored his first NFL touchdown as a member of the Atlanta Falcons. He would later go on to play in a World Series and then two Super Bowls, winning them both. Some loved him, others hated him, but there was no denying that Sanders was a monstrous talent with a flair for the dramatic. He was young, rich and seemingly on top of the world.

So why, then, did he try to end it all by driving his black Mercedes over a 30-foot cliff? Because nothing mattered to the game's biggest showman, neither the fame nor the money. His life had an emptiness that he couldn't fill with the richest contract or the hottest car.

"When I hit bottom," wrote Sanders in his autobiography, *Power, Money & Sex: How Success Almost Ruined My Life*, "the car started sliding awkwardly, rocking back and forth, until I came down hard and slid to the bottom of the hill. Miraculously, I walked away without a scratch."

He was not, however, unchanged.

Sanders considers himself a happy man these days, more relaxed and fulfilled. His faith has given him the depth of character to match the many feats he accomplished as his era's greatest two-sport athlete.

As the trash-talking, brash and bejeweled Prime Time, Sanders was larger than life. In his MLB career he played for four teams, including the 1992 Atlanta Braves, who made it to the World Series. In the Fall Classic against the Toronto Blue Jays, Sanders batted .533 with eight hits, two doubles, four runs and an RBI, all while playing with a broken bone in his foot.

In football he was vastly, outrageously superior. He ran back kicks and punts, intercepted passes and was as dangerous a scoring weapon as any of the Falcons' receivers. In fact, Sanders would occasionally line up at wide receiver and race downfield to catch passes. In his five years in Atlanta he scored 10 touchdowns: three on interceptions, three on kickoff returns, two on punt returns and two on pass receptions. He overcelebrated every one of them.

"How do you think defensive backs get attention?" asked Sanders, who played multiple sports at Florida State University. "They don't pay nobody to be humble."

Sanders was equally a braggadocio when he high-stepped his stuff for the San Francisco 49ers and Dallas Cowboys. He won Super Bowl XXIX with the 49ers and Super Bowl XXX with the Cowboys. (Sanders had become such a pain in the Cowboys' neck that when the time came to sign him as a free agent, Dallas owner Jerry Jones asked his players if it was okay to do that. They said yes.)

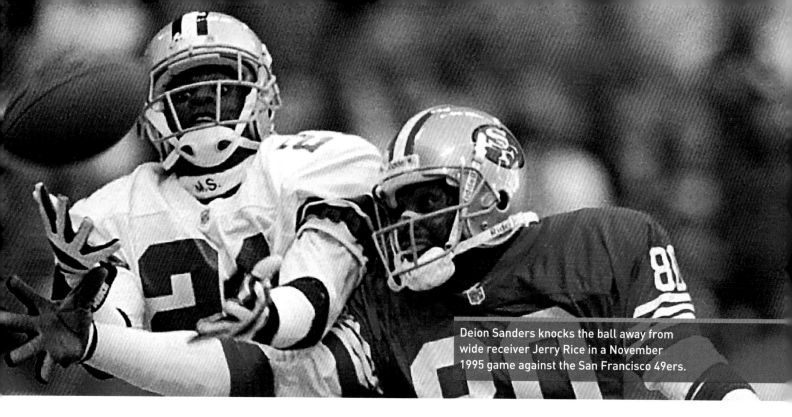

Deion Sanders knocks the ball away from wide receiver Jerry Rice in a November 1995 game against the San Francisco 49ers.

Sanders was so dominant on defense that some teams wouldn't even bother to throw his way.

"It was part of our game plan to keep the ball away from him," said New Orleans Saints receiver Michael Haynes at the time.

With the Cowboys, Sanders continued to strut and be well-paid for his bravado. He could shut down entire offenses and intercept passes before taunting his former teammates as he ran down the sidelines en route to an easy touchdown, as he did against Atlanta. In 1996 he was on the field for 50 percent of the Cowboys' offensive plays and 80 percent on defense. He was living the dream life, even performing a rap song entitled "Must Be the Money." Everywhere you looked, there was Neon Deion, smiling, shilling, playmaking. He was a one-man corporation. Then came the crash landing in 1997.

Sanders's wife had sued him for divorce and refused to bring their children to Cincinnati, where he was playing baseball for the Reds. Suddenly the money no longer mattered.

"I had just had the best season of my career. Everything I touched turned to gold," Sanders wrote in his autobiography. "But inside, I was broken and totally defeated ... I remember sitting at the back of the practice field one afternoon, away from everybody, and tears were running down my face. I was saying to myself, 'This is so meaningless. I'm so unhappy. We're winning every week and I'm playing great, but I'm not happy.'"

After driving his car over a cliff and surviving, Sanders began to reshape his life through religion. He learned to separate Prime Time from real time. He left Dallas and signed with the Washington Redskins. A year later he retired, then un-retired to join the Baltimore Ravens for the 2004 season. That year he intercepted a pass and brought it back for a touchdown, the ninth interception return touchdown of his career, tying him for second behind Rod Woodson (12).

After re-retiring, this time for good, Sanders worked as a football commentator before finding some solace in charitable deeds. He mentored two young football players: Devin Hester, the Chicago Bears high-speed kick returner, and U.S. college running back Noel Devine. He raised money for victims of Hurricane Katrina by challenging professional athletes in football, baseball, basketball and hockey to donate to relief efforts.

The new Deion Sanders is happier than ever. His life isn't a mix of conflicting sports, juggled schedules and empty desperation. It's calmer.

And Sanders can handle that. ∎

College: Florida State University
Drafted: 1989, Atlanta Falcons, 5th overall
Years active: 1989–2005
Top honors: First Team All-Pro (1992–1994, 1996–1998), NFL AP Defensive Player of the Year (1994), Super Bowl champion (1994, 1995)
Hall of Fame induction: 2011

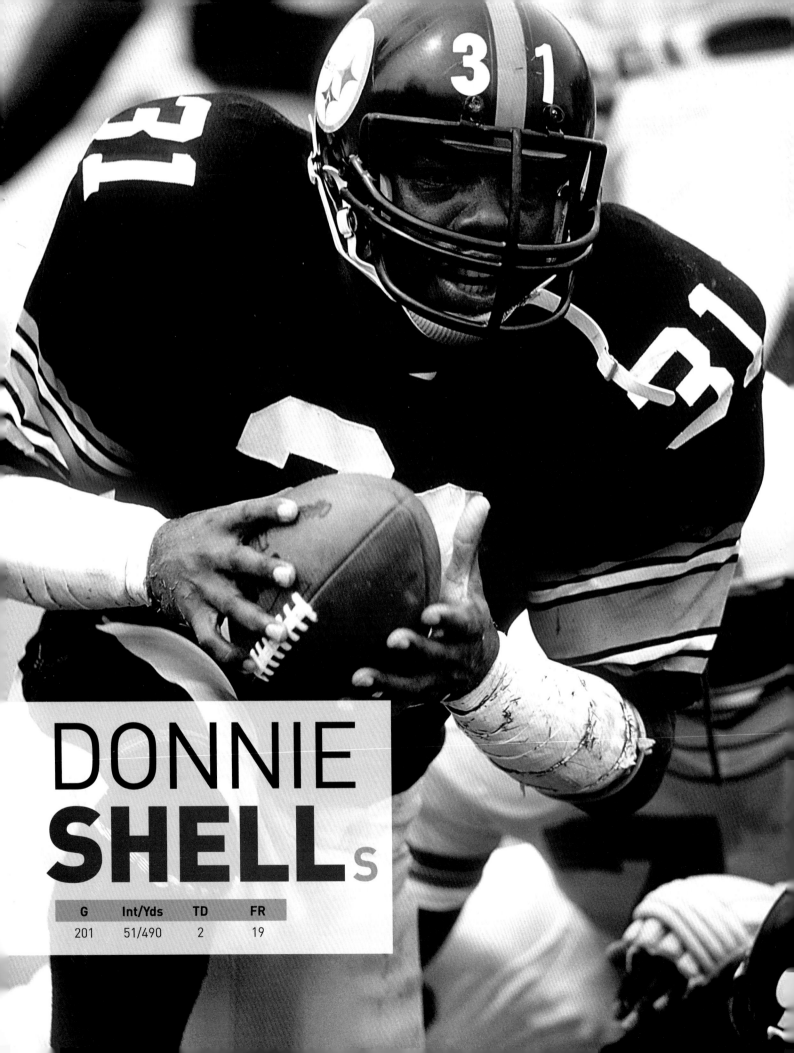

DONNIE
SHELLs

G	Int/Yds	TD	FR
201	51/490	2	19

DONNIE SHELL WAS SO STONE-COLD stunned by the news that all he could muster was, "Wow. Wow. Wow."

If you followed his career and retirement from the Pittsburgh Steelers, you'd appreciate why he was at such a loss for complete sentences. At 67, having seen so many of his teammates inducted into the Pro Football Hall of Fame, he figured his chances of joining them were infinitesimally slim.

Then, less than a month into 2020, his phone rang and Shell was suddenly where he always wanted to be — in a place where the best of the greats are honored, where an improbable story can come to a magnificent conclusion.

He was, after all, a key rivet in Pittsburgh's Steel Curtain. He played behind a defensive front anchored by Joe Greene, a linebacking crew that featured Jack Lambert and Jack Ham, and a secondary led by Mel Blount — all of them Hall of Famers, some of whom had been campaigning to get Shell enough votes to earn his spot in the Canton, Ohio, shrine.

Based on statistics alone, there was a compelling case to be made for him. But after the 1974 NFL Draft had ended, both Shell's name and his school, South Carolina State, had not been called — and that year's talent lottery went a full 17 rounds.

Shell's university coach, Willie Jeffries, told him there were tryouts available for him in Denver, Houston and Pittsburgh. Jeffries told Shell he had to go with the Steelers because they were looking for character players who worked hard, just like Shell. The former university linebacker turned strong safety took that to heart. The instant he stepped onto the Steelers' practice field, he began hustling and making plays as if he'd been in the NFL for years.

Of course, it helped that the veterans were on strike, still negotiating a new collective bargaining agreement with the league. That afforded the rookies more time for practice repetitions, and no one used that added opportunity better than Shell.

"I felt good enough to think I would have made the team even if the veterans had been there [right from the start of training camp]," Shell told NFL.com. "I didn't know we'd win a Super Bowl in my rookie year." And in his second year with the Steelers, too.

The more Shell played and the more experience he earned, the better he became. His role as strong safety was to cover every type of receiver the opposition threw his way, from the bigger tight ends to the fastest deep threats to running backs who slipped out of the backfield and into the defensive secondary.

Shell also showed how he could manhandle the NFL's powerhouse rushers. The Shell highlight reel includes a 1978 "wow" collision involving the Steelers' defensive back and the Houston Oilers' semi-trailer, Earl Campbell. On this play, the 233-pound Campbell was carrying the ball past the Pittsburgh defensive line into open field when the 190-pound Shell shocked everyone by stopping Campbell on the spot, lifting him off the turf then slamming him down like a bag of cement.

That hit damaged one of Campbell's ribs and finished him for the rest of the game.

He was, after all, a key rivet in Pittsburgh's Steel Curtain.

"That's the one time I was happy to see Earl leave," admitted Greene. "I wasn't happy to see him get hurt, but I was happy to see him leave."

That was always the goal of the Steelers' defense — make the other side feel even its best players were no match, not that day, not ever. With that in mind, Shell put together a formidable list of accomplishments. He played in 201 games, second only to center Mike Webster's franchise best of 220. Shell had 19 fumble recoveries and a career count of 51 interceptions, a record for NFL strong safeties.

The number that mattered most, though, was four. As in, four Super Bowl championships in six seasons. It was a triumph that made the Steelers the team of the 1970s and lifted its players to all-star, Hall of Fame distinction. For Shell, it just took a lot longer.

"Don't give up on your dreams and aspirations," he said of his journey to the top of the sport. "I believe God created everybody and gave them certain talents and gifts. Some had to work harder to make those gifts come out, and I was one of those people." ∎

College: South Carolina State University
Drafted: undrafted
Years active: 1974–1987
Top honors: Super Bowl Champion (1974, 1975, 1978, 1979), First Team All-Pro (1979, 1980, 1982)
Hall of Fame induction: 2020

MIKE
SINGLETARY LB

G	Int/Yds	Sk	FR
179	7/44	19	12

THE EYES OF MIKE SINGLETARY WERE INDEED THE windows to his soul. They looked as if they were going to pop right out of his head. Right out of his helmet, too. They burned with intensity. One scorching look from Singletary, and wild animals would have run for cover.

Singletary's soul was no less passionate. He wanted to be the best middle linebacker in the game. The best teammate. The best husband. The best father. Everything worth doing was worth doing to its fullest; that was Singletary's guiding principle. "If you want to be the best, if you want to be the best at something, you will not be denied," he said. "You're not going to quit. You're not going to stop. You're going to keep fighting."

Singletary was a never-quit fighter who overcame his lack of size (6-foot, 230 pounds) with a crackling disposition. His tackles bordered on assault and battery. One of his all-time favorite targets was Los Angeles Rams running back Eric Dickerson. In a 1985 playoff showdown in Chicago, Dickerson took a handoff on third and one and looked to have room running through the right side of the Bears' defense. Singletary charged in, stopped Dickerson dead in his tracks, then threw him for a loss. To celebrate, Singletary began barking like a dog.

A bemused linebacker, Wilbur Marshall, said after Chicago's 24–0 win, "Dickerson didn't know where he was at."

Chicago head coach Mike Ditka had a better story about that playoff game. The day before, he was talking to the offense while Singletary was addressing the defense in a room next door. As Ditka tells it, what started out as a calm and rational speech quickly turned into a Knute Rockne rant, complete with Singletary screaming and his defensive mates turning over tables and trashing chairs.

With his determination and his smarts, Singletary was the defensive catalyst of the Bears' 1985 season, which saw them go 15-1. In the ensuing playoffs, Chicago dominated from start to finish, ravaging the New England Patriots in Super Bowl XX. That season, Singletary recorded 109 solo tackles, three sacks, one interception and three fumble recoveries. He also knocked down 10 passes. He was named the NFL's Defensive Player of the Year.

Singletary's need to be the best was forged in childhood. He was born the last of 10 children in Houston, Texas. When he was five years old, his brother Dale died. When he was 12, his parents divorced and his dad, a Pentecostal

pastor, left. That same year another brother, Brady, was killed in a car crash.

Singletary was lost, with "no confidence ... no self-esteem," he said. His mother sat him down and told him he could accomplish anything he wanted because there was greatness in him. She told Singletary to trust in his faith and believe in its values. Singletary said that as soon as his mom finished her talk, he went to his room and wrote down his goals: "Find a way to get a scholarship to go to college; become an All-American in college; get my degree; go to the NFL; and buy my mom a house and take care of her for the rest of my life."

Singletary went to Baylor University and was a two-time All-American. The Bears drafted him in the second round in 1981 and, by the seventh game of his rookie season, Singletary was giving opponents fits with his crazy-eyed look and samurai warrior attacks.

In 12 seasons in Chicago, the voracious defender appeared in 10 Pro Bowls, made 1,488 tackles and was voted to both the Pro Football and College Football Halls of Fame.

It was his wife, Kim, who met Singletary while they were attending Baylor in the late 1970s, that introduced him as a Pro Football Hall of Fame inductee. He called her his best friend.

"A lot of people think I'm corny," Singletary told the *Chicago Tribune*. "I want it that way, and I like it that way. You watch me as close as you can, and I'll do my best to teach you something."

Corny, keen, a natural leader — those qualities served Singletary well in his post-playing career, where he coached in different capacities and tutored stars such as Ray Lewis and Patrick Willis. For a time, Singletary worked as a senior advisor to the NFL's football operations department. He later returned to coaching in the since-folded Alliance of American Football. Whatever is next for him, bet on Singletary imparting his wisdom to young defensive players looking to be better.

Offensive stars of tomorrow, be warned. ▪

> ## *Singletary's soul was no less passionate. He wanted to be the best middle linebacker in the game. The best teammate. The best husband. The best father. Everything worth doing was worth doing to its fullest; that was Singletary's guiding principle.*

College: Baylor University
Drafted: 1981, Chicago Bears, 38th overall
Years active: 1981–1992
Top honors: First Team All-Pro (1984–89, 1991), NFL AP Defensive Player of the Year (1985, 1988), Super Bowl Champion (1985), NFL Walter Payton Man of the Year (1990)
Hall of Fame induction: 1998

BRUCE
SMITH DE

G	Sk	Tkl	FF	FR
279	200.0	1,224	43	15

TOMMY KRAMER WAS THE FIRST TO go down, in 1985. Jesse Palmer became the record-breaker in 2003. In between, the list of victims included John Elway, Joe Montana, Phil Simms, Dan Marino, Steve Young and 70 others, including Ken O'Brien, who was hunted down and bagged more than a dozen times by Bruce Smith.

It's no wonder that O'Brien, a Pro Bowl quarterback for the New York Jets, didn't jump like a startled cat at the mention of Smith's name. The Buffalo Bills defensive end had that effect on quarterbacks. He had the same effect on his teammates.

With the Bills trailing the Kansas City Chiefs in a key AFC matchup, Smith stomped into the offensive meeting at halftime and yelled at his teammates, "Gosh darn it, stop turning over the football." (Okay, he didn't say 'gosh darn it.') Aware Smith would be even angrier if the game ended the same way it began, Buffalo's offense held onto the ball, scored 17 points and easily defeated Kansas City.

"I'm not a very outspoken person until the time comes," said Smith afterward. "If I step on somebody's toes, I'm not sorry about it because it's the truth and it hurts."

Smith stepped on toes, rammed helmets and did whatever he could to make quarterbacks worry and wince. He chased lesser-knowns such as Browning Nagle and Dave Brown as unremittingly as he hounded Drew Bledsoe and Donovan McNabb. As a harasser of quarterbacks, Smith was an equal opportunist.

"I watched my first NFL game in Detroit in 1934 when I was a kid, and I think Bruce Smith is the best defensive lineman I have ever seen," said the late Bills owner Ralph Wilson. "I'm not saying that because he's a Buffalo Bill. I'm saying that because I have seen all the great ones, and I don't think anyone was ever better."

Buffalo's first-overall selection in the 1985 draft, Smith was the team's all-time sack leader by 1989 (52) and one of the Bills' undisputed leaders. With Jim Kelly, Andre Reed and Thurman Thomas holding onto the ball on offense, Smith inspired a defense that backstopped Buffalo to a record four consecutive Super Bowl appearances in the 1990s.

In 13 of his 19 seasons, Smith recorded 10 or more sacks. His best showing came in 1990, when he got to the quarterback 19 times and earned his first of two Defensive Player of the Year awards. The same year he was voted to the Pro Bowl, an honor he would receive 11 times. Virtually each time the ball was snapped, he was double-teamed by offensive linemen and blocking backs.

"There are five players in this league who can take a team on their shoulders and make a difference," said New York Jets quarterback Boomer Esiason. "Barry Sanders, Jerry Rice, Emmitt Smith, Thurman Thomas and Bruce Smith."

Buffalo fans wanted Smith to retire as a Bill, but it wasn't to be. In 1999 he was released to free up salary-cap room and, two days later, signed with Washington, which was close to his hometown of Virginia Beach. Smith managed 29 sacks in four seasons with the Redskins, including the 199th of his career to lift him ahead of Reggie White for the all-time record.

Smith's pursuit of the record wasn't well-received in all corners. Several sports columnists and commentators criticized him for staying in the game longer than he should have and for taking a roster spot that should have gone to a younger player. He was called selfish and record-hungry. And when Redskins coach Steve Spurrier benched him, Smith spoke out, saying he was still the team's best pass rusher even at age 40.

Toward the end of Smith's final season, one newspaper quoted an unnamed NFL scout as saying, "Bruce Smith is just limping toward that sack record. The first four games he seemed to be pumped up, but the last two weeks he looks bad."

While he wasn't the player he once was, Smith was good enough to set the record, which may stand for some time. It happened on December 7, 2003, at Giants Stadium. Smith had knocked New York's starting quarterback, Kerry Collins, out of the game and, in the fourth quarter, was able to tackle his replacement, the Canadian-born Palmer, for a 7-yard loss.

The Redskins players rushed onto the field to congratulate Smith, who was given the game ball. Later in the Washington dressing room, he opened a gift that had been given to him by his tailor. It was a burgundy-colored robe with the Redskins' logo on the back and "All Time" written across the front.

He wore it with pride — the all-time hunter content at last. ∎

College: Virginia Polytechnic Institute and State University
Drafted: 1985, Buffalo Bills, 1st overall
Years active: 1985–2003
Top honors: NFL AP Defensive Player of the Year (1990, 1996)
Hall of Fame induction: 2009

MICHAEL
STRAHAN DE

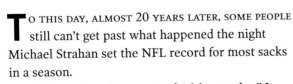

G	Int/Yds	Tkl	Ast	Sk	FR
216	4/124	854	188	141.5	15

To this day, almost 20 years later, some people still can't get past what happened the night Michael Strahan set the NFL record for most sacks in a season.

Said the critics, "It wasn't a legitimate play." It was an act, a contrivance between Strahan and his target, Green Bay Packers quarterback Brett Favre. The fix had to be on, since Favre rolled right without any blockers and left himself unprotected against an incoming Strahan. It was a cream-puff tackle, but a sack just the same. And it gave the New York Giants defensive end 22.5 for the 2001 season, bettering New York Jet Mark Gastineau's record of 22 set in 1984.

But while fans and media picked away at the merits of the play, Strahan explained it in a rational way. He pointed out that he didn't have a sack in the first three weeks of the season. That meant he rang up 22.5 sacks in 13 games — an astounding bit of work that has gone unappreciated.

"That's hard to match, and I've never spoken like this about it because I've always kind of taken it," Strahan told the NFL Network of what he's faced over the years. "I always have to say, 'If you don't like it, then break it.'"

That he was even in a position to approach the sack record comes with a story all its own. Before Strahan took on a leadership role with the Giants, he studied Lawrence Taylor and how he oversaw the dressing room. It took close to a decade for Strahan to earn the trust of the general manager, the coaches and his teammates. And he had a lot of time to make up for.

For much of his youth, Strahan barely played the game. His father, Gene, was in the military and moved his family to a US Army base in Germany. Strahan was a linebacker with the Mannheim Bison youth team. When that season ended, Michael flew to Houston to live with his uncle Art, a former NFL defensive lineman, and play at Westbury High School.

Based on one season of high school football, Texas Southern University offered Strahan a scholarship, which he happily accepted. By his senior year, he was being scouted by NFL personnel who liked Strahan's quickness and his ability to shed blockers and get to the quarterback. He had a Texas Southern–record 19 sacks and drew a slew of awards as the Division 1-AA Defensive Player of the Year.

The Giants took him with the 40th pick overall in the 1993 NFL Draft. He improved as an NFL player and managed 18 sacks, but that was a combined count over four years. By 1997 the time had come for Strahan to live up to his potential and, at long last, he was ready to create some honest-to-goodness bedlam.

In 1997 he was credited with 68 tackles and 14 sacks. The following season, he had 15 sacks and an interception that he returned 24 yards for a New York touchdown. Things got so good for Strahan that from 2001 to 2003 — a span of 48 regular-season games — he topped out at 52 sacks.

With everything he had won in his career, Strahan could have retired with few regrets. But the missing link was all about winning an NFL championship. In his first Super Bowl appearance, Super Bowl XXXV, his dream was crushed by a 34-7 loss to the Baltimore Ravens that left Strahan wondering how much longer he could play at a high level and still have a chance at winning the Vince Lombardi Trophy.

His second shot at the Super Bowl seven years later didn't look any easier when the Giants' opponent turned out to be the 18-0 New England Patriots, out to make history by surpassing the perfect 17-0 Miami Dolphins of 1972.

When the game began, Strahan vowed to relax and not fret over every bounce of the ball. "I've been uptight in the Super Bowl, and it didn't work," Strahan said. The game plan was to play hard and enjoy the moment. Surely they enjoyed how disruptive they were to the Patriots and their ace quarterback Tom Brady.

With the fabled helmet catch by receiver David Tyree, combined with a defense that allowed Brady only 14 points, the Giants handed New England its first loss in 19 games. Strahan celebrated like it was his last game, which it was.

After announcing his retirement, Strahan took a job as a member of *Fox NFL Sunday*'s pregame crew. His on-air partners include Terry Bradshaw, Howie Long and former head coach Jimmy Johnson. With his upbeat personality and his gap-toothed smile, Strahan has maintained his popularity — which means he's going to keep hearing about the sack that set the record. Was it real or really tainted?

Consider it one for the mystery books. ▓

> *With everything he had won in his career, Strahan could have retired with few regrets. But the missing link was all about winning an NFL championship.*

College: Texas Southern University
Drafted: 1993, New York Giants, 40th overall
Years active: 1993–2007
Top honors: First Team All-Pro (1997, 1998, 2001, 2003), NFL AP Defensive Player of the Year (2001), Super Bowl Champion (2007)
Hall of Fame induction: 2014

TERRELL
SUGGS LB

G	Int/Yds	TD	Sk	FR
244	7/144	1	139	15

FOR 16 SEASONS, HE ESTABLISHED HIMSELF IN THE SAME position with the same team. He became a franchise leader in a number of statistics, the most fun being quarterback sacks. Nothing made Terrell Suggs happier than manhandling the other team's starting pivot. Come to think of it, hauling down the backup quarterback wasn't bad, either.

Then things changed. The Baltimore Ravens, who had once made Suggs the highest-paid linebacker in the NFL, offered a deal — but so did the Arizona Cardinals. They offered a one-year, $7 million package, and Suggs took it. Then things changed again. Arizona put Suggs on waivers, and the Kansas City Chiefs claimed him three days later.

Kansas City wanted the former Defensive Player of the Year after losing a pair of defensive ends to injuries. Suggs and his pass-rushing skills were hurried in to provide depth and to help the Chiefs win Super Bowl LIV. That was how head coach Andy Reid had it planned, and that was precisely how it played out in the 31–20 final.

"First, you want to know if he can still play. Then you want to know how he'll fit in with your team," said Reid of Suggs. "We have strong leaders, some very good veterans. [Suggs] added to that."

The biggest risk with signing Suggs was his age (then 37). It was the same story for the start of the 2021 season when he waited for teams to call and make an offer. Having not played a down since that Super Bowl win with the Chiefs, it was easy to understand why Suggs had disappeared from the NFL's radar.

Not that long ago, he was drawing all kinds of attention but for the wrong reason.

In a 2012 mini-controversy, Suggs tore his Achilles tendon in his right foot while working out in an Arizona fitness center — at least, that was his story. Another story was that he blew out his Achilles tendon playing basketball, an activity the Ravens wanted their Defensive Player of the Year to avoid. It was even written into the "don't do that" section of the contract he signed.

The fallen Suggs vowed to get back up in a hurry. On October 21, 2012, against the Houston Texans, Suggs returned to the amazement of many and took his place in the Ravens' defensive unit. Not only did he return, he contributed four tackles and a sack. That he needed a mere five-and-a-half months to recover from having his Achilles tendon surgically repaired made him both a prophet and a medical marvel.

"I wasn't surprised for the simple fact that everybody in the building knew I could do it, I could come back," Suggs told the Baltimore Sun. "It was just all a matter of when."

Tough as tungsten, with a voracious appetite for hunting ball carriers, Suggs showed those traits well before being the 10th pick overall in 2003 out of Arizona State, one of the youngest players (at age 20) ever drafted on the defensive side of the ball. The Ravens chose the Sun Devils star to team with the marauding Ray Lewis, who was on the verge of becoming one of the greatest linebackers of all time.

Ironically, along with a few other 2003 blue-chippers expected to be high picks in that draft, Suggs had appeared in commercials for Madden NFL 2004, with all the soon-to-be rookies seen doing menial chores for

Lewis. In his bit, Suggs was seen lugging the Ravens linebacker's bags.

"The first thing I thought about [after being drafted by Baltimore] was me and Ray Lewis doing that commercial, and how he made me do his laundry," said Suggs at the time. "And now it's actually going to be a reality."

Over the intervening seasons, Suggs became more than just a Lewis sidekick. In each of his first four pro games, Suggs set an NFL record by recording a sack. In 2011 he was at his zenith, especially when Lewis was sidelined with a toe injury. In the four games Lewis missed, the Ravens won every outing, with Suggs recording seven sacks. Baltimore finished 12-4 and won the AFC North title, with Suggs taking AFC Defensive Player of the Year laurels.

That set the stage for an even more memorable 2012.

After damaging his Achilles and then reclaiming his spot on the defense, Suggs aided Baltimore's run through the playoffs. Even with a second injury — a torn biceps muscle picked up late in the regular season — he had two sacks, 10 tackles and a forced fumble against the Denver Broncos in the divisional playoffs. He continued to help lead the push to the Super Bowl when the Baltimore defense held the New England Patriots scoreless in the second half of the AFC Championship Game. Afterward, Suggs dialed down his frequent criticisms of Patriots superstar quarterback Tom Brady: "You gotta play perfect to beat him, and we played perfect."

Suggs wasn't as domineering weeks later in Super Bowl XLVII, but his teammates did their part in a 34–31 victory over the San Francisco 49ers that gave Suggs his first NFL title. It was a long wait for a guy who was once the youngest player in the NFL.

When Super Bowl LIV ended with another ring for the linebacker, a smiling Suggs did countless interviews, most of them asking if his championship relationship with Kansas City had another year or two left in it. All Suggs would say is that the Chiefs were an option, and so was retirement.

That's the kind of scenario all football players dream about — the opportunity to leave the game after winning its ultimate trophy. And better yet, winning it twice. ■

College: Arizona State University
Drafted: 2003, Baltimore Ravens, 10th overall
Years active: 2003–present
Top honors: NFL AP Defensive Rookie of the Year (2003), NFL All-Rookie Team (2003), First Team All-Pro (2011), NFL AP Defensive Player of the Year (2011), Super Bowl Champion (2012, 2019)
Hall of Fame induction: N/A

JACK
TATUM DB

G	Int/Yds	FR
136	37/736	10

HE USUALLY WORE BLACK, WHICH MADE PERFECT sense. He played "safety," which didn't.

There was always something bordering on visceral in the way Jack Tatum used to summon every ion in his body to slam headlong into the opposition.

"My idea of a good hit," Tatum once said, "is when the victim wakes up on the sidelines with train whistles blowing in his head."

This was clearly a proponent of the legendary Vince Lombardi line: "Ballet is a contact sport. Football is a collision sport."

There was always something bordering on visceral in the way Jack Tatum used to summon every ion in his body to slam headlong into the opposition.

Tatum took that philosophy to a whole different level during his nine seasons in Oakland, and what he accomplished as a Raider was considerable. By the time of his trade to the Houston Oilers in 1980, where he ended his career after one season in Texas, he'd intercepted 30 passes while modeling black-and-silver and played in three Pro Bowls.

Born in Cherryville, North Carolina, Tatum's rise to the pros began during his years at Passaic High School in New Jersey. He arrived in the NFL following a Hall of Fame-worthy collegiate career at Ohio State. Initially recruited by coach Woody Hayes as a running back, Tatum's switch to the defensive secondary helped the Buckeyes to an unbeaten season and a national championship in 1968. Over Tatum's three seasons as the competitive consciousness of the secondary, Ohio State went 27-2 and collected two Big Ten titles. Tatum was then selected by the Raiders in the first round in the 1971 NFL Draft.

Never a wait-and-see kind of player, Tatum quickly made a name for himself in his rookie season after knocking both Baltimore Colts tight ends, John Mackey and Tom Mitchell, with crushing hits.

The following year Tatum returned a fumble a record 104 yards for a touchdown (since tied by Aeneas Williams in 2000).

That season, Tatum was also an unwitting part of the one of the most celebrated plays — the Immaculate Reception. With only 22 seconds remaining in the 1972 AFC divisional playoff and Oakland set to move on, Steelers quarterback Terry Bradshaw aimed a pass at tailback John "Frenchy" Fuqua. Tatum arrived at the same time as the pass, and the ball caromed into the air. It dropped into the inviting hands of Pittsburgh's Franco Harris, who appeared out of nowhere and lugged the rock 42 yards for the winning touchdown.

On a team noted for its outlaw swagger, Tatum fit in perfectly. The apex of his career arrived on January 9, 1977. With 103,000 fans crammed into the Rose Bowl, Oakland crushed the Minnesota Vikings 32–14 in Super Bowl XI. One of the most replayed moments of that game is a colossal thump by Tatum on Minnesota's Sammy White that blew the receiver's helmet clear off his head.

The most telling game of Tatum's career, however, was by then three years in the past. On August 12, 1974, in an exhibition versus New England, Tatum and Patriots wide receiver Darryl Stingley collided as Stingley was elevating for a pass on an inside slant route. In trying to lessen the impending impact, Stingley lowered his helmet and slammed into Tatum's shoulder. Tatum, as always, gave no quarter. The force of the collision severely damaged Stingley's spinal cord, severing his fourth and fifth vertebrae. He was left paralyzed from the neck down.

The hit wasn't penalized, nor did the league take disciplinary action after a review. The repercussions, though, were wide-ranging.

Tatum's longtime nickname, the Assassin, once seen as a positive for flat-out physical football, took on a wholly different tone. The fact that Tatum never apologized for the hit, citing it as part of the game, branded him a villain to many. Stingley forgave him, in time. Others would not.

"It was tough on him, too," said Tatum's good friend and former Ohio State teammate John Hicks. "He wasn't the same person after that. For years he was almost a recluse."

In one of his three autobiographies, Tatum wrote, "When the reality of Stingley's injury hit me with its full impact, I was shattered. To think that my tackle broke another man's neck and killed his future."

Stingley passed away on April 5, 2007, of heart disease and pneumonia complicated by quadriplegia. Three years later, after years of suffering from diabetes that cost him all five toes on his left foot before losing the remainder of the leg due to circulation problems, Tatum died of a heart attack while awaiting a kidney transplant.

The two men had never spoken face-to-face since the hit. ■

College: Ohio State University
Drafted: 1971, Oakland Raiders, 19th overall
Years active: 1971–1980
Top honors: Super Bowl Champion (1976)
Hall of Fame induction: N/A

BOBBY
WAGNER LB

G	Int/Yds	Sk	TD	FR
151	11/187	23.5	1	9

DISTILLED, BOBBY WAGNER IS PART LEONARDO — tactical, courageous, a born leader — and part Raphael — the aggressive conscience of his group.

Over the years, as he's blossomed into one of the game's most dominating presences on the defensive side of the ball, the Seattle Seahawks' stellar middle linebacker's devotion to the Teenage Mutant Ninja Turtles franchise has been well documented.

Wagner's Turtle-mania runs so deep, is so entrenched, that back in 2014 when his car was broken into and ransacked, the only item that he publicly asked to be returned was a turtle shell backpack from the comic-book ninjutsu warriors.

That backpack didn't just carry odds and ends; it was a treasure trove of memories. It had been a present from his mom, Phenia, who had died of a heart attack five years before the theft. The two of them would watch the TV series together when Bobby was younger.

His plea was answered. The beyond-price item was returned.

Gaze at Wagner's accomplishments up to this point in his pro career — Super Bowl winner, three-time NFL tackles leader, eight-time Pro Bowler, six-time First Team All-Pro selection, highest-paid middle linebacker in the league, the Seahawks' all-time tackle leader, and so on and so on — and it's difficult to wrap your head around the fact that, heading into college, he was tendered only one scholarship offer, and that was by Utah State.

Over four seasons at Maverick Field, he set a standard for all to follow in the Mountain West Conference. A superb MVP Senior Bowl performance, in which he racked up a combined 22 tackles, caught the attention of

A starter since arriving in Seattle, Wagner has continued to up the ante year after year.

the NFL scouts in Mobile, Alabama. A bout of pneumonia kept Wagner from attending the 2012 NFL Combine, but his full range of abilities were on display at Utah State's pro day.

The Seahawks were impressed and intrigued enough to select Wagner in the second round, 47th overall, in the 2012 NFL Draft. It turned out to rank among the shrewdest selections in franchise history.

A starter since arriving in Seattle, Wagner has continued to up the ante year after year. In 2014 he played in his first of six (and counting) consecutive Pro Bowls. In five of eight seasons to date, he's recorded at least 80 solo tackles, including a career high of 97 in 2017.

The 2013 season proved a high-water mark for both the franchise and its defensive linchpin. After posting a 13-3 regular-season record, the 'Hawks ran the playoff table, hiding the Denver Broncos 43–8 in Super Bowl XLVIII. Sidekick and outside linebacker Malcolm Smith enjoyed a monster game, with a pick and returned fumble for a touchdown to collect Super Bowl MVP laurels. No matter — Wagner had his ring.

Seahawks coach Pete Carroll certainly understands the seismic dynamism Wagner injects into his defense. "The thing I love about looking at great players is, do they show that ability to do it year after year after year," commented Carroll in 2018. "I think that's what greatness

is all about. Bobby's put together a résumé of really Hall of Fame stuff.

"This is the kind of guy that gets there someday. To add on to that, the leadership that he's brought and the direction and focus that he's brought on a regular basis — really, he has been a perfect Seahawk throughout the whole time he's been here."

That perfection was rewarded prior to the 2019 campaign. Negotiating his own deal, Wagner finalized a three-year, $54 million contract extension.

Wagner responded to the pay hike and praise by delivering 159 combined and 86 solo tackles as Seattle finished 11-5 in the NFC West. The Seahawks knocked off the Philadelphia Eagles in the postseason before falling 28–23 to the Green Bay Packers, just one step from another Super Bowl appearance.

Although the 2020 and '21 seasons didn't end the way fans in Seattle had envisioned — a 30–20 wild-card playoff loss to the L.A. Rams and a no-postseason 7-10 record, respectively — Wagner continued to excel, contributing 81 and 92 solo tackles, respectively.

"I would love Bobby to play here forever," confessed Carroll, as Wagner entered the final year of his contract amid much speculation. "He's been as solid as you could ever want a player to be and we've kind of grown up as Seahawks together here in this program over the years and I'd love for him to be here. I don't see why we'd be thinking anything else."

He's still at the summit of his profession. Wagner's total of 170 tackles in '21 — combined and solo — led the league.

But on March 8, 2021, the Seahawks triggered a seismic shift in their organizational aspirations in order to free up sizable cap space, trading franchise QB Russell Wilson to Denver and later that night releasing Wagner outright, after 10 seasons, 151 games and eight first-team Pro Bowl selections.

"Thank you, Seattle, for everything," Wagner tweeted in true Ninja Turtle style. Days later, he signed with the LA Rams for $50 million over five years. ▪

College: Utah State University
Drafted: 2012, Seattle Seahawks, 47th overall
Years active: 2012–present
Top honors: NFL All-Rookie Team (2012), Super Bowl Champion (2013), First Team All-Pro (2014, 2016–21)
Hall of Fame induction: N/A

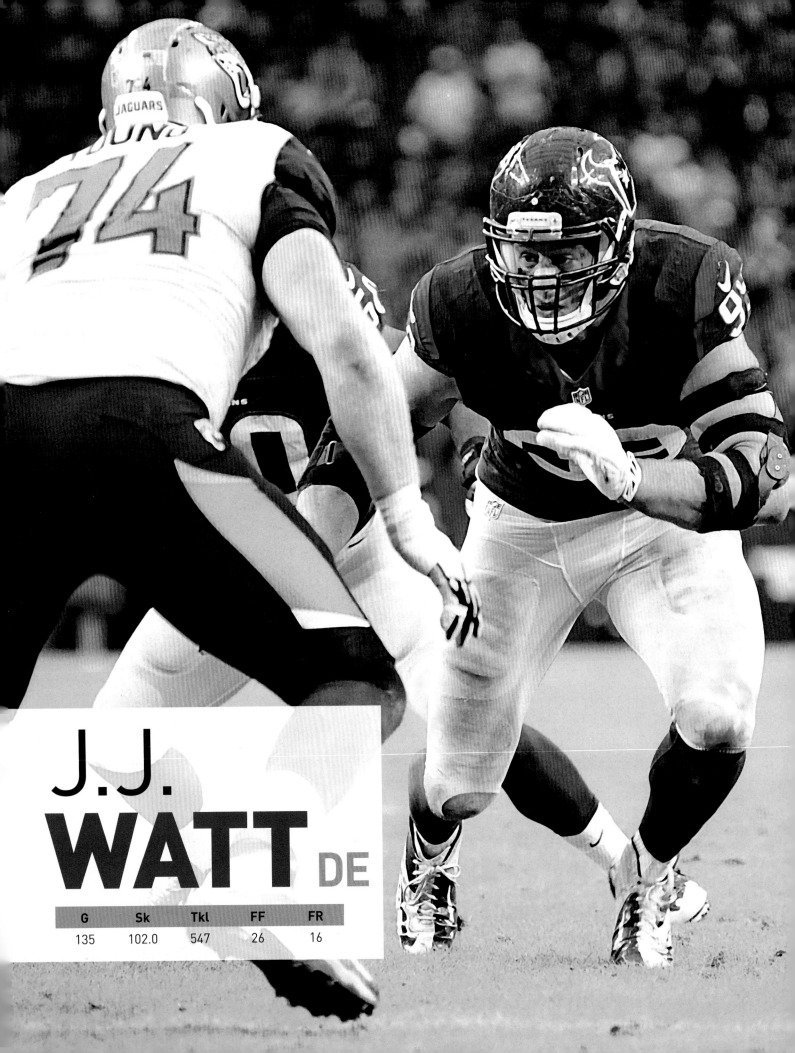

J.J. WATT DE

G	Sk	Tkl	FF	FR
135	102.0	547	26	16

I T HAD THAT ONE-FOR-THE-AGES storybook feel about it.

The 32-year-old surefire first-ballot Hall of Famer, returning to active duty only three months after surgery, having torn the labrum, biceps and rotator cuff in his left shoulder in a game against his first love, the Houston Texans.

With J.J Watt in harness for his introductory season in Tempe, the Arizona Cardinals had burst out of the gate 7-0.

After he was injured, they went 4-6 the rest of the way.

Yet there he was, back in the nick of time, the spitting image of a superhero, eager to help power the Cardinals to victory on January 17, 2022, and then on to further playoff glory.

Sometimes, though, the ending of a story doesn't live up to its promise.

"It was a massive failure," Watt told the *Arizona Republic* in the dark, dank aftermath of a 31–14 wild-card beatdown by the L.A. Rams on January 17, 2022.

"I mean, from what we were capable of doing and what we showed we can do, to what we showed today.

"We put up an embarrassing performance. There's no other way to put it, really."

That degree of withering honesty is a part of how you become one of the greatest defensive ends of forever, a three-time NFL Defensive Player of the Year, a five-time All-Pro and Pro Bowler.

"Success isn't owned," Watt once said. "It's leased. And rent is due every day. Every single day someone's coming for your job. Someone's coming for your greatness."

Married to pro soccer star Kealia Ohai, recipient of an honorary doctorate from Baylor College of Medicine, one-time *Saturday Night Live* guest host and a grand marshall of the Daytona 500, Watt is constantly searching for more, looking for any way to get better and be greater.

After all, you can take the boy out of Pewaukee, Wisconsin, but you can't totally take Pewaukee out of the boy. Even a boy who's 6-foot-5 and 288 pounds.

After accepting a scholarship at Central Michigan University, Watt played sparingly at tight end and was asked to switch to offensive tackle. Instead, he applied to the University of Wisconsin and played at defensive end. There he found his niche. After wowing the scouts at the 2011 NFL Combine, Watt was drafted by Houston in the first round and went on to make the All-Rookie Team.

In 2012 Watt racked up 20.5 sacks, two shy of Michael Strahan's single-season record (showing that predatory instinct can run in a family, his younger brother T.J. of the Pittsburgh Steelers would tie the Strahan record in 2021), and won his first of three Defensive Player of the Year awards. His second came in 2014 when he had another 20.5 sacks. That year, incredibly, he become the first defensive lineman to score five touchdowns in a season since 1944.

By then Mega Watt was so well established that opponents were running out of ways to praise him, let alone block him. Hue Jackson, the Cincinnati Bengals' offensive coordinator at the time, offered up three words about facing Watt: "Lord. Have. Mercy."

Back surgery and a fractured left tibia limited Watt to starts over the 2016 and 1017 seasons.

But the accolades kept coming, this time for his work off the field.

In 2017 Houston was reeling from the devastation wrought by Hurricane Harvey, and Watt set out to raise funds to help. He targeted $200,000. Over 200,000 people responded, donating $41 million. For his efforts, *Sports Illustrated* named him a cowinner of its Sportsperson of the Year award.

"All I did was give people a way to help," said Watt. "If I'm going to get an award, I feel like over 200,000 other people should, too."

Healthy again, Watt rebounded with 14 sacks in 2018. The following season he made a miraculous recovery from a torn pectoral muscle to prod the Texans into the playoffs.

Watt had built such a unique connection with Houston fans over 10 years that when he left the Texans to sign a two-year, $31 million deal with Arizona in February of 2021, the people of the Lone Star State didn't — couldn't — hold it against him.

"The one thing I can promise," he told Cardinals partisans, "is that I'm going to work my ass off every day to make you proud."

A rare person and player. A quarterback hunter for the ages, as well as an old-school hero for a new age. ▪

College: University of Wisconsin–Madison
Drafted: 2011, Houston Texans, 11th overall
Years active: 2011–present
Top honors: NFL All-Rookie Team (2011), NFL AP Defensive Player of the Year (2012, 2014, 2015), First Team All-Pro (2012–2015, 2018), NFL Walter Payton Man of the Year (2017)
Hall of Fame induction: N/A

RANDY
WHITE DT

G	Sk	FR
209	52	10

H E BECAME KNOWN OVER TIME AS THE MANSTER.
Half man. Half monster.

As well as — and this simply cannot be understated — *all* Cowboy.

Randy White was a 6-foot-4, 257-pound defensive lineman that could grapple a gator or chase down a cheetah — whichever needed doing on any given play. Exploding off the edge, White was a key member of the Doomsday Defense that included the likes of Thomas "Hollywood" Henderson, Jethro Pugh, Ed "Too Tall" Jones, Charlie Waters and Mel Renfro.

"His performances range anywhere from spectacular to spectacular," Cowboys' boss Tom Landry once noted. "He could outmatch anybody's intensity from game to game."

Born in Pittsburgh, Pennsylvania, White was recruited out of high school by the University of Maryland and began life in collegiate football as a fullback. An undistinguished fullback.

Only after Jerry Claiborne, who came over from Virginia Tech, took up the reins of the program prior to White's sophomore season did White switch to the defensive line.

His senior year proved to be a study in accomplishment. He collected the Outland Trophy as best collegiate interior lineman and the Lombardi Award as best collegiate player, and he was named Atlantic Coast Player of the Year. Despite losing the Liberty Bowl to the Tennessee Vols, White capped his Maryland career by being named the game's most valuable player.

White was selected second overall in the 1975 NFL Draft, behind University of California quarterback Steve Bartkowski, who went to the Atlanta Falcons, and two picks in front of a North Carolina running back by the name of Walter Payton.

"Here was this guy who weighed 240 pounds, big and strong, who can run a 4.7 40," Dallas personnel director Gil Brandt would later recall. "You hear about guys like that. But you just don't see them very often."

Initially slotted in at middle linebacker, playing behind the magnificent Lee Roy Jordan, White worked mainly on special teams his first two seasons. But after being shifted to the defensive line, at right the defensive tackle position, he emerged as a force to be reckoned with.

"It was just like somebody took the handcuffs off, and I could go play," White recalled.

His breakout year three performance would begin a run of nine consecutive Pro Bowl and seven First Team All-Pro team selections. What set White apart from his peers was his deadly combination of muscle and hustle.

"Strength is important," he said. "You need a combination of strength, speed and mobility or agility.

"I know I have good strength but without the speed and agility to go with it, I would not be playing major-league football."

White had been largely a spectator when the Cowboys lost to the Pittsburgh Steelers in Super Bowl X. By Super Bowl XII, though, he had emerged as an integral part of a magnificent defense. Dallas' Doomsday unit made quarterback Craig Morton's life a living hell that day at the Louisiana Superdome, as part of a comprehensive 27–10 Cowboys triumph over the Denver Broncos. Denver's longest play from scrimmage

Randy White squares off against the St. Louis Cardinals in 1987.

that afternoon would measure only 21 yards, coming during their first possession of the game. But White snuffed out the danger of the drive by sacking Morton for an 11-yard loss that pushed the Broncos out of field-goal range.

The defensive domination was absolute as Denver was limited to just nine first downs, only one via the pass, and 152 net yards. Hounded relentlessly by the Big D front all day, Morton finished with a pauper's 39 yards through the air, converting only one first down via the pass, and was picked off four times.

So impregnable was the Dallas resistance that White — credited with six tackles along with the sack — shared game MVP honors with Harvey Martin, his bookend on the flip side of the defensive line. This is the only time in Super Bowl history that has happened.

And on White's 25th birthday, no less.

The 'Boys would return to the Big Dance the very next season, facing the Pittsburgh Steelers at Miami's Orange Bowl. Once again the Steelers beat the Cowboys, 35–31.

As the years accumulated, injuries — shoulder surgery, a bulging disc in his neck — began to compromise White's effectiveness.

Following the 1988 season, his 14th on behalf of America's Team, Randy White called it quits at age 33. Symbolically, Landry — the only head coach he'd ever played for — stepped down that off-season, too.

"Physically," White confessed on that bittersweet day, "I played at a certain level, and I just don't think I can perform at that level anymore."

That certain level — a level few others can dream of, let alone achieve - enshrined Randy White in the College and Pro Football Halls of Fame and earned him a place of distinction on the NFL's 100th Anniversary Team. ■

College: University of Maryland
Drafted: 1975, Dallas Cowboys, 2nd overall
Years active: 1975–1988
Top honors: NFL All-Rookie Team (1975), Super Bowl Champion (1977), Super Bowl MVP (1977), First Team All-Pro (1978, 1979, 1981–85)
Hall of Fame induction: 1994

Super Bowl History

Super Bowl I — Jan. 15, 1967
Memorial Coliseum, Los Angeles, California
Green Bay Packers 35
Kansas City Chiefs 10
MVP: Bart Starr, QB, Green Bay

Super Bowl II — Jan. 14, 1968
Orange Bowl, Miami, Florida
Green Bay Packers 33
Oakland Raiders 14
MVP: Bart Starr, QB, Green Bay

Super Bowl III — Jan. 12, 1969
Orange Bowl, Miami, Florida
New York Jets 16
Baltimore Colts 7
MVP: Joe Namath, QB, New York

Super Bowl IV — Jan. 11, 1970
Tulane Stadium, New Orleans, Louisiana
Kansas City Chiefs 23
Minnesota Vikings 7
MVP: Len Dawson, QB, Kansas City

Super Bowl V — Jan. 17, 1971
Orange Bowl, Miami, Florida
Baltimore Colts 16
Dallas Cowboys 13
MVP: Chuck Howley, LB, Dallas

Super Bowl VI — Jan. 16, 1972
Tulane Stadium, New Orleans, Louisiana
Dallas Cowboys 24
Miami Dolphins 3
MVP: Roger Staubach, QB, Dallas

Super Bowl VII — Jan. 14, 1973
Memorial Coliseum, Los Angeles, California
Miami Dolphins 14
Washington Redskins 7
MVP: Jake Scott, S, Miami

Super Bowl VIII — Jan. 13, 1974
Rice Stadium, Houston, Texas
Miami Dolphins 24
Minnesota Vikings 7
MVP: Larry Csonka, RB, Miami

Super Bowl IX — Jan. 12, 1975
Tulane Stadium, New Orleans, Louisiana
Pittsburgh Steelers 16
Minnesota Vikings 6
MVP: Franco Harris, RB, Pittsburgh

Super Bowl X — Jan. 18, 1976
Orange Bowl, Miami, Florida
Pittsburgh Steelers 21
Dallas Cowboys 17
MVP: Lynn Swann, WR, Pittsburgh

Super Bowl XI — Jan. 9, 1977
Rose Bowl, Pasadena, California
Oakland Raiders 32
Minnesota Vikings 14
MVP: Fred Biletnikoff, WR, Oakland

Super Bowl XII — Jan. 15, 1978
Superdome, New Orleans, Louisiana
Dallas Cowboys 27
Denver Broncos 10
Co-MVPs: Randy White, DT, Dallas
Harvey Martin, DE, Dallas

Super Bowl XIII — Jan. 21, 1979
Orange Bowl, Miami, Florida
Pittsburgh Steelers 35
Dallas Cowboys 31
MVP: Terry Bradshaw, QB, Pittsburgh

Super Bowl XIV — Jan. 20, 1980
Rose Bowl, Pasadena, California
Pittsburgh Steelers 31
Los Angeles Rams 19
MVP: Terry Bradshaw, QB, Pittsburgh

Super Bowl XV — Jan. 25, 1981
Louisiana Superdome, New Orleans, Louisiana
Oakland Raiders 27
Philadelphia Eagles 10
MVP: Jim Plunkett, QB, Oakland

Super Bowl XVI — Jan. 24, 1982
Pontiac Silverdome, Pontiac, Michigan
San Francisco 49ers 26
Cincinnati Bengals 21
MVP: Joe Montana, QB, San Francisco

Super Bowl XVII — Jan. 30, 1983
Rose Bowl, Pasadena, California
Washington Redskins 27
Miami Dolphins 17
MVP: John Riggins, RB, Washington

Super Bowl XVIII — Jan. 22, 1984
Tampa Stadium, Tampa, Florida
Los Angeles Raiders 38
Washington Redskins 9
MVP: Marcus Allen, RB, Los Angeles

Super Bowl XIX — Jan. 20, 1985
Stanford Stadium, Palo Alto, California
San Francisco 49ers 38
Miami Dolphins 16
MVP: Joe Montana, QB, San Francisco

Super Bowl XX — Jan. 26, 1986
Louisiana Superdome, New Orleans, Louisiana
Chicago Bears 46
New England Patriots 10
MVP: Richard Dent, DE, Chicago

Super Bowl XXI — Jan. 25, 1987
Rose Bowl, Pasadena, California
New York Giants 39
Denver Broncos 20
MVP: Phil Simms, QB, New York

Super Bowl XXII — Jan. 31, 1988
Jack Murphy Stadium, San Diego, California
Washington Redskins 42
Denver Broncos 10
MVP: Doug Williams, QB, Washington

Super Bowl XXIII — Jan. 22, 1989
Joe Robbie Stadium, Miami Gardens, Florida
San Francisco 49ers 20
Cincinnati Bengals 16
MVP: Jerry Rice, WR, San Francisco

Super Bowl XXIV — Jan. 28, 1990
Louisiana Superdome, New Orleans, Louisiana
San Francisco 49ers 55
Denver Broncos 10
MVP: Joe Montana, QB, San Francisco

Super Bowl XXV — Jan. 27, 1991
Tampa Stadium, Tampa, Florida
New York Giants 20
Buffalo Bills 19
MVP: Ottis Anderson, RB, New York

Super Bowl XXVI — Jan. 26, 1992
Metrodome, Minneapolis, Minnesota
Washington Redskins 37
Buffalo Bills 24
MVP: Mark Rypien, QB, Washington

Super Bowl XXVII — Jan. 31, 1993
Rose Bowl, Pasadena, California
Dallas Cowboys 52
Buffalo Bills 17
MVP: Troy Aikman, QB, Dallas

Super Bowl XXVIII — Jan. 30, 1994
Georgia Dome, Atlanta, Georgia
Dallas Cowboys 30
Buffalo Bills 13
MVP: Emmitt Smith, RB, Dallas

Super Bowl XXIX — Jan. 29, 1995
Joe Robbie Stadium, Miami Gardens,
  Florida
San Francisco 49ers 49
San Diego Chargers 26
MVP: Steve Young, QB, San Francisco

Super Bowl XXX — Jan. 28, 1996
Sun Devil Stadium, Tempe, Arizona
Dallas Cowboys 27
Pittsburgh Steelers 17
MVP: Larry Brown, CB, Dallas

Super Bowl XXXI — Jan. 26, 1997
Louisiana Superdome, New Orleans,
  Louisiana
Green Bay Packers 35
New England Patriots 21
MVP: Desmond Howard, KR-PR,
  Green Bay

Super Bowl XXXII — Jan. 25, 1998
Qualcomm Stadium, San Diego,
  California
Denver Broncos 31
Green Bay Packers 24
MVP: Terrell Davis, RB, Denver

Super Bowl XXXIII — Jan. 31, 1999
Pro Player Stadium, Miami Gardens,
  Florida
Denver Broncos 34
Atlanta Falcons 19
MVP: John Elway, QB, Denver

Super Bowl XXXIV — Jan. 30, 2000
Georgia Dome, Atlanta, Georgia
St. Louis Rams 23
Tennessee Titans 16
MVP: Kurt Warner, QB, St. Louis

Super Bowl XXXV — Jan. 28, 2001
Raymond James Stadium, Tampa,
  Florida
Baltimore Ravens 34
New York Giants 7
MVP: Ray Lewis, LB, Baltimore

Super Bowl XXXVI — Feb. 3, 2002
Louisiana Superdome, New Orleans,
  Louisiana
New England Patriots 20
St. Louis Rams 17
MVP: Tom Brady, QB, New England

Super Bowl XXXVII — Jan. 26, 2003
Qualcomm Stadium, San Diego,
  California
Tampa Bay Buccaneers 48
Oakland Raiders 21
MVP: Dexter Jackson, FS, Tampa Bay

Super Bowl XXXVIII — Feb. 1, 2004
Reliant Stadium, Houston, Texas
New England Patriots 32
Carolina Panthers 29
MVP: Tom Brady, QB, New England

Super Bowl XXXIX — Feb. 6, 2005
Alltel Stadium, Jacksonville, Florida
New England Patriots 24
Philadelphia Eagles 21
MVP: Deion Branch, WR, New England

Super Bowl XL — Feb. 5, 2006
Ford Field, Detroit, Michigan
Pittsburgh Steelers 21
Seattle Seahawks 10
MVP: Hines Ward, WR, Pittsburgh

Super Bowl XLI — Feb. 4, 2007
Dolphin Stadium, Miami Gardens,
  Florida
Indianapolis Colts 29
Chicago Bears 17
MVP: Peyton Manning, QB,
  Indianapolis

Super Bowl XLII — Feb. 3, 2008
University of Phoenix Stadium,
  Glendale, Arizona
New York Giants 17
New England Patriots 14
MVP: Eli Manning, QB, New York

Super Bowl XLIII — Feb. 1, 2009
Raymond James Stadium, Tampa,
  Florida
Pittsburgh Steelers 27
Arizona Cardinals 23
MVP: Santonio Holmes, WR, Pittsburgh

Super Bowl XLIV — Feb. 7, 2010
Sun Life Stadium, Miami Gardens,
  Florida
New Orleans Saints 31
Indianapolis Colts 17
MVP: Drew Brees, QB, New Orleans

Super Bowl XLV — Feb. 6, 2011
Cowboys Stadium, Arlington, Texas
Green Bay Packers 31
Pittsburgh Steelers 25
MVP: Aaron Rodgers, QB, Green Bay

Super Bowl XLVI — Feb. 5, 2012
Lucas Oil Stadium, Indianapolis,
  Indiana
New York Giants 21
New England Patriots 17
MVP: Eli Manning, QB, New York

Super Bowl XLVII — Feb. 3, 2013
Mercedes-Benz Superdome, New
  Orleans, Louisiana
Baltimore Ravens 34
San Francisco 49ers 31
MVP: Joe Flacco, QB, Baltimore

Super Bowl XLVIII — Feb. 2, 2014
MetLife Stadium, East Rutherford,
  New Jersey
Seattle Seahawks 43
Denver Broncos 8
MVP: Malcolm Smith, LB, Seattle

Super Bowl XLIX — Feb. 1, 2015
University of Phoenix Stadium,
  Glendale, Arizona
New England Patriots 28
Seattle Seahawks 24
MVP: Tom Brady, QB, New England

Super Bowl 50 — Feb. 7, 2016
Levi's Stadium, Santa Clara, California
Denver Broncos 24
Carolina Panthers 10
MVP: Von Miller, LB, Denver

Super Bowl LI — Feb. 5, 2017
NRG Stadium, Houston, Texas
New England Patriots 34
Atlanta Falcons 28
MVP: Tom Brady, QB, New England

Super Bowl LII — Feb. 4, 2018
U.S. Bank Stadium, Minneapolis,
  Minnesota
Philadelphia Eagles 41
New England Patriots 33
MVP: Nick Foles, QB, Philadelphia

Super Bowl LIII — Feb. 3, 2019
Mercedes-Benz Stadium, Atlanta,
  Georgia
New England Patriots 13
Los Angeles Rams 3
MVP: Julian Edelman, WR,
  New England

Super Bowl LIV — Feb. 2, 2020
Hard Rock Stadium, Miami Gardens,
  Florida
Kansas City Chiefs 31
San Francisco 49ers 20
MVP: Patrick Mahomes, QB,
  Kansas City

Super Bowl LV — February 7, 2021
Raymond James Stadium, Tampa,
  Florida
Tampa Bay Buccaneers 31
San Francisco 49ers 9
MVP: Tom Brady, QB, Tampa Bay

Super Bowl LVI — February 13, 2022
SoFi Stadium, Inglewood, California
Los Angeles Rams 23
Cincinnati Bengals 20
MVP: Cooper Kupp, WR, Los Angeles

Additional Captions

Page 2: Chicago Bears running back Walter Payton charges up the field in an October 1985 game against the Tampa Bay Buccaneers.

Page 6: New York Jets quarterback Joe Namath during the 1972 season.

Page 10: Cleveland Browns running back Jim Brown looks on from the sideline in 1963.

Page 12: Tom Brady warms up before an October 2019 game against the New York Jets.

Page 16: Jim Brown during an NFL game circa the 1960s.

Page 20: Dick Butkus eyes New Orleans Saints quarterback Archie Manning during an October 1971 game.

Page 24: David "Deacon" Jones of the Los Angeles Rams is seen in 1966.

Page 28: Joe Montana in 1993 with the Kansas City Chiefs.

Page 32: Walter Payton in action.

Page 36: Jerry Rice catches a pass during a December 2000 game against the New Orleans Saints.

Page 40: Lawrence Taylor smiles from the sidelines during a December 1985 game versus the Green Bay Packers.

Page 44: Johnny Unitas playing for the Baltimore Colts.

Page 48: Reggie White in action against the Minnesota Vikings in September 1997.

Page 52: Los Angeles Raiders running back Marcus Allen carries the football in this photo from the 1980s.

Page 58: Marcus Allen in 1984.

Page 60: Lance Alworth catches a pass during a game at San Diego Stadium in 1966.

Page 62: David Bakhtiari in action against the Indianapolis Colts in November 2016.

Page 68: Drew Brees delivers a pass in a December 2019 game against the Carolina Panthers.

Page 72: Eric Dickerson runs upfield during a game against the Detroit Lions at Anaheim Stadium on October 2, 1983.

Page 80: Zach Ertz straight arms Buffalo Bills safety Duke Williams during a December 2015 game.

Page 84: Larry Fitzgerald makes a catch in a December 2013 game versus the Seattle Seahawks.

Page 88: Antonio Gates runs with the ball during an October 2010 game against the New England Patriots.

Page 90: Rob Gronkowski catches a pass in a September 2018 game between the Patriots and the Jacksonville Jaguars.

Page 96: Tyreek Hill scores on a reception in the AFC championship game between the Kansas City Chiefs and the Tennessee Titans in January 2020.

Page 102: Bo Jackson in action during a November 1990 game against the Kansas City Chiefs.

Page 104: Julio Jones runs with the ball in a December 2018 game versus the Arizona Cardinals.

Page 106: Alvin Kamara during a November 2019 game against the Tampa Bay Buccaneers.

Page 108: Travis Kelce makes a reception and runs upfield during a playoff game against the Indianapolis Colts during January 2019.

Page 110: Steve Largent catches a pass during a November 1978 game between the Seattle Seahawks and the Oakland Raiders.

Page 114: John Mackey in action in 1971.

Page 120: Dan Marino in a game against the New England Patriots.

Page 122: Bruce Matthews in action during an October 1994 game versus the Los Angeles Raiders.

Page 126: Randy Moss runs with the ball in a September 2003 game against the Green Bay Packers.

Page 128: Anthony Munoz in action with the Cincinnati Bengals.

Page 134: Terrell Owens charges up the field in a September 2003 victory against the Chicago Bears.

Page 138: Aaron Rodgers looks to pass during a snowy December 2019 game versus the New York Giants.

Page 140: Ben Roethlisberger sets up to throw a pass in a 2019 preseason game against the Tennessee Titans.

Page 144: Gale Sayers races upfield in a November 1967 game versus the Green Bay Packers.

Page 146: O.J. Simpson runs the ball against the Baltimore Colts.

Page 150: Bart Starr throws a pass in a 1965 game.

Page 154: Lynn Swann battles Cleveland Browns cornerback Clarence Scott in a September 1978 game.

Page 158: Thurman Thomas runs with the ball during an AFC championship game against the Denver Broncos in January 1992.

Page 160: LaDainian Tomlinson finds a hole up the middle during a game against the Tampa Bay Buccaneers.

Photo Credits

Front cover:

J.J. Watt: Randy Litzinger/Icon Sportswire
Reggie White: Cliff Welch/Icon Sportswire
Tom Brady: Ian Johnson/Icon Sportswire
Dan Marino: Tom DiPace/AP Photo
Emmitt Smith: John Cordes/Icon Sportswire
Jerry Rice: Greg Trott/AP Photo

Back cover:

Stephon Gilmore: Gregory Fisher/Icon Sportswire

Interior:

Associated Press (AP Photo)

Al Messerschmidt: 47, 57, 58, 149, 218
Associated Press: 22, 24, 60, 101, 131, 162, 172, 252–53
Charles Tasnadi: 153
Chuck Solomon: 158
David Durochik: 6, 44, 133, 174, 187, 220, 228
David F. Smith: 27
David Stluka: 83, 143
Eric Gay: 217
Greg Trott: 36, 39
Harold P. Matosian: 194
Harry Cabluck: 93
Jim Mone: 157
Lou Krasky: 71
Mitchell B. Reibel: 192

NFL Photos: 166, 201, 202
Paul Abell: 94
Paul Spinelli: 40, 43
Perry Knotts: 108
Peter Read Miller: 72
Pro Football Hall of Fame: 113
R.C. Greenawalt: 154
Reed Saxon: 236–237
Steve Luciano: 9
Todd Rosenberg: 55
Tom DiPace: 2, 48, 222
Tony Tomsic: 10, 16, 19, 20, 50, 67, 114, 146, 150, 170, 214
Vernon J. Biever: 32, 34, 144, 209, 210
William Straeter: 197

Icon Sportswire

Andrew Dieb: 77, 242
Andy Lewis: 80, 206
Bryan Lynn: 140
Chris Williams: 182
Christopher Mast: 231
Cliff Welch: 14, 28, 120, 128, 160, 177, 235
Dannie Walls: 191
David Rosenblum: 90, 137
Dilip Vishwanat/Sporting News: 126
Doug Murray: 184
Frank Mattia: 104
Hector Acevedo/Zuma Press: 119
Icon Sportswire: 88
Jeff Carlick: 134
Jeffrey Brown: 62
John Cordes: 79, 102, 122, 168
John McCreary: 68

John W. McDonough: 30, 245
John Rivera: 232
Joshua Sarner: 12
Joshua Weisberg: 84
Kevin French: 246–247
Kevin Reece: 52
Leslie Plaza Johnson: 99
Michael Workman: 164
Owen C. Shaw: 75, 87, 125
Rich Graessle: 138
Rich Kane: 198, 224
Robin Alam: 65, 178, 181, 205
Roy K. Miller: 106
Scott Winters: 96, 188, 227
William Purnell: 117
Zuma Press: 212

Acknowledgments

George Johnson

Any time a chance arises to work on a project alongside Al Maki, I am all in. Immediately. I've been in this wacky business of writing for over 40 years, and he's one of the best I've seen. Period. End of sentence. I'd help reinterpret the phone book if Al asked me to.

Add Steve Cameron of Firefly Books to the mix, as well as editors Julie Takasaki (patient enough to answer each and every angst-tinged e-mail) and NFL freelance fact-checker *par excellence* Ronnie Shuker and how could a guy go wrong? On this project, I was one lucky old scribbler. I hope that shows in the finished product.

Allan Maki

In many ways, updating *NFL Heroes* was like falling back on an enjoyable routine. This time, though, there were some new voices on the conference calls and back-and-forth emails, which kept things interesting.

Firefly's Julie Takasaki started the project but was moved into the managing editor's role. She turned things over to Darcy Shea, who quickly proved himself an all-pro editor with his Joe Montana-ish cool under pressure — at least he was whenever we called to say Russell Wilson/Tyreek Hill/Davante Adams/etc. had been traded while Aaron Rodgers re-upped with the Green Bay Packers and Tom Brady retired then unretired faster than you can spell Rob Gronkowski.

The best part of this exercise was being able to work again with columnist George Johnson. He's the prolific pro's pro of prose. He's talented, able to produce quality work on extreme deadlines, and his style is a treat to read, especially when it came to the players he followed as a kid, such as Dick Butkus, Johnny Unitas, Ray Nitschke and Joe Namath. Great stars chronicled by an outstanding writer.

My heartfelt acknowledgment and thanks definitely go to my wife, Jeanne, who was ever so tolerant of my constant researching, writing and rewriting. She understands me well enough to know that when I say I need five more minutes to finish a story I'm really talking about an hour.

Index